TECHNOLOGY ILLUSTRATED,

BEING A SERIES OF

TREATISES ON THE CONSTRUCTION OF ROADS, BRIDGES, CANALS, HYDRAULIC ENGINES, FLOURING AND SPINNING MILLS,

AND ON THE

PRINCIPAL PROCESSES

IN

COTTON MANUFACTURE, COINING, MINING, METALLURGY, AGRICULTURE, &c.

WITH

An Atlas of Thirty-five Steel Plates,

CONTAINING ELEVEN HUNDRED ILLUSTRATIONS.

NEW YORK:
D. APPLETON AND COMPANY,
346 & 348 BROADWAY.
1856.

CONTENTS

OF

TECHNOLOGY.

(The numbers refer to the bottom paging of the text.)

CONTENTS OF THE PLATES (X. Nos. 1—35)

TO

TECHNOLOGY.

*** The references for explanations of the subjects are to the bottom paging of the text.

TECHNOLOGY.

PLATES X. 1—35.

INTRODUCTION.

THE first effort of man is to procure his food and the most indispensable necessaries of life; when these are supplied he endeavors to make his existence more comfortable, and to obtain various physical and mental enjoyments. For the attainment of these objects a great variety of different kinds of labor is required, which are sometimes quite simple, but more frequently complicated, requiring much knowledge and skill. The totality of knowledge by which we learn to transform and prepare the products of nature, the raw material, so as to serve for the use and pleasure of man, we call *Industrial Science* or *Technology*. In other words, technology comprises the knowledge of the various arts and manufactures by means of which the different materials are adapted to our uses, and the knowledge of all the substances and auxiliaries which serve for that purpose. It is evident that the field of Technology is one of vast extent, there being no branch of human industry into which it does not enter.

However crude technology must have been in its beginnings, being at first limited to the preparation of food, the construction of secure dwellings, and the manufacture of arms and clothing, it has yet risen to a high degree of development in the course of centuries. While the first inhabitants of the earth were content with a rude preparation of the products of nature, using only the power of their hands, we call to our aid the elementary forces of nature, and have subjected them to our rule; the most sagacious discoveries in mathematics, physics, and chemistry, the experience of centuries and the most distinguished results of human ingenuity are united for the purpose of saving power, time, and human labor, while at the same time the results are more perfect than it is possible for them to become by mere manual labor. The knowledge of those implements and machines which have been invented for working raw materials constitutes therefore one of the principal branches of industrial science. In order to treat of the latter in its full extent it would be necessary to compile a voluminous work with countless plates. This, however, could not be the design of the present treatise, which only forms a subdivision of a more comprehensive work; and we have therefore selected the most important and interesting subjects and discussed them more at length, in preference to giving something of all without treating fully of any.

One of the principal means of advancing civilization is facility of communication, by which men are brought together and the products of one region are speedily and safely transferred to another; the interchange of ideas as well as the exchange of the productions of nature and industry being thus promoted and facilitated. We therefore place at the head of our treatise the means of communication.

I. MEANS OF COMMUNICATION.

Means of communication include the construction of highways on land and water. The welfare of a state is greatly promoted by a well regulated system of roads and inland navigation, and it is easy to discover the difference in the civilization, industry, and general opulence of two countries, in one of which communication in all directions is made easy and convenient, while in the other cities and villages are in a measure isolated by the bad condition or want of highways. How much has been effected in this respect by the construction of railroads in the greater part of Europe and in the United States need scarcely be mentioned. We will now proceed to consider the different kinds.

1. The Construction of Roads.

The natural surface of the ground, unless it be rock, when used as a road, is soon brought to such a condition by the action of the weather and of vehicles as to offer great obstacles to convenient communication. On this account artificial roads have been constructed since very ancient times, and remains of such which have been preserved to the present time show how carefully and judiciously they were designed. The first highroads of which we have any knowledge were built by Semiramis, and one of them led from Susa to Sardis, a distance of 2100 miles. The Carthaginians also had artificial roads, and the oldest in China were built so durably as to be still available. The Greeks, especially the Athenians, constructed excellent roads, particularly for their religious processions, as for instance the sacred road of Eleusis, and that to Delphi; there was also such a one near Cyrene.

The Romans, especially in the reigns of Augustus, Vespasian, and Trajan, constructed causeways from the city of Rome to all parts of the empire, however difficult the ground, all of which radiated from a central column (*milliare aureum*) and were divided into miles of eight stadia each. They were built with extreme care, and remains of these Roman roads are found in almost all parts of Europe. They have below a bed of mortar (*substratum*) of about one inch in thickness; on this rests a stratum ten inches in depth, of flat stones (*statumen*) laid in mortar and breaking joints, which serves as a support for the second stratum of 8–10 inches, composed of concrete (*rudus*) or small pebbles cast in cement. The third layer consists of a mass of lime and brick-dust (*nucleus*), on which finally was placed a stratum of gravel or a stone pavement (*summum dorsum*). In this way the body of the road was something over three feet in depth. Besides these roads they had others of less importance, consisting of two gravel-ways twenty feet in width.

In the middle ages the Roman roads were suffered to fall into decay, and no new ones were constructed except in France by Queen Brunehild, for which reason causeways are even now called *chemins brunehauds* in Belgium. In modern times causeways were first built in Holland, and subsequently in Spain, England, Germany, and France.

A. Streets in Cities.

Streets in cities are paved with stones almost without exception, and only in some cities the streets in the suburbs are made in the manner of causeways as we shall describe them below.

The paving of streets may be done in two ways; that most commonly in use is represented on *pl.* 1, *fig.* 5. There are others, however, constructed in the manner shown in *fig.* 3. Every street should have side-walks along the houses (*figs.* 3, 4, 5, 6) from three to eight feet wide, covered with flags of granite, or paved with bricks; the latter, however, should only be used where nothing better can be obtained. Some years ago asphaltum was very much advocated; it was mixed with very fine gravel and spread in a semi-liquid state over the side-walks, when after cooling it presented a smooth surface similar to granite. The idea was soon given up, however, as the wear of the asphaltum was very great, and it became soft in very warm weather.

The carriage-way of the street should be elevated in the centre (*fig.* 3) and slightly arched, so as to turn the water to both sides, where it runs off more readily in gutters (*a*, *fig.* 3, and *g*, *fig.* 5), which must have a longitudinal descent. In cities provided with sewers which run along under ground usually in the middle of the streets, and carry off the rubbish from the houses as well as the water from the streets, the latter may be much less arched; the gutters are in that case provided with conduits covered with grating, through which the water enters the sewers; these also have openings through which they may be entered from the street and cleaned.

In places where the soil is firm and the seasons generally dry, the pavement itself may be made in the manner shown in *pl.* 1, *fig.* 3 being a section, and *fig.* 4 a ground-plan. Here the tracks of the wheels only, *c c* (*fig.* 3), and EF (*fig.* 4), are laid with closely fitted stones, and the spaces *b*, *d*, and *b* (*fig.* 3) are covered with well-rammed gravel. In most cases, however, the pavements are made as shown in *figs.* 5 and 6, where the whole street is paved with round stones (pebbles) fitted together as closely as possible. The wheel-tracks should in any case be laid with flat stones, *ff* (*fig.* 5), and the spaces *ee* paved with small pebbles, on which the horses have a safer hold. Sometimes long stone sleepers are employed for the wheel-ways, jointed together as seen at *figs.* 7 and 8. Another mode of joining the stretchers, by Mathews, is shown in *fig.* 9, by which not only the lateral displacement but also the lifting of the ends is to be prevented. This is effected by the introduction of a key-stone, *d*, which may either be shaped as in *fig.* 10, *cde*, or else as in *fig.* 11, *cde*.

In order to avoid the disagreeable noise and diminish the dust attendant on stone pavements, it was proposed in England and France to use instead of the paving-stones blocks of wood of equal size, placed with the transverse section of the fibres on the surface.

This idea was favorably received, and trials were made by paving whole streets in this manner, on which, however, many drawbacks and imperfections became apparent, the most important among which were the great cost and the action of moisture, which by swelling the wooden blocks deranged their position and destroyed the pavement. On this account wooden pavements have gradually disappeared, but they are frequently applied in passages, covered ways, and stables, where they are found to answer very well. There are many different modes of constructing wooden pavements, and we will proceed to consider some of them.

The simplest kind of wooden pavement consists of cubical blocks of wood placed so as to break joints on an even and firm foundation of sand, and firmly pressed together by a curb-frame; but such a pavement is too much affected by changes of temperature and moisture to remain in order long, and with any unequal yielding in the foundation it will become uneven. It was therefore proposed so to shape and arrange the blocks as to support each other, similar to the voussoirs of an arch. Of this kind is the pavement represented in *pl.* 1, *fig.* 21 *b'*. It consists of blocks of wood (*fig.* 21 *a*) the tops of which are regular hexagons, as the dotted lines *bb'* (*fig.* 21 *a*) show, while the lower sides are irregular hexagons of three long and three short sides, *a* and *a'*. *Fig.* 21 *a* shows how according to this construction the sides of the blocks form warped surfaces, which, when the blocks are arranged as in *fig.* 21 *b*, will hold and lock them in such a manner that no single one can be removed. Grooves are cut into the upper surface in order to afford a safe footing for the horses.

Arranged on a similar plan is the construction of Laves of Hanover. *Fig.* 13 represents a walk for foot passengers; *fig.* 12, a carriage-way; *fig.* 14 is a cross-section and *fig.* 15 a longitudinal one of the latter. Here the wooden blocks rest on the cross-sill *c* and the longitudinal beams or sleepers *a* and *b*; their upper surfaces are regular squares, while the sides are cut obliquely in different forms, and in such a manner that the several prisms form, as it were, voussoirs of a flat arch, which are held immovably against each other by a key-prism. The latter is fastened by screw-bolts to the sleepers. When the pavement gets wet and the prisms swell, the pressure which they exert upon each other, and which otherwise raises the pavement in the form of an arch, is thus directed downwards, in which direction no displacement is possible.

An improved construction has been sometimes used, which is shown in *pl.* 1, *figs.* 16–20. Here we have first a substructure, which of itself is a wooden pavement, through which, however, the moisture that penetrates from above is drained off into the bed of sand below. *Fig.* 16 shows this substructure, which can be conveniently taken up when water or gas pipes, &c., are to be laid. Two or more sills are placed lengthwise at suitable distances from each other and united at intervals by cross-ties. On these sills rest short pieces of plank, *a a a*, bevelled at both ends in opposite directions (*fig.* 17), the piece *d* remaining, however, which prevents the pieces of plank from being pushed closely together, thus leaving the interstices *c c c* (*fig.* 16), which serve as drains. Those pieces which abut against the curb of the pavement (*fig.* 16, left side) are fastened to the sill. No further fastening is required, as any pressure acting on the substructure will only serve to bring its several parts more closely together. The prisms for the pavement itself are made of various forms, some of which are represented in *figs.* 18, 19, 20, and 21. Of these *figs.* 18 and 19 show a pavement which is very suitable where the ascent is considerable and the horses require a very secure footing. The perspective view (*fig.* 19) shows the form of the single blocks as well as the manner in which they are alternately so placed as to afford a firm step both in ascending and descending. *Fig.* 21 shows a combination of blocks which also forms a very firm pavement. They are truncated pyramids, alternately inverted, and two such courses will support themselves entirely.

Great attention is at all times to be bestowed on the cleanliness of streets, and especially of wooden pavements, but the cleaning when done by human labor is too expensive and slow. Many attempts have been made in England and France to perform this labor by machines, and one of the most effective of these is represented in *fig.* 27. It is a street-cleaning machine made by Whitworth & Co. of Manchester, where as well as in London it has for some time been successfully in use. Two horses with a driver can work with a machine of the dimensions given below with a speed of 100 feet per minute, and thus can sweep thoroughly in one hour 120 yards of a street 50 feet in width.

The machine consists of a cart provided with an apparatus which sweeps the street, and carries the dust and rubbish into the interior of the cart, when it is moved. In this consists its superiority over other machines of this kind, which only move the dirt aside, and leave it to be carted away separately. It operates equally well on all kinds of pavements and roads.

The machine represented in *fig.* 27 consists of a two-horse cart, A, of ordinary size, with two large wheels, B; the body of the cart hangs low between the wheels, and consists of two parts, the lower one of which can be taken off when full and exchanged for another. For this purpose it is suspended by chains passing over pulleys, K. Both pulleys are on the same axle, which also carries a cog-wheel that is moved by an endless screw, which may be turned by a crank or key in a place accessible to the driver. In this way the lower part or box which, when in use, is fastened by bolts, may be exchanged for another when required, and thus when the place of deposit is at a distance, the full boxes may be left and afterwards carried off together in a frame-cart. Through the bottom of A passes a pipe, the upper end of which reaches a little above the top of the full load of solid dirt; in the cart the fluid and solid parts will separate, and the former may be drained off into the sewers by opening the bottom of the pipe.

At the top of the back part of the cart there is an axle movable in fixed bearings, carrying two pulleys, D, of 1 foot diameter, at a distance of 3 feet 4 inches apart; outside of these pulleys movable about the ends of the axle are two light wrought-iron frames, which carry at their lower ends the bearings for another axle, on which also two pulleys, E, are fixed. Round the pulleys D and E pass two parallel endless chains, F, on which are fixed, at regular intervals, thirty rows of brooms, 3 feet 4 inches in length. On the top of the frame is a light cover of sheet-iron; below is a wide trough resting with its upper end on the top edge of the lower cart-box. On the axle D there is finally a pinion into which works a large cog-wheel on the inner face of one of the cart-wheels; and thus when the cart is drawn by the horses the system of brooms is made to move in the direction of the arrows, each broom successively touching the street and carrying the dirt up the trough into the box. When the lower box is to be changed, or the full cart is to be drawn away, the whole broom-frame is raised into a horizontal position. For this purpose it is provided with the sector, I, over which passes a chain that winds up on the pulley H; the latter is also moved by a crank, endless screw, and cog-wheel. On the axle of H is another pulley, over which also passes a chain, to the end of which weights may be applied in order partially to balance the weight of the broom-frames, and thus to regulate the pressure used in sweeping. An apparatus for counting the revolutions may also be attached to the axle D, which is advantageous when the work is contracted for by the square yard.

B. Roads.

Roads connecting places of importance, and forming the great arteries of the country through which they pass, are constructed with great care; they are regularly graded, drained, secured from inundation, and covered with gravel or broken stone, so as to be easily and safely travelled at all seasons.

The grade of a road, *i. e.* its inclination to the horizon, should in no place be so steep as to require heavy wagons to take additional teams, or in descending to lock their wheels; it should not exceed 3–5 per cent. The road should be sufficiently wide to allow two wagons to pass each other conveniently without encroaching upon the foot-way; the width of the roadway should therefore be at least 24 feet. In regions subject to inundation, safety requires that the road should be above the level of the highest water, and guarded against its pressure by bridges and breakwaters. In order to allow the rain-water to run off rapidly, a transverse convexity is given to the road-way, *e f i m* (*pl.* 1, *figs.* 1 and 2); the footpaths *d e* and *m n* should also have a slight lateral slope towards the side-channels. The depth of the latter is 3–4 feet, and when the road is on a level with the adjacent ground, as in *fig.* 1, the slopes of the side-channel *a b c d* may be 1 base to 1 perpendicular. When the road is on an embankment, as in *fig.* 2, its side slope should be 1½ base to 1 perpendicular, and the same slope, or even a less inclination, is required for the sides of excavations. The bottom *b c o p* of the drains is two feet in width. At intervals walled drains, termed *culverts*, built of stone or brick, and usually arched at the top, pass under the road, and convey the water to the main drains which communicate with the natural courses. Shade-trees should not be planted on the road itself, as they are apt to keep it damp.

When a road is to be made, the country through which it is to pass is carefully surveyed and mapped; profiles of the surface are obtained by means of the spirit-level, and from these data the location of the road is determined on, and estimates made of the required structures, such as bridges, culverts, and side-walks, and of the number of cubic yards of embankment and excavation. The line of road being thus marked on the ground, the grading and draining are done according to the plan proposed; on each side of the road from 3 to 6 feet are marked off for the footpaths *de* and *mn* (*figs.* 1 and 2), and two rows of curbstones placed at *e* and *m*. The paved bottom road covering (*fig.* 1) is formed of three layers of stone. The bottom layer, *h*, consists of small blocks of stone, about 6 inches high, packed together as closely as possible, the interstices being filled with small stones compactly set with a hammer. The second layer, *g*, of broken stone, is made four inches high, and the convexity of the carriage-way is begun to be formed. The third layer, *f*, should consist of the hardest broken stone, of the size of a pigeon's egg, and should again be from 4 to 6 inches high. A coating of clean gravel, two inches thick, termed a *binding*, is spread on the surface, and levelled by means of a road-roller. The elevation of the centre of the carriage-way is about one eighteenth of its width. The foot-paths are also covered with gravel, and serve as abutments for the body of the road.

In order to diminish the wear and tear of the road as well as of the conveyances, *summer roads* are sometimes laid out on the sides of stone roads. They are not covered with stone, and are closed by gates in wet weather and in winter.

The materials for a good road-covering are the harder kinds of stone, quartz, the scoriæ of iron-furnaces, poor iron-ore, &c. Sandstone and all kinds of slate are too friable for the purpose. In Holland the so-called klinker roads are made, which are covered with brick baked very hard, called *klinkers*.

Another mode of forming the road-covering was first brought into notice by McAdam; roads made according to his system are called *Macadamized*, and have been adopted in many states on account of the economy in their first construction. *Pl.* 1, *fig.* 2, represents a road of this kind; the covering consists entirely of broken stones, those of the bottom layer being about as large as hens' eggs, and those on top of the size of a hickory-nut; gravel when it can be procured is preferable for the top-coating. Roads of this kind will only answer when the subsoil is very firm; they require much care during the first years, as deep ruts are readily made, which must be constantly filled up, but after some time the whole mass will attain a high degree of compactness and durability.

We have mentioned above that after the superstructure of stones is spread on the road, it is pressed and smoothed down by a road-roller. Formerly huge cylinders of granite were employed for this purpose; the axle, which passed through the centre, rested on bearings in a square frame, which was drawn by ten or twelve horses. In modern times cylinders of cast iron are used, and we will notice two of the various forms which have been given to these rollers.

The road-roller of Schattenmann consists of a hollow cast iron cylinder of 4 feet diameter and 4 feet width. On each side is fastened by screws a cross of cast iron, through the centre of which the axle passes. On the ends of the axle rest cast iron bearings which are attached to the under side of the frame which carries a box 6 feet long, 5 feet wide, and 2 feet high, capable of being loaded with three tons of stone. Attached to the frame are two scrapers of plate iron, two brakes which can be pressed against the cylinder by screws, and four rings through which levers can be pressed to prevent the roller from upsetting on inclined grades or very soft ground. At each end of the frame is a pole and below it a runner, in order to be able to reverse the motion without turning the roller round. The cast iron cylinder with arms and axle weighs about two tons, the frame and box about one ton, and, by loading the roller, the weight of the whole may be increased to six tons. *Pl.* 1, *fig.* 22, is a side view of this machine, and *fig.* 23 a part of the section of the cylinder with its arms and axle. A is the cylinder, B the frame, C the box, D the brakes, E the adjusting screws for the same, F the scrapers, G the runners, H the poles, shown in part, I the arched floor of the box, K the bar supporting the latter. The roller is drawn by six or eight horses, and is at first passed over the road several times without additional load, after which the box is gradually loaded to the full extent. In one working-day 2,500 sq. yards may be worked in this way; the road must be kept moist, however, the whole time.

The road-roller by Schæfer is loaded within the cylinder. *Fig.* 24 represents a side view of it, *fig.* 25 a section of the cylinder, and *fig.* 26 a horizontal section of the whole machine. The axle rests in bearings on the frame EF, to which the pole B is attached. In the interior of the cylinder is a hexagonal system of boxes, *i*, *i*, *i* (*fig.* 25), which are held by the arms *f*, *f*, and the knees *d*; these boxes or cells are loaded when required with bars of lead or iron, through the openings *m*, *m*, which are closed by covers and bars, *b*, *b* (*fig.* 24). This roller has the advantage that the axle and frame are not loaded as much as in the preceding one, the pressure being more immediately upon the road; the axle may therefore be of less diameter, and less force will be required to move the roller.

C. Tunnels.

Tunnels are subterranean roads which are excavated through mountains, under rivers, or under structures, in order to avoid the obstacles presented to their passage on the surface. The ancients appear to have made tunnels at early date, for in Babylon an arched way 500 feet long, 15 feet wide, and 6 feet high, passed under the bed of the Euphrates connecting the two palaces. The grotto of Pausilippo near Naples is also a structure of this kind. In modern times tunnels have been excavated in most civilized countries. In Germany we name the tunnel near Tübingen in Wirtemberg, by means of which the river Ammer is carried through the Oesterberg; also the tunnel near Reichenau in Austria, 1,362 feet long, and 3,700 feet above the level of the sea, through which a stream is made to pass for the purpose of floating wood to Vienna. In France the canal of Languedoc is carried through a mountain. Between Gravesend and Rochester in England is a tunnel of about two miles in length, through which passes a canal connecting the river Medway with the Thames. The Bridgewater canal passes through a tunnel near Manchester, and various other tunnels for similar purposes exist in England. Of Railroad tunnels we shall speak below.

The most remarkable tunnel is the celebrated Thames tunnel, of which we have given representations in *pl.* 1, *figs.* 28–34. It was built by Sir I. Brunel, a French engineer, who on seeing a ship's keel hollowed out entirely by the worm, had conceived the idea that a large tunnel might be made by driving a number of small tunnels close to each other. For this purpose he constructed his so-called shield, of which a single field is represented in *fig.* 33. These fields, of which there are twelve in all, as *fig.* 31 shows, consist of the bottom-plates, *f*, *f*, the side-faces, *d*, composed of several pieces, and the top-plates, *c*, *c*; each has three compartments, in each of which a man can work erect. The openings in the side-plates allow the workmen to assist each other. The forward face of the field is composed of a number of iron plates, *a*, *a*, 6 inches wide and 2 inches thick, each of which is supported by two screws against the side pieces, when the shield is placed against the earth wall that is to be perforated. The earth is thus sustained while the shield itself abuts at its head and foot plates against the masonry, and can be moved forward by screws. *Fig.* 32 shows this plainly. When the work is to proceed each workman takes out one of the foot-plates, *a*, and removes the earth immediately before it to exactly the depth of 6 inches, after which he inserts the plate again and presses it firmly against the new wall by means of the screws. He then takes up the next plate and proceeds as before, until he has pushed forward all its plates, when six inches will have been gained on the whole face of the tunnel, and the shield can be moved forward by that amount. The newly gained space is immediately closed by the arches (*figs.* 31 and 32), while the thirty-six workmen in the shield proceed to excavate another 6 inches. In this manner the pressure of the earth is supported at all times, except at the small spaces where the earth is just being moved, and these may be closed at once should any portion suddenly give way. The form and dimensions of the arches are shown in *fig.* 31.

The success of the work is wholly due to the use of this shield and Brunel's unflinching perseverance. The shield, which is entirely his invention, has been set up by the proprietors of the tunnel as a monument in honor of the distinguished engineer.

The tunnel is situated between Wapping and Rotherhithe (see the plan, *fig.* 28) at the only point between London Bridge and Greenwich where it could be driven without endangering the foundations of the bridges across the Thames. The banks of the river at this place are but 1200 feet distant from each other. Formerly it was necessary to make a circuit of four miles to pass from one side of the river to the other.

The joint-stock company which constructed the tunnel was formed in 1824, and the work was commenced in the following year by the construction of a cylinder of brick, fifty feet in diameter, three feet thick, and forty-two feet high, on the Rotherhithe shore, 150 feet from the river. This cylinder rested on a cast iron ring, sharp on its lower edge, and its masonry was well connected by iron rings and anchors. On its top was erected a steam-engine of thirty horse-power for the purpose of elevating the earth and water from the excavation; the earth being dug away from under the cylinder, it gradually descended until in this manner a walled shaft of sixty-five feet depth was obtained; a second shaft eighty feet deep was sunk in the first one, to serve as a reservoir for the water. The tunnel commences at a depth of sixty-three feet; it was excavated thirty-eight feet wide and twenty-two and a half feet high, as it was to afford room for two arches, each fifteen feet high, and having a footway besides the carriage-way (*pl.* 1, *fig.* 30). The entrance to the tunnel from the shaft is shown in *fig.* 34. The excavation of the tunnel was commenced on the first of January, 1826. For every foot in length about 45–50 tons of earth were removed and delivered at the head of the shaft by the steam-engine, and 5,500 bricks were required for the masonry. Although the tunnel descends about three feet in every hundred, yet it approaches the bed of the river near the middle to within ten feet (*fig.* 29). Still no accident happened until the 18th of May, 1827, when at a distance of 544 feet from the shaft the water broke in with such violence that within fifteen minutes the tunnel was filled with water and about 1,000 tons of sand. On examining the break with the diving-bell it was found that the arches had not been damaged, and that the shield remained in its place. The break was filled with 3,000 earth bags, each containing a ton of clay, and the water being pumped out, the work was re-commenced in September, but progressed very slowly, as the workmen were much inconvenienced by fire-damp, and the work was often dangerous. Fifty-two feet more were completed when, on the 12th of January, 1828, the water broke in a second time and filled the tunnel in ten minutes. On this occasion six workmen lost their lives. This break having also been closed by means of 4,000 tons of clay in bags, the water was again pumped out; but the work stopped here for want of funds. Seven years afterwards, when government agreed to advance all the funds required, the work was taken up again, but progressed very slowly on account of the difficulties of the ground. Three more breaks also occurred, but one life only was lost. In January, 1841, the tunnel had reached the opposite bank, a distance of 1,140 feet, and on the 13th of August of the same year Sir I. Brunel walked for the first time below the Thames from one shore to the other. On the 25th of March, 1843, the tunnel was completed with the exception of the descending road for the carriages, and was opened for foot passengers. The carriage road on each side is forty feet wide and descends fifty-seven feet in two turns of a spiral of 200 feet in diameter, the grade being thus very moderate. The archways are lighted by gas, and the temperature in them is but little different from that of the open air.

The whole cost of the work, originally estimated at $800,000, amounted to $3,000,000, on account of the breaks and many other accidents; and the excavation and removal of a cubic yard of earth cost on the average $16. According to a moderate estimate the income of the tunnel amounts to $100,000 annually.

D. Railroads.

Roads with wheel-tracks of large blocks of dressed stone closely fitted were used early by the Egyptians and Indians in order to transport with more facility the great burdens they used in their structures, and a stone road of that kind led from Palmyra to Baalbec through the desert. The Romans had similar stone-tracks, for which they used granite, porphyry, and syenite; but still the blocks were frequently crushed by the immense loads transported over them, and on that account stone-tracks gradually fell into disuse.

About 300 years ago the first wooden railroads were built in Germany, in the mines of the Hartz mountains. The track consisted of two parallel beams or sleepers of timber, between which the wheels ran on planks. The roads affording great facility, Queen Elizabeth employed German miners to construct similar ones in England in iron and coal mines. It often occurred that the carriages were thrown off the track by stones and other impediments, in order to obviate which iron tires with exterior flanges were put on the wheels. The rapid wear of the wooden rails, which did not last over six years, caused in 1738 the employment of flat bars of cast iron, which were secured with spikes to the wooden rails. In 1770 the continuous wooden support was replaced by stones and the flat rails by prismatic ones (*edge rails*), and next came the Vignole or T-rails. In 1776 Carr proposed to support the rails on wooden cross-sills, and in 1797 Barnes employed blocks of stone in place of the latter. Since 1810 wrought iron has been used for rails instead of cast iron, and the rails may thus be made 15–18 feet long, and much lighter than before when they were but 3–4 feet long.

At first railroads were only introduced to facilitate the transportation of burdens by horse-power, one horse drawing as much on the railroad as eight on a common road. After the invention of the steam-engine, Dr. Robinson suggested in 1750 that it might be used as a motive power on railroads, but the idea was ridiculed as insane; it was however pursued by Watt in 1769, and by Evans in North America in 1786, but without any practical attempt. It was only in 1802, after the invention of the high pressure steam-engine, that the inventors Trevithic and Vivian undertook the construction of a locomotive steam-engine, and in 1804 they obtained a patent for one to move carriages on a railroad. The first engine drew on the Merthyr-Tidwyl road five carriages of iron-ore weighing eleven tons, a distance of nine miles in $1\frac{3}{4}$ hour. At the same time Oliver Evans constructed a locomotive in the United States, but it was not until 1824 that Stephenson built the first successful locomotive for the Stockton and Darlington railroad, by which at length passengers were transported in 1826. It still remained doubtful whether preference was not due to the employment of stationary steam-engines, until in 1829 Stephenson's locomotive "Rocket" was victorious in all trials. When in 1830 the Liverpool and Manchester railroad succeeded beyond expectation, and Stephenson's tubular boilers proved to be as safe as advantageous, the railroads at once rose to that high degree of importance which has ever since continued to increase. From that time no branch of industry has been so much the object of new inventions as railroads; the most ingenious men surpassed themselves in constantly adding new improvements to their engines. Self-acting inclined planes and stationary steam-engines were employed for overcoming steep grades, and new forces were sought in order to replace steam by a less expensive motive power, of which however atmospheric pressure was the only one practically attempted, in 1839, but has since been abandoned.

After England the United States were the first to introduce railroads with locomotive steam-engines. The first railroad in France was that from St. Etienne to Lyons, built in 1827; in Germany that from Nürnberg to Fürth, in 1835. Since then railroads have been constructed in all the European States, and in a few years a connected system of railways will be spread over all Europe.

After this brief historical review we will now proceed to treat of the construction of railroads and the motive power employed on them.

1. Location of a Railroad. The location or first determination of a railroad line is a matter of the greatest importance, as the success and value of the work are in a great measure dependent on a judicious selection of the line, and the highest qualities of talent and knowledge are required in the engineer who undertakes the task. The considerations that must mainly guide in the location are, the object of the road, the grades and curvatures, the physical conditions of the country, and the relative cost of the road in different locations.

The objects of railroads may be various. A main line which is intended to connect distant parts of a country and to serve as a basis for a system of branch roads which are to intersect the country in every direction, will be made to pass through the most important places only, pursuing its general direction without reference to minor towns. If a road in a sparsely populated country is intended to serve as a means of promoting its colonization, the physical conditions of the country will be the prevailing consideration, and the road will pass through those regions the agricultural or mineral products of which promise the greatest success. Again the object of a road may be to transport passengers and freight by the same power as rapidly as possible from one terminus of the road to the other; in this case the straight direction of the road would be a main condition, which, however, would have to yield if unfavorable grades occurred, or the direct line could only be obtained by a disproportionate expenditure.

An important point to be kept in view in the location of a road is the distribution of excavations and embankments, which should, if possible, be so arranged that the amount of earth to be moved in either case is nearly equal. Opportunities of using the earth from neighboring hills for embankments must also be regarded; the surplus of excavated earth must either be disposed of by augmenting the side slopes of the embankments or else a suitable place of deposit must be provided near the road. Of still greater importance are the grades of the road, and great changes of direction or even the abandonment of a particular route may be occasioned by the unfavorable nature of the country. It is generally received that from 8 to 9 lbs. per ton is the resistance of friction on a level road, so that 1 in 280 is about the inclination at which the action of gravity equals the resistance of friction.

Descending grades should be carefully avoided when the point to be reached is higher than the point of departure. When favorable gradients cannot be obtained, we must at least endeavor to cross valleys on their highest ridges and hills on their lowest depressions, or else, if a satisfactory line cannot thus be obtained, the obstacles must be overcome by stationary steam-engines or by tunnels. The admissible grades on a railroad will be determined by the probable amount of transportation and the power which may be available in each case. The gradients may either conform in general to the face of the country and undulate with the same, or else the elevation to be overcome may be concentrated in some few places, where in consequence the grades will be short and steep, requiring the employment of additional locomotives or of stationary engines, while for the remainder of the road much more favorable grades and partial levels will be obtained. A road laid out on the first system requires in general less capital, and less labor on the part of the engineer, while the second system calls for the exertion of the highest powers on the part of the latter, and frequently involves a much larger capital; but on the other hand the speed will be much more uniform and the wear and tear of locomotives will be less than on the undulating grades, the varying power on which is very injurious to the engines. To which of these systems the preference is due in any particular case must be determined by existing circumstances, the value of a railroad depending mainly on the amount of transportation of freight and passengers. Whether the road is mainly to be used for travel or for transportation of freight will materially influence the choice of location, as in the former case speed, in the latter power, are the chief considerations. In cases where the bulk of transportation is in one direction, as on roads carrying coal from the mines to market, ascending grades in that direction will, if possible, be avoided altogether.

Another essential point to be kept in view in the location of a railroad line are the curves arising from changes of direction. Independently of the increase in length of the road the curves exert a very injurious influence on the locomotives and cars. In turning a curve the flanges of the wheels will impinge against the rails, and the outside wheels must pass over a longer space than the inside wheels, and therefore are dragged a certain distance over the rail, which causes great friction and torsion in the axles. It has been attempted to diminish the dragging of the exterior wheels and the friction of the flanges by giving a conical form to the tire of the wheels and elevating the exterior rail in curves by a certain amount, by means of which the force of gravity will counteract the tangential velocity to some extent. Nevertheless the resistance of friction remains very prejudicial in practice, and its amount depends on the length of the radius of curvature, on the width of the track, on the length and weight of the train and its speed. It will become still more sensible if faults exist in the laying of the rails and in the construction of the cars.

2. Construction of a Railroad. In proceeding to the actual work of construction after having perfected the plans, the attention of the engineer must be directed to a great variety of points, all of which are essential to the ultimate success of the road. We will now follow the several steps of the construction of a railroad.

a. Grading. In railroads the principle that they should be dry and secure from inundation is of still greater importance than in common roads, as it is essential to the duration of the superstructure.

In order to give solidity to embankments the newly filled earth must always be spread equally over the road. Embankments of no great depth may be made solid by ramming and rolling, but if they are considerable, the filling should be done in layers and the material so spread as to produce a firm combination of the masses of earth. If the earth is to be moved but a short distance, wheelbarrows may be employed, but for distances of any considerable length two-wheeled carts are used, which are often made to run on temporary railroad tracks. Embankments should not be formed by filling from one side to the other, raising the whole at once (*side-forming*), but rather by embanking out from one end in the whole width of the bank, by which some solidity is given to the lower portion by the pressure of the superincumbent earth as well as that of the carts and workmen. When side-forming is resorted to it should be done as indicated in *pl.* 2, *fig.* 1 (that is to say, the filling should be commenced from the bottom for some distance along the embankment, by means of a guide-way, *b*, supported on trestles, *c c*, filling first the part *ad* of the slope, next *de*, and so on. The core of the profile is considerably solidified in this manner, but the method is expensive and slow). For very wide embankments (*fig.* 2), the two outside portions *bc* and *fg* may be completed first with the aid of temporary tracks, and the interior part *de* filled afterwards. All embankments are at first to be made higher than the required grade of the road by the probable amount of settling of the earth. Very high banks should be allowed at least a winter season to settle before the superstructure is laid, a precaution to be recommended for all embankments. The inclinations of the side slopes should always be less than that which the earth naturally assumes; it will generally be from 1 upon 1 to 1 upon 1½, and according to circumstances even 1 upon 2 and less.

The width of the roadway will depend on the number of tracks, but it is advisable always to grade for two tracks, even where only one is to be laid at first; because a subsequent widening of the embankments is always attended with a want of firmness, which is not counterbalanced by the advantage of transporting the material on the finished track. The distance between two tracks is made a little greater than the width or *gauge* of the track. From 4 to 5 feet are generally allowed from the end of the supports of the track to the beginning of the side slopes. In cuttings, at least 4 feet should be left between the longitudinal supports of the rails and the side-drains. To preserve the side slopes they should be sown in grass seed or sodded; low bushes may also be planted to advantage.

In order to keep the road dry, drains are made along the foot of embankments. In excavations, drains are necessary not only by the sides of the roadway, but also above the side slopes, in order to carry off the surface water. *Pl.* 2, *fig.* 3, gives an idea of such an arrangement when walled drains, *b d f e*, run along the road *i h i; k* is the ordinary ditch, *l* a second one on the hill side. In England gutters of earthenware or other drains, *g*, are sometimes used under the middle of the track to carry off the water from the superstructure.

Cross-drains or culverts are constructed in various ways, of which some examples are given in *figs.* 4, 5, 6, and 7. In wet or marshy soil drains must be made under the body of the road emptying into the side drains; an example of this is given in *fig.* 3.

In localities where land is very expensive, and stone can be obtained at moderate cost, the extent of the side slopes both in cutting and filling may be diminished by building *sustaining walls*, of which *figs.* 11 and 12 show examples. They may be built of dry masonry, and should have a batter of at least 1 upon 10.

The best materials for embankments are gravel, sand, and clay; clay, which mixes very readily with water, and earth containing vegetable substances, are least adapted to the purpose. In marshy localities it is often requisite to remove the upper stratum to the depth of several feet, and to fill in solid material, such as gravel. When this is not sufficient, and the subsoil will not sustain the weight of the road and trains, it is best to drive wooden piles on which the superstructure for the railroad is placed. *Fig.* 24 shows a road partially sustained by piles.

In regions where timber is abundant, the use of wooden trestles or truss-work in the place of embankments is sometimes resorted to. Structures of this kind are required to be very firm in order to withstand the racking caused by the passage of the trains. Embankments are generally filled in afterwards to take the place of the woodwork as it decays, and this system is found very suitable in cases where the funds for the construction of a road are not abundant, and it has to be built in part from its income. *Pl.* 2, *figs.* 13, 14, and 15, represent a structure of this kind; *fig.* 13 is a side view, *fig.* 14 a top view without the superstructure, and *fig.* 15 a cross section. The sleepers *a a* support the three uprights *b b b*, sustained by the side-braces *d d*, which form a kind of truss with the cross-tie *c c;* on the latter rest the timbers *e e* which support the track; *f f* are the stringers on which rest the longitudinal sleepers of the track or the rails; *g g* are side railings.

As railroads frequently cross common roads, regard must be had to these crossings in arranging the grades of the road. If the highway is to pass above the railroad, which consequently is in excavation, the depth of the cut, as well as in all cases the importance of the road, will determine the manner of bridging. The clear space between the bridge and the rails should in general not be less than 16 feet, in order to allow a free passage for the chimneys of the locomotives. When the cut is of a less depth, the required elevation must be attained by making an embankment on the highway on each side of the bridge, the grade of which must not be steeper than 1 in 15. A separate chapter will be devoted to the construction of bridges; but to illustrate road-crossings, we have given in *pl.* 2, *figs.* 16, 17, and 18, a viaduct of masonry; *fig.* 16 is a side view on the left, and a longitudinal section on the right; *fig.* 17 is a ground plan of an abutment, and *fig.* 18 a horizontal section below the roadway. *Fig.* 19 shows a perspective view of a viaduct of very similar construction.

When, on the other hand, the grade of a railroad is at a considerable elevation above a highway, the former must cross on a bridge, which, whether built of wood or stone, must have strong abutments and wing walls of stone to sustain the embankments on both sides. *Fig.* 20 shows a viaduct of this class; *fig.* 21 is the ground plan of an abutment, and *fig.* 22 a horizontal section below the roadway. In cases where the railroad crosses a valley on a viaduct, no especial construction will be required for a road-crossing, except perhaps a slight change in the direction of the highway, in order to make it pass through one of the bays of the viaduct. When the elevation of the railroad is not sufficient to allow the highway to pass under it, the latter is brought to the level of the former by means of embankments. Road-crossings on a level are prohibited by law in England. They are, however, very frequent in the United States and in Germany, and no accidents appear to have occurred at such crossings where proper care has been used. An elevated pavement of wood or stone must be laid at such crossings, even with the top of the rails, as shown in *figs.* 45, 46, and 47. The edges of the pavement next to the rails are covered with flat iron bars, *b b'*; they must not approach the rails on the inner side nearer than about two inches, in order to leave the spaces, *c* (*fig.* 47), for the flanges of the wheels. They are either even with the rails (*fig.* 46) or elevated above them as in *fig.* 47; the latter arrangement has the advantage that the wheels of the carriages crossing the railroad will not touch the rails, while on the other hand it has the disadvantage that dirt accumulates easily on the rails, causing great friction, and sometimes even throwing the cars off the track; constant attention, therefore, is required in such places.

Rivers and streams are crossed by railroads on bridges built either of stone, wood, or iron, and requiring various modifications of construction according to the length and angle of the crossings. The chapter on *bridge-*

building will give the details on this subject. Drains and small water-courses are crossed by means of *culverts*, which are also bridges on a small scale. An arched culvert is represented in *pl.* 2, *figs.* 8, 9, and 10, in front view and cross-sections. When the elevation of the track is not sufficient to admit of an arched stone culvert, iron plates may be employed; and when locomotives only are used, it is not necessary to cover the drain, longitudinal string-pieces being laid across the opening to support the rails.

When the line of a railroad is interrupted by rocks or hills where an excavation is impracticable, and the location of the road cannot be changed, it becomes necessary to pierce the obstacle by *tunnels*, which are driven according to the principles of mining, and which if very long require to be ventilated by shafts from above. *Fig.* 23 shows the mouth of a railroad tunnel in a mountainous region.

b. The Superstructure. The durability and safety of a railroad are altogether dependent on the quality of the rails, and on their being firmly fastened to solid supports imbedded below the roadway surface. These supports may either be of wood or stone, and may continue without interruption along the track, or support the rails only at certain intervals. The first railroads had continuous supports and flat bar rails, called *plate* or *tram rails;* but the difficulty of procuring the large quantities of timber required for that kind of superstructure, and its great cost, together with the extensive manufacture of iron in England, soon led to the adoption of rails of sufficient strength not to require a continuous support, but capable of bearing the load when sustained only at intervals by stone or wooden sills to which they were attached by iron *chairs*.

The stone used for supports should be of the densest and hardest kind; a block intended for the support of one chair should measure at least 2 feet each way, but generally the top face only need be dressed. Those blocks on which the ends of two rails meet should be still longer, as on them the load is not sustained by the rigidity of the rails. To fasten the chairs to the stone supports, holes are drilled by machinery into the blocks 6 inches deep and 1 or 1½ inches in diameter, to correspond exactly with the holes in the chairs. The blocks are generally not simply sunk into the roadway, but a bed of dry masonry 1 to 3 feet thick is carefully laid under each track, of the width of the supports. On this bed the blocks are accurately adjusted to the level of the road and firmly packed with gravel, after which the road is filled up with earth, gravel, or broken stone, to the level of the blocks, and well rammed. The top layer is made with a transverse convexity for the better drainage. *Pl.* 2, *fig.* 30, shows a ground plan of this arrangement, *fig.* 31 a section. The distance from centre to centre of the supports varies from 3 to 5 feet; it appears, however, unadvisable to exceed the measure of 3 feet 4 inches, by which a rail of 15 feet length has five supports. A distance of 3 feet is still preferable, but more expensive. In order to prevent the lateral displacement of the rails more effectually than could be done by a large number of supports for single chairs, large stone sills have been employed extending entirely across the track and receiving two chairs, as may be seen in *figs.* 30 and 31.

As all embankments settle more or less according to their depth, it becomes necessary to re-adjust the level of the stone blocks by packing gravel underneath, which, on account of their weight, is very expensive. In order to avoid this, wooden cross-sills are generally first used on embankments for the time of their duration, after which they are replaced by stone blocks, as the road will have become settled by that time. *Fig.* 29 shows one of these wooden sills. They have great advantages when placed sufficiently near each other. The best kinds of wood are used for the purpose, generally oak, which sometimes is *kyanized.* They should be twelve inches wide, from 4 to 6 in thickness, and 6 feet long, and are generally flattened on top, or else only notched to receive the rails. They are laid on beds of broken stone, and should not be more than 3 feet apart from centre to centre. Opinions differ as to the proper height of the filling between and outside of the tracks. Some keep it below the top of the sills in order to keep the rails clear of earth, and to air the wood, which they suppose assists its preservation; while others prefer to fill up as high as can be done without interfering with the flanges of the wheels; because wood, especially oak, is in fact better preserved by being entirely covered with earth than when partially exposed to the air; and because such filling protects the wood from being set on fire by coals dropping from the locomotives: and besides, in case of the locomotive or any carriage running off the track, the revolution of the wheels will be gradually stopped, diminishing very much the breakage and danger attendant upon such accidents.

The fastening of the chairs on stone supports is shown in *pl.* 2, *fig.* 33, which illustrates the method used on the London and Birmingham road. First holes are drilled of 1½ inches diameter, to correspond with those in the chair; on the bottom of the holes iron or wooden wedges, *e*, are placed with the edges upwards, and oaken pins, split at the lower end and tarred, are driven into the holes and cut off even with the chair. The iron spikes *d*, chisel-shaped at the lower end, and sometimes barbed, are then driven home, and confine the chair firmly to the support. The rail *a* is then placed into the chair and fastened to it by the wedge *c*. We must not omit to mention that the stone-blocks are frequently split by the successive driving of the pins and spikes, and afterwards by the swelling of the pins by moisture. Between the chair and stone-block must be placed a plate of wood, or else a piece of felt, ¼ inch thick, and soaked in oil, in order to break the rebounding which would otherwise be intolerable and ruinous to the cars.

The first rails were of cast-iron, and it was not until 1820 that at Birkingshaw, under the direction of J. Stephenson, wrought-iron rails were produced. Those of cast-iron had the double disadvantage of being necessarily very short, and so brittle as to break readily when not continuously supported. They can be used only on roads where the superstructure is made as is shown in *figs.* 25 and 26, where the rails, *d*, are supported by longitudinal sills, *b*, which rest on the cross-sills, *a*; or as in *figs.* 27 and 28, where the rail-stringers, *c c*, rest on stone-beds, *a*, which have supporting walls at the junctions of two rails. The use of cast-iron rails has been almost entirely abandoned since the advantages of wrought-iron rails have been fully recognised.

The requisites of a good rolled rail are the following: 1. It must be rolled at an equal temperature throughout, and be entirely free from flaws. 2. The profile must be precisely the same at both ends, in order to allow perfect fittings to be made. 3. The rail must be perfectly straight, and must have a suitable form. 4. It must offer sufficient surface to the driving wheels without at the same time producing too much friction; the surface is therefore generally slightly convex, in order to fit the conical tire in some measure. 5. That cheek of the rail which is exposed to the greatest pressure must be sufficiently strong not to break, and somewhat rounded, in order to correspond to the flange of the wheel.

For the system of interrupted supports (*pl.* 2, *fig.* 32), the form and weight of the rails depend on the weight of the locomotives to be employed, their required speed, and the distance between the supports, as no flexure should take place. Various forms of rails have been used; those most generally employed now have a broad base, an oval top, and are from 3 to 5 inches high. A weight of 16 or 17 pounds per foot is generally deemed sufficient; rails of much less weight have been employed on roads over which no very heavy trains are transported. The usual length of rails is 15 or 18 feet, and the ends meet at right angles, although an angle of 45° would be preferable, as diminishing the shock in passing from one rail to the next.

The fastening of the rail and chair has been effected in many different ways; at present it is simply done by fastening the rails to the sills by means of spikes, the heads of which lap over the base of the rail, and at the ends only iron plates with projections that hold down the rail are used. Some of the more complicated chairs are shown in *pl.* 2; *fig.* 33 is a cast iron chair of the London and Birmingham road, the manner of fastening which has been referred to above; *fig.* 34 shows Hartley's chair for the Manchester and Bolton Road, which is fastened with spikes, *c*, the dotted lines showing the fastening between the chairs; the rails here weigh 20 pounds per linear foot. *Fig.* 36 represents the chair and rail on the Northern road in Austria, where the rail *a* is held in the chair *b* by the heads of screw-bolts *c*. *Fig.* 37 is a cast-iron bridge-rail and chair of the Providence (R. I.) road. The shape of the spikes is shown in *fig.* 35. *Fig.* 42 shows Stevenson's attachment of chair and rail by which he intended to obviate the existing imperfections, but which was found too complicated and requiring too much accuracy in the execution for practical use, although well calculated to answer its purpose; *a* is the rail, *b* the chair, *c* the wedges, *d* the spikes, &c.

The method of fastening the rails in the chairs by means of wedges of wrought-iron has proved to be imperfect, the wedges being loosened by the vibration of the track caused by the passage of the trains. The wedges in *fig.* 33 are of oak-wood prepared with a solution of corrosive sublimate (*kyanized*) and compressed by hydraulic pressure; these also are found to become loosened, and require constant driving, besides having other disadvantages. Wedges of tempered cast-iron have been employed with the best success.

The foundation for a superstructure on the plan of *continuous support* for the rail is generally a uniform layer of broken stone, into which the sleepers are imbedded and firmly settled with beetles until no sensible sinking takes place. The cross-sills are rough hewn in order to remove the sap-wood, and their ends generally project 12–18 inches beyond the sleepers. The longitudinal sills are let into the cross-sills, and are either wedged or fastened by means of chairs. In the South it is best to use yellow pine for these, as that wood warps and cracks less from the effects of the heat than oak.

The arrangement of the timber is shown in *pl.* 2, *figs.* 25 and 26, with a rail as in *fig.* 39. The longitudinal sills or stringers will have a depth of from six to ten inches, according to the strength of the rail and the proposed burdens; the supports may be four feet apart, and the length of each stringer should not be less than twenty feet in order to avoid too frequent breaks, which in one track should always be opposite the middle of a stringer on the opposite track. In the same way the joints of the rails should never correspond with those of the stringers.

Superstructures of this kind being very expensive in countries where timber is scarce, they have not been introduced to a great extent in Europe; even in the United States the lower sleepers have frequently been dispensed with on that account, the cross-sills resting in beds of broken stone. In the place of wooden supports a stone superstructure has also been employed, consisting of two continuous parallel walls of stone, connected by cross-ties of stone, which may be replaced by wooden sills of one foot square, or else by iron rods and binders, where stones of sufficient length cannot be obtained. The direct attachment of the rails to stone being very injurious, as stated above, wood must be interposed between the rail and the support. Plank of two inches in thickness will suffice for rails of two inches depth, but heavier string-pieces will be required for rails of less size. Grooves of the width of the wooden stringers are cut into the stone of such a depth that the top of the rail is at least two inches above the rough-dressed stone surface, in order to allow room for the flanges of the wheels. The fastening of the rail may be done as in *pl.* 2, *fig.* 33; *figs.* 27 and 28 show a superstructure of this kind.

The rails used with continuous supports are of very different forms and sizes, varying from three pounds to eight and even thirteen pounds per linear foot. The ends are generally cut off at an angle of 45°, sometimes also in the form of a *mitre joint* (*fig.* 40), which is preferable. The rails are fastened to the supports by spikes or screws, the holes for which are one eighth of an inch longer than required, in order to allow for the effect of temperature upon the iron. Under the joints are placed plates of zinc or iron, to prevent the ends of the rails from being pressed into the wood. An excellent form for the flat rail is that shown in *fig.* 39, weighing nine pounds per linear foot, which was devised for the New Orleans and Nashville railroad. *Fig.* 41 shows the ordinary flat rail. Of many other different forms we only instance that proposed by Strickland, the *bridge* or U-*rail* (*fig.* 38), weighing 13½ pounds per linear foot, and a similar one by J. K. Brune (*figs.* 43 and 44), which has a more convex bearing surface than the preceding.

Pl. 3, *fig.* 28, is a plan of the superstructure of the Baltimore and Ohio Railroad; *fig.* 23 is a longitudinal section; *fig.* 27, a cross-section of the same. *Fig.* 26 shows the attachment of the rail to the sill by plates and screw-bolts; *fig.* 24 is a top view and *fig.* 25 a side view of the chair. The whole forms an excellent arrangement.

In laying the rails the effect of changes of temperature upon their length must be paid attention to. The difference in length at extremes of temperature is from $\frac{1}{8}$ to $\frac{3}{21}$ of an inch in a rail of 18 ft., and if the rails were laid close to each other at a low temperature the track would inevitably be torn up by an increase of heat. In order to avoid this, pieces of iron gauged to thicknesses corresponding to the existing temperature are interposed between the ends of the rails while they are being fastened to the supports.

The distance between the inner edges of two opposite rails is called the *gauge* of the track. On the first railroads in the coal-mines the gauge was from 3 ft. to 3 ft. 6 inches, but on the introduction of locomotives the gauge was increased, and Stephenson first introduced the gauge of 4 ft. 8½ inches on the Stockton and Darlington road. The success of his locomotives caused them to be employed everywhere, and thus the above gauge of 4 ft. 8½ inches came to be almost universally adopted. A wider gauge was subsequently considered by Stephenson himself preferable for the more powerful engines built since then; and Brunel proposed a gauge of 7 ft. for the Great Western Railway, which was adopted. In Russia and in Baden a gauge of 6 ft. was introduced, but in the latter state it was found necessary to lay extra tracks for the narrow gauge in order to accommodate trains from adjoining roads. The broad gauge is also used on the Atlantic and St. Lawrence Railroad in Maine.

The distance between the rails must be greater by about ¾ of an inch than that between the flanges of the wheels, so as to allow a play of ⅜ of an inch for each wheel, without which the friction would be too great. A larger play would prove destructive to the road and to the carriages, by allowing the latter to rock violently from side to side. The flanges (*pl.* 5, *fig.* 14 *c* and *fig.* 12 *a*) are on the inside of the wheels, and guard the carriages against sliding off the rails.

On railroads consisting of a single track provision is made for allowing two trains to pass each other by an arrangement called a *siding* or *turnout*, consisting of a portion of a track laid by the side of the main track, at a suitable distance from it, and connected with it at each extremity by a curved portion, which is so arranged by means of a movable part that the cars can either continue on the main track or enter the turnout, as circumstances may require. The curved portion must be composed of two arcs of circles, one tangent to the main track, the other tangent to the siding, and both tangent to each other midway, but convex in opposite directions. The movable portion by means of which the cars may be made at pleasure to take either track is called a *switch*. A simple arrangement for turning out to the right is shown in *pl.* 2, *fig.* 48, where *a a* are the rails of the main track, *b b* those of the turnout; the latter do not come close up to the former, but leave a space of 1½ or 2 inches in order to allow the flanges to pass when the train continues on the main track. Two rails of the main track are connected by the iron bars *c c*, and are attached as usual to chairs at the ends furthest distant from the turnout; each rests on a cast-iron plate provided with shoulders, *e e*, and is movable by means of a lever attached to the end of the bar *d*, its elasticity allowing it to be bent so as to be on a line with *b*, the shoulder *e* limiting the extent of the motion. When it is desired to turn out on either side of the main track, the switch is arranged as in *fig.* 51, where the rails *e h* turn out to the left and *g k* to the right.

Another kind of switch is shown in *fig.* 50; the movable rails and the tongue *s* turn on pivots, and are placed in the desired position by means of a lever attached to *m*. The construction of such a lever is seen in *pl.* 3, *fig.* 29; it is contained in a box, *ghkl*, which is partly imbedded in the earth. The lever *d* turns on the pivot *c* and moves the switch by means of the bar *b*, attached at *a*; it is also connected by the band *e* with a spring, which is compressed when the lever is brought from the position *p* into the position *q*, when the switch is aligned with the side-track. When the pressure on the lever is relinquished, the action of the spring will replace the switch in its position in the main track. The switch just described is used on the London and Greenwich Railroad. When the guide-rails do not move on pivots, but are only bent, they will of their own accord return to their former position as soon as the pressure on the bar is relinquished. Another switch for a turnout is shown in *pl.* 2, *fig.* 49, which is an excellent plan.

An arrangement similar to a siding, termed a *crossing*, is made on roads with double tracks to enable trains to pass from one track to the other. *Fig.* 52 represents a crossing connecting the two tracks CE and DF in every direction; *ab*, *cd*, *ef*, *gh*, are the rails of the tracks; *ik*, *lm*, *no*, *pq*, *rs*, *tu*, *vw*, *xy*, those of the crossing. $\alpha\beta$ and $\gamma\delta$ are two rails 6 ft. in length, forming part of the main tracks and held together by ties as the figure shows; they can be moved about a pivot in the centre so as to form the connexion between any set of corresponding rails, as may be desired. Cast-iron plates, called *crossing-plates* or *frogs* (*fig.* 54), are laid where the rails cross each other; *d*, *e*, *f*, *g*, are the ends of the rails; the piece *abc* of wrought-iron is riveted or screwed on the plate, and the cheeks *m* and *n* prevent the wheels from sliding off. It may be preferable to weld the rails together in the requisite form, as in *fig.* 53, and to lay the pieces *p* and *q* at the sides to keep the flanges in the proper direction. For unimportant crossings short tongues of wrought-iron, fastened on wood and brought into the required position with the foot, are generally sufficient.

Pl. 3, *fig.* 9, represents a switch with a counterpoise, *u*, which causes the switch to assume its position in the main-track whenever left to itself. The switch in use on the Magdeburg and Leipsic road is represented in *figs.* 10, 11, and 12. It is moved by a crank, *h*, *h* (*fig.* 12), or an eccentric in the box, *e*, and the position of the target, *n* (*fig.* 11), to the right or left always indicates the position of the switch, the two sides of the target being, moreover, painted of different colors.

When two tracks diverge at a considerable angle where there is no room for curves, as at the stations, horizontal disks of wood or iron, called *turn-tables*, which revolve about a centre, are employed to transfer cars from one track to the other. The turn-table is crossed by rails on which, when in line with one of the tracks, the carriage is drawn; the table is then revolved until the rails are in line with the other track, when the carriage can be moved on. Turn-tables are also used to reverse the position of the locomotive on the track.

The upper part of *pl.* 3, *fig.* 4, shows the top view, the lower part the substructure; *fig.* 5 a section of a turn-table of wrought and cast iron, which is in very general use. It revolves about the centre pin, A, on eight cast-iron rollers, B, B, ten inches in diameter, carried by the rods, *c*, *c*, which centre in a wrought-iron ring, D, that turns about the centre pin. The bearings of the rollers and of the centre pin are plainly seen in *fig.* 5. The whole is inclosed by a cast-iron ring, E, cast in four pieces. The disk consists of four arms, I, I, crossing it at right angles, and four others, K, K, which radiate from the centre; the spaces between the arms are filled with an iron grating. On the top of the table are two tracks crossing each other at right angles, and corresponding exactly with the track of the road in gauge and level. Turn-tables of this construction have generally not more than 16 feet diameter. A turn-table calculated to receive a locomotive and tender of 30 feet in length is represented in *pl.* 3, *fig.* 1, as seen from below; *fig.* 2 is a cross-section on the line A′, B′; *fig.* 3 a longitudinal section on A, B. It revolves in a circular well, and consists only of a zone just wide enough to receive the track, in order to be as light as possible; it is readily moved by two men when loaded with the engine and tender.

c. Stations. The arrangement and size of the buildings at railroad stations depend of course on the amount of travel and transportation at each station. Stations of importance have besides the hall for the arrival and departure of the cars, a ticket-office, a sitting-room for passengers, a restaurant, baggage-room, &c.; warehouses for goods, locomotive and car houses also belong to main stations, together with offices for the transaction of the business of the road. On *pl.* 3, *fig.* 30, is a view of the Leipsic station of the Saxon and Bavarian railroad.

At proper distances along a line of railroad are water-stations for the supply of the tender. The water is contained in an elevated reservoir from which it is carried to the tender by a pipe. *Fig.* 6 shows a water-pipe of improved construction; the pipe issues from the reservoir, and is closed by the stop-cock D; when this is opened the water rises in the column A to the valve H, which is closed by the weight *b*, and opened by means of the lever *d*, when the tender is brought under the supply-pipe F, which can be turned in all directions on the support B, E, having a water-tight joint at G. *Fig.* 6 *a* is a section on the line 3, 4; *fig.* 7 one on 1, 2, and *fig.* 8 one on 5, 6. Arrangements for warming the water in the reservoir in winter are necessary in cold climates.

3. Motive Power on Railways. The power by which loads are trans-

ported on railways is that of horses, steam, atmospheric pressure, or gravity. The employment of horses on railroads differs from that on ordinary roads only in their being able to draw much heavier loads. We therefore proceed at once to the consideration of the locomotive steam-engines and cars. The employment of atmospheric pressure or gravity requiring special modes of construction, we shall treat of them under separate heads.

a. Locomotives. The general features of a locomotive, aside from the tender which carries the supply of fuel and water, are the following: A tubular boiler is supported on a frame with four, six, or eight wheels wedged firmly on their axles, which turn in bearings. Below the boiler or on both sides of the frame are two cylinders, the piston-rods of which cause the axles of the driving-wheels to revolve either by means of cranks or by wrists on the outside of the wheels. The other wheels either revolve independently, in which case they are smaller than the drivers, or they are coupled with the latter by connecting rods, when they must be of exactly the same diameter.

Pl. 4, *fig.* 1, is a side view of a locomotive, *fig.* 2 a vertical section through one of the cylinders, *fig.* 3 a horizontal section in the plane of the sliding-valves, and *figs.* 4, 5, and 6, represent the apparatus for working the valves and reversing the motion in different positions of the eccentrics. A is the boiler, C the fire-box, F the smoke-box, and G the chimney. The boiler is cylindrical, and is made of sheet-iron of about $\frac{5}{16}$ of an inch in thickness, riveted steam-tight with $\frac{3}{8}$ inch rivets. It is covered by a casing of strips of inch plank, hooped together to diminish the radiation of heat.

The fire-box has double sides, the inner being of sheet copper; it descends about two feet below the bottom of the boiler. The grating is in the middle of the bottom part. It is seen by *fig.* 2 that the fire-box is surrounded by water in all parts but the door and the grating. The tubes or flues extend from the fire-box to the smoke-box, and are entirely surrounded by water; there are from sixty to one hundred and eighty flues in a boiler, and it is the large amount of heating surface gained by this arrangement that constitutes the superiority of the tubular boilers over all others in the production of steam. If any of the flues collapse, the water will enter the fire-box and put out the fire, but no explosion will ensue.

Below the smoke-box are the two steam-cylinders VV. About the fire-box is the steam-dome D, into which the steam rises before passing on to the cylinders, in order to deposit the particles of water which it carries with it. The steam then descends as the arrow shows through a funnel, and passing along the pipe S arrives at the cylinders, as shown by the second arrow. The enlarged portion of the steam-pipe is screwed into a corresponding opening at the back of the fire-box, which is covered by a plate provided with a packing-box, through which passes the spindle of the regulator or steam valve. By this valve the quantity of steam admitted into the cylinders is regulated, and it is constructed in various ways. In the engine before us it is what is called a disk valve, consisting of a circular plate, from which two segments are cut, working steam tight against a similar plate at the entrance of the main steam-pipe S; when the movable plate is turned by the crank so that its openings correspond with those in the stationary one, the way is opened for the steam from D to S; if the movable plate be turned a quadrant, then the openings are closed and the steam is shut off from S.

The main steam-pipe S passes through the forward end plate of the boiler, and is connected with two descending pipes which carry the steam to the steam-boxes U U, whence it is delivered by the slide-valves to the cylinders; the cast-iron steam-boxes are situated immediately over the cylinders, and are screwed fast at their ends to the boiler plates. The slide-valves also communicate with the exhaust-pipe F, which conducts the steam after it has operated upon the pistons into the chimney G, as indicated by the arrows (*pl.* 4, *fig.* 2). This almost unceasing stream of steam into the chimney creates a powerful draught, which in stationary engines is accomplished by the height of the chimney. Rods connected with the slide-valves, and passing through stuffing-boxes in the steam chambers, which are actuated in a manner hereafter explained, serve to bring the valves in a proper position to throw the steam alternately upon one side or other of the pistons. When the slide-valve is in the position seen in *pl.* 4, *fig.* 4, the steam is thrown upon the back of the piston, while the space in front of the piston is opened to the exhaust-pipe. When a contrary motion takes place in the slide-valves, then the space at the back of the piston is thrown open to the exhaust-pipe, and the steam rushes out from this side of the piston. The piston passes through a stuffing-box in the head of the steam-cylinder, to prevent leakage of the steam and the consequent loss of power. The end of the piston-rod is attached to a cross-head which runs upon ways, and is connected by a joint with a connecting-rod, which embraces at its other end the crank upon the shaft of the main driving-wheel, which thus receives its motion from the piston.

We come now to the apparatus which serves to regulate the motion of the slide-valves; in general this is accomplished by eccentrics, of which at least two are necessary in the locomotive, as there are two cylinders to be operated. These eccentrics are seen at *e*, in *figs.* 3, 4, and 5, and give motion to the connecting-rods *e f*, which operate the double-armed levers *l i*, connected with the rods *m*, which move the slide-valves. The eccentrics are so arranged that they admit the steam to the cylinder just before the piston reaches the end of its stroke; the steam thus operates as a cushion to receive the blow of the piston, and prevent the injury which would otherwise result to the machinery. This is called the *lead* of the engine. *Fig.* 6 shows an arrangement of double eccentrics, for the purpose of reversing the motion of the engine.

The wheels are an important part of the locomotive; they are constructed in a great variety of ways. In the machine before us two kinds of wheels are used. The middle or driving-wheels have no flange, and a diameter of 6 feet; the other two pair, the running-wheels, are 4 feet in diameter, and are furnished with flanges, which serve to retain the locomotive upon the rails. The rim of the wheels consists of two concentric hoops. The interior, to which the spokes are secured, is of cast-iron; the exterior is of wrought-iron shrunk on while hot. The wheels are all secured fast to their axles, which project out beyond the wheels, and run in composition-boxes which have their seats upon the cheeks or pendent arms, seen in *fig.* 1, formed of strong plate iron, with which the wooden frame of the locomotive is covered. Upon the top of each of the journal-boxes rests the end of a vertical rod, the other end of which is connected with the spring, which for the driving-wheels is placed above the main frame of the engine, and for the running-wheels below; the springs are all secured to the main frame, and each bears its share of the weight of the locomotive.

The boiler is secured to the main frame by six iron knees. P is the man-hole, to enable the inside of the boiler to be cleansed. O is the safety-valve, and upon the steam-dome there is another, immediately under the control of the engineer, while the other is beyond his reach. The valve at the back of the engine is connected with a lever secured to a spring balance, which serves to show at any moment the pressure of the steam within the boiler. Upon the top of the boiler, near to the position of the engineer, is the steam-whistle, for the purpose of giving signals; this consists of two hollow metallic half globes or balls, the upper one of which has a sharp edge, and is placed immediately over the lower one. Within the lower half globe is another slightly smaller, so arranged that between the two there is a narrow opening or slit all round the edge.

Steam is admitted from the boiler between the two cups of the lower half globe, and rushes out of the opening between them against the sharp edge of the upper cup, and the well known whistle is produced.

Upon the end of the boiler, near the fire-door, is a glass indicator for showing the height of the water in the boiler.

To soften the concussions of the cars with each other, and with the engine while in motion, and also as a measure of safety in case of accidents, both the locomotive and the passenger cars are furnished with *buffers*, *a* (*pl.* 5, *fig.* 19). These are cushions stuffed with horse-hair or other elastic substance, either alone or in conjunction with steel springs. They are seen at the extreme forward end of the locomotive carriage in *pl.* 4, *fig.* 1.

The locomotive is always accompanied by its tender, which carries a supply of fuel and water; it is seen in *pl.* 5; *fig.* 9 is a side view, *fig.* 10 a longitudinal section, *fig.* 11 shows one half of the upper portion of the tender in plan. Upon the frame P, running upon four or six wheels B, rests a horse-shoe formed body, which serves to contain the water for the supply of the locomotive. This water receptacle is made of sheet-iron, and is entirely covered in upon top, where there are three holes closed by valves or covers; the centre one Q receives the water, and the others communicate with spaces separated from the water-chamber, and which are used to carry tools and other articles which may be required during the journey. The vacant space left by the peculiar form of the water-box serves to carry the fuel. The water is fed to the locomotive through the tube A′, having flexible joints to enable it to accommodate itself, without breaking, to the motion of the locomotive and tender. The tender is connected with the locomotive by chains and hooks seen hanging from the buffer in *fig.* 9.

A cock in the supply-pipe K (*pl.* 4, *fig.* 3), within reach of the engineer, serves to regulate the supply of water to the engine; and there is also a cock upon the tender to shut off the water entirely. The supply-pipe terminates in a chamber K (*fig.* 2), from which the water is taken by a pump which forces it into the boiler.

Pl. 5, *fig.* 1, is a longitudinal section of Stephenson's locomotive with variable expansion; *fig.* 2, front view of the same, the end plate of the engine being removed; *fig.* 3 *a*, is a horizontal section of the cylinders; *fig.* 4, a vertical section of the same; *fig.* 5 is a view of the pump; *fig.* 6, section of the end of the exhaust-pipe; *fig.* 7 *a*, section through one of the slide-valves; *fig.* 7 *b*, a plan of the same; *fig.* 3 *b*, view of the piston with metal packing, seen in section in *fig.* 3 *c;* and finally, *fig.* 8 illustrates the position of the different parts of the valve-gearing during the operation of the machine. As we have already explained the construction of a locomotive, it will be sufficient to enumerate those parts which differ essentially from the one already described. A is the main frame of the machine. The springs C rest upon the rods D, as already explained, the whole weight of the locomotive being carried by the rods E; l^3 is the dome, which is furnished, instead of a cock, with a slide-valve n', the rod L of which passes through a stuffing-box in the steam-dome, and thence to the position of the engineer, where it is managed by the levers *I I'*. Upon the pipe which carries the steam from the boiler is a safety-valve, beyond the reach of the engineer, kept down by a spiral spring, as seen in *fig.* 1. G is the lower end of the chimney, O' is the man-hole, H are the steam cylinders. The cylinders F F have their valves upon the inside, close to each other; this is rendered necessary, as we shall presently see, by the expansion arrangement. The exhaust-valves of both cylinders open into a common chamber T (*fig.* 4), whence the steam passes by the two side pipes to the exhaust-pipe K, which by means of a double-angled lever may be more or less closed by the engineer as required. The steam may also be thrown into a chamber U, whence it is blown out beneath the locomotive through a slide valve Q (*figs.* 4–7 *a* and 7 *b*), also manageable by the engineer without leaving his station. The pistons *j j* (*fig.* 3 *a*) are furnished with spring metal packing, as seen in *figs.* 3 *b* and 3 *c*. The piston-rods O are connected with the cranks upon the driving-wheel shafts. The steam-pipe K carries the steam from the steam-dome to the valve-chest and cylinders, as in the former case, the valves receiving their motion from the shaft of the driving wheels, which have already been set in motion by the pistons. The *variable expansion* was effected by Stephenson by what is technically called *link motion*. For each valve there are two eccentrics by the side of each other, and so placed upon the main driving-shaft that one of them will drive the valve-rod forwards and the other backwards. The forward ends of these connecting-rods are united by a link, which has a slat in the middle, in which plays a pin connected with the end of the valve-rod. By this simple and effective arrangement the forward or backward motion is effected, without the necessity of uncoupling the eccentrics; all that is necessary being to change the lever I′ from one extreme of the arc in which it moves to the other, which, through the levers *k′ h′*, so change the position of the slotted link that it either lies at its top or bottom, and receives motion from either one or other of the eccentrics. If the lever I′ is in a vertical position, then neither of the eccentrics will predominate, the slide-valve will remain stationary, and no steam will be admitted to the cylinders. The working by expansion is effected in the following manner. In the vertical position of the lever I′, although the driving-shaft may continue to revolve, no steam is admitted to the cylinder; when, however, this lever is at either extreme of its motion, the valve-rod makes its full stroke, the valve opening its entire passage to the cylinder; consequently the nearer the lever I′ is to its vertical position, the shorter will be the stroke of the valve-rod, and the sooner the steam will be cut off and permitted to act by expansion. Thus the engineer has it within his power, by operating the lever I′, to work his engine with any degree of expansion, forwards or backwards. The feed pump is at P, *fig.* 1, and in detail *fig.* 5; *fig.* 2 shows the arrangement of the tubes in the boiler.

Of the numerous improvements which have been made in locomotives, we will mention only one, which has caused quite a revolution in their construction. William Norris, of Philadelphia, ran the connecting rods to crank-pins in one of the arms of the driving-wheels, in place of attaching them to cranks upon the axles. The advantages of this modification are very great, and most of the European locomotives are now built upon this plan. In the Norris locomotive the cylinders, with their valve chests, lie outside of the main frame upon both sides of the boiler. By the whole arrangement a double advantage is gained. Where the crank was upon the driving-axle it described a circle equal to the half stroke of the piston, added to the thickness of the crank-wrist; consequently the stroke could not be lengthened without raising the boiler. This is not now necessary, and the diameter of the boiler may be increased, and consequently the number of the flues and the extent of heating surface, as well as the length of stroke of the pistons. The axles being now perfectly straight, are stronger and more durable with the same weight of iron. The working parts are more exposed to view, more easily controlled, and in case of injury or accident, are more easily repaired.

b. Passenger Cars. Railroad cars require an entirely different construction from ordinary carriages to enable them to run with the necessary velocity and safety. We shall notice first the wheels and axles, then the trucks, brakes, and couplings. The wheels and axles are of primary importance both as regards the safety of passengers and the durability of the cars. Constant efforts have been made to obtain a cast-iron car-wheel without flaws, and of sufficient strength to withstand the shocks to which it is exposed; but it would seem that this has never yet been accomplished, although the desired end has doubtless been approached. It is necessary in the first place that the rim or tread of the wheel be very hard, otherwise it would soon wear uneven from constant contact with the rails, and become useless; on the contrary, it is necessary that the other parts of the wheels, the naves, spokes, &c., should be annealed, to avoid the constant breakage which would otherwise result. It has been attempted to accomplish these two ends by casting the tire or tread of the wheel in contact with a ring of iron, which *chills* and very much hardens this part of the wheel, while the spokes and nave were cast in sand and permitted to cool gradually, the ring or band of iron called the *chill* being laid into the mould of sand, so that the whole wheel was cast together. The unequal contraction of the iron, however, in the rim and spokes in wheels cast in this manner has thus far prevented the attainment of a perfectly safe cast-iron wheel. Cast-iron wheels have been hooped with a tire of wrought-iron, shrunk on while hot, or secured with screws or bolts. The wheels have also been made entirely of wrought-iron, by uniting the separate portions of the wheel by welding or otherwise; sometimes the tire has been made of steel, at others the body of the wheel has been made of wood suitably combined with iron; indeed countless combinations of wood, steel, wrought and cast iron have been tried in the effort to obtain a cheap, durable, and safe wheel. *Pl.* 5, *fig.* 13, is a portion of a wrought-iron wheel and axle; *b c* is the axle, *a* a spoke welded to the nave, which is made in one piece with the axle. These wheels are safe but expensive, and are much used upon passenger cars in England. In America cast-iron is very generally used; it is more durable upon the tread, but more liable to break than wrought-iron. *Fig.* 14 is a section through a wheel in which wooden spokes *b* are introduced between the rim *c* and nave *a*, a plan not now much used. The diameter of car-wheels is usually three feet, with a thickness upon the tread of three or four inches.

Railroad axles are of wrought-iron, and require to be carefully proved before being put in use, as a small flaw may cause a breakage, and consequently loss of life and property.

The bearings or gudgeons are turned cylindrical and run in composition boxes, which must be capable of carrying a supply of oil for lubricating the bearing parts and preventing undue friction. When this has not been attended to with care, the heat has become so excessive as to melt the brass bearings above the journals.

Pl. 5, *fig.* 15, represents a journal-box of approved construction in longitudinal section. Here the oil is placed in a vessel in the top of the box, and is permitted to drop slowly upon the axles through the hole *h* in the bearing, from the end of a wick, the other end of which is in the oil-box above. The oil that drips from the journal is drawn off from the bottom of the box and may be used a second time. *Pl.* 5, *fig.* 16, shows a method of keeping the journal always lubricated without the use of the wick and without waste of oil; the ring *g* is turned upon the journal and descends into the box below the level of the surface of the oil, which is poured in at the opening *i*.

The bodies of the cars are variously constructed according to the use to which they are to be put, whether they be for the transportation of passengers, freight, or animals. The passenger-cars are differently constructed upon almost every railroad. In Europe there are three or four classes of cars, and the most convenient arrangement is there thought to be a division of the car into three or more separate apartments, holding eight to ten persons each, as seen in *pl.* 5, *figs.* 24 and 25. In the United States, however, most of the cars at the present time have but one apartment, the seats being arranged transversely two upon each side of a centre passage. In Europe the first-class cars are fitted up with great elegance. *Fig.* 29 shows the interior of the Duke of Brunswick's car upon the Brunswick railroad, and *fig.* 30 Queen Victoria's car upon the London and Dover railroad.

For the transport of merchandise which must be protected from the weather long tight cars closed on every side are used, as seen in *figs.* 27 and 28. For the transport of sand and other materials not injured by the weather, cars are used with low sides and without roof; *figs.* 22 and 23 show a car for the transport of wood. For the transport of animals cars formed of slats or grating are used; they are also furnished with rings to which to secure the animals.

The car *trucks* are of the same size in all passenger cars. The height of the wheels is always 3 ft., and the carriage frame rests upon springs which are secured to the journal-boxes, as shown in *pl.* 5, *figs.* 22-24 and 27. A species of spring much preferred at the present time is seen in *fig.* 18; this spring gives a particularly easy motion to the cars. The spring *b* consists of a single piece of steel and is secured to the main frame *f* at *g* by means of a link-joint, and to the axle-box at *c; dd* are chains which unite the ends of the springs and secure them to the axle-box. At first it was presumed that these springs would be easily broken, and to guard against this, the additional springs, *e*, were applied.

Pl. 5, *fig.* 26, shows a portion of the frame of a passenger car as sometimes constructed; it consists of the timbers, *ff* and *g*, strengthened longitudinally by the centre beam *dd*, and also by the diagonal braces *e;* the steps *i i*, for the accommodation of passengers, are secured to the frame. To neutralize the effect of the concussions of one car against the other while in motion the so-called *buffers* are applied to each end of the carriage frame; these are leather cushions upon the ends of rods, *b*, which rods are attached to springs, *a*, beneath the body of the carriage. The buffers receive the shocks and prevent them from annoying the passengers. In freight wagons the springs are dispensed with, and only the leather cushions are used. In eight-wheel cars it is necessary that the wheels be permitted to accommodate themselves to the curves of the track, to a degree which would be impossible were the axles secured rigidly to the car-frame. Without some provision of this kind great friction and a speedy destruction of the rails and wheels would result. To effect this flexibility the wheels are secured in small frames called *trucks*, upon the centre of which the main car-frame is permitted to pivot, as seen in *pl.* 5, *fig.* 27; *figs.* 17 *a* and 17 *b* show an arrangement for accomplishing this purpose, contrived by Ross Winans, an American engineer, at the time of the introduction of eight-wheeled cars; *fig.* 17 *a* is a bolster secured beneath the main frame of the car with the king-bolt *d* projecting downwards, and into a cavity in a corresponding bolster (*fig.* 17 *b*), which is secured to the centre of the wheel-truck. This arrangement permits the wheels to accommodate themselves to the curves of the track, without reference to the main body of the carriage.

In order to arrest the cars when it is necessary to stop, or to check their progress in descending inclinations upon the road, *brakes* become necessary; they consist of blocks of wood which are pressed against the rim of the wheels by an arrangement of levers, or in any other manner, and thus produce sufficient friction to arrest or at least to retard the motion of the cars. The simplest form of brake is seen in *pl.* 5, *fig.* 22; the lever, *b*, is so connected with the brake block, *c*, that when the lever is depressed the block is pressed against the wheel, but when the lever is raised to the position indicated by the dotted lines the block is removed from contact with the wheel, which is left free to revolve.

A brake of different construction is seen in *fig.* 9, in which motion is communicated to the break blocks *ff* by the lever G, through the joints *cd*, the one being pressed forwards and the other backwards. In this manner by a slight modification all the brakes of a six or eight-wheeled car may be applied at once; in *fig.* 27 is seen a brake of this description. *Fig.* 19 shows a brake of different construction; *kk* are the brake blocks, secured to the rack bars *ii*, which engage with a cog-wheel upon the upright axle *h*; upon this axle there is a bevel wheel, which gears with a similar bevel wheel upon the shaft *f*, which is in a similar manner connected with the crank *e* above, and thus upon turning the crank the brakes are applied to the wheels, the one forwards and the other backwards. In this same figure is seen a peculiar method of applying springs to buffers. The buffer-rod *a* is attached to the bent lever *b*, one arm of which is connected with the spring *d*, through the rod *c*. When two cars strike together, the rod *a* is forced in, and by means of the bent lever and connecting-rod the force of the blow is transmitted to the spring *d*, which thus neutralizes the shock and returns the buffer to its place when the pressure is removed.

In order to connect several cars into one train, coupling bars or chains become necessary; sometimes these are attached immediately to the car frames, at others to springs upon the frame as in *pl.* 5, *fig.* 26; the coupling-chain is hooked into the hole *h* upon the end of the bar *d*, which is attached to the small pair of semi-elliptical springs which afford a certain degree of elasticity to the connexions, and prevent the disagreeable jars which are experienced in starting and stopping where the couplings are rigid. Sometimes the chain couplings are drawn together by means of screws until the buffers touch, in order in passenger cars to diminish the unpleasant jolting of the cars against each other; at the short turns in the road this arrangement, however, has a tendency in conjunction with the centrifugal force to throw the cars off the track, or at least by increasing the friction to injure the roads, cars, and locomotives. A plan of this coupling is given in *pl.* 5, *fig.* 20, and a side view in *fig.* 21; *aa* are the coupling-chains attached to the end hooks of the car at *d*; the buffers *b* are brought in contact and the arm *t*, attached to a right and left screw, is turned until the semi-elliptic springs (*fig.* 26) are slightly strained, and the lever is suffered to fall into a vertical position, the weight *w* upon its end keeping it from rising.

4. Inclined Planes. Where a considerable rise is to be overcome in a railroad route, it is often preferable to concentrate the ascent at the termination of the route, instead of equalizing it through the whole length of the road. Various methods have been adopted for overcoming these steep ascents, and we will describe some of the most usual of them.

a. Self-acting Roads. Where loaded cars descend an inclined plane they are often made to bring up the empty cars; such roads are called by the English self-acting roads. The motion is communicated by means of a rope or chain to which the cars are attached. This rope or chain runs in the middle of the road upon rollers (*pl.* 4, *fig.* 14, G), and upon the upper end it passes over a drum or wheel (*fig.* 13) which lies beneath the surface at the top of the ascent. This wheel is from 6 to 16 feet in diameter, and revolves in a masonry chamber, over which are strong timbers which serve to carry the rails. Usually there are two roads side by side upon the ascent; when therefore the loaded cars are upon the left track at the top, the empty cars are upon the right track at the bottom, and as soon as the full cars are permitted to descend, they draw the empty ones up upon the other track. If the descent is so steep that danger is to be apprehended from the accelerated motion of the descending cars, a brake is applied to the large drum at the top, by means of which the motion is moderated and controlled. The rollers upon which the rope runs are formed in a variety of ways: *pl.* 3, *fig.* 19, is a plan of a roller used upon the Düsseldorf and Elberfeld inclined plane; *fig.* 17 a side view of the roller and the box in which it runs; *fig.* 18 is a longitudinal section upon A B of *fig.* 19; *fig.* 20, cross-section on C D, *fig.* 19. The case, *a*, is secured to the timbers, *e*, *e*, and contains the bearings, *c*, of the roller *b*, which is of cast-iron, the axle being of wrought-iron, and of a size according with that of the rope which it has to carry. The size and quality of the ropes upon an inclined plane are of the first importance. Wire ropes are at the present time almost exclusively made use of, and as these may sometimes break, it is necessary to have the means at hand instantly to stop the descent of the cars; this is accomplished by brakes. To the ascending cars, however, a self-acting arrangement is applied in the following manner: behind the last car hang one or more bars, 6 to 7 feet long, and 3 inches square, suspended to the car at one end, and shot with iron at the other. These bars trail after the car; and in case the latter attempts to descend, the point of the bar enters the ground and holds the car stationary.

b. Inclined Planes with Stationary Engines. It is almost exclusively in mines that a counter-weight can be depended upon to modify the motion of the descending cars; in other cases, where a loaded train of cars is to be raised or lowered, some other power must be resorted to, and this is usually steam. A short distance from the top of the plane is a drum, *o* (*pl.* 3, *fig.* 16), lying horizontally with its axis perpendicular to the direction of the rails; attached to this drum is a cog-wheel which engages with a pinion, upon the shaft of which is a fly-wheel and clutch; the shaft is driven by a steam-engine. The drum turns upon a cylindrical axis, from one end to the other of which it may be moved by a lever; it has also a brake attached to it, by which its motion may be controlled.

If the inclined plane has only a single track, as seen in *pl.* 4, *fig.* 7, turnouts must be arranged at the top, the middle, and foot of the plane, that the ascending and descending cars may cross each other. When loaded cars are to ascend the plane the end of the rope is attached to them, the drum is turned, and as the rope is wound upon it the cars ascend.

When cars are to descend the plane, whether they be loaded or empty, they are in like manner attached to the rope and suffered to descend, the drum being uncoupled from the engine and the motion regulated by the brake.

When the inclined plane has a double track, as is necessary upon roads where there is a great deal of travel, two drums are required, the one for the ascending trains, the other for those descending. The arrangement of the tracks is the same as for self-acting planes.

Where the plane has so little inclination that the descending cars cannot move the heavy cable, it becomes necessary to attach a second rope to the foremost of the descending cars, while the other end, after passing over a roller at the foot of the ramp, is secured to the last of the ascending cars, and thus the engine carries the ascending cars up, and the descending ones down.

A similar plan is adopted upon the inclined plane in the great Liverpool tunnel, to move the cars in each direction (*fig.* 12). An endless cable passes first around the vertical drum, A, which has two grooves upon its surface, thence diagonally to a smaller drum, *a*, then half round the pulley, *c*, past the pulley, *a*, again, and diagonally across to the lower groove in the pulley A, thence along the centre of one of the tracks, over the large wheel, B, and along the centre of the other track again.

The cable, by the hygrometric changes of the atmosphere, is liable to contraction and expansion, to compensate for which, and to keep it constantly tightened, the roller, *c*, is placed upon a carriage running on rails, which is drawn back by a heavy weight, the suspending cord of which passes over the pulley, *d*, and thus the cable is kept uniformly tight through all weathers, moist and dry.

A steam-engine at the top of the ramp gives motion to the drum A, and the cable receives a constant motion up one track and down the other. The cars are attached to the cables by smaller ropes.

In a similar manner a line of horizontal road may be worked with stationary engines.

The road is divided into distances of 500 to 600 rods, and at the termination of each stretch there are a double track and a stationary engine. The drums at the stations A B C (*fig.* 11) are run alternately first in one direction, then in the other. D and E are the trains drawn in the direction of their arrows by the cables *h* and *k*, upon the drums *o* and *q*, and dragging after them the cables *i* and *g* from the drums *m* and *n*, which are uncoupled from their respective engines A and B.

Instead of running the two drums of each machine one after the other, they may be run at the same time, but then a double track with crossings becomes necessary, as seen in *fig.* 10.

Pl. 3, *fig.* 13, shows the engine-house of the Düsseldorf and Elberfeld inclined plane, *fig.* 14 a plan of the same, *fig.* 16 a view from above of the main drum and parts connected therewith, and *fig.* 15 a cross-section on the line, C′ D′, of *fig.* 16. Here the drums do not lie in the prolongation of the plane, as in *pl.* 4, *figs.* 9 and 10, but perpendicular to the same; *o*, is the main drum, driven by the steam-engine; from this drum the cable runs over the two inclined intermediate wheels, *p* and *q*, and thence over the rollers, *c r* (*fig.* 15), to the railroad track. *Figs.* 17, 18, and 19, are the cable-rollers, as already more particularly described. In *fig.* 14 are seen upon the left the two steam-engines which operate upon the crank-axle, *k*, upon the other end of which is the fly-wheel, *n*, and the main drum, *o*. *b c d e*, are water and steam-pipes to and from the boiler-room and the well, *a*.

5. Suspended Railroads. These were first suggested in England by Palmer, but have never been introduced to any extent. A road of this kind was used at the building of the military works at Posen, and as its construction is peculiar, we will give a short description of it. *Fig.* 21 is a side-view of the car and road; *fig.* 22 an end view of the car, with a section of the rail. At *y* in *fig.* 21 is seen the end of a second car attached to the first. The road consisted of a continuous wooden sleeper or beam, B, having an iron rail, C, upon its top, and supported upon posts, A. The cars were balanced upon each side of the road, and were supported upon the top rail, C, by a grooved roller, H. To the sides of the posts, A, were secured bars, G, having each an iron rail, J, in its centre, against which the body of the cars rests either with or without friction-rollers. Where horses are the moving power, they are to travel one upon each side of the road.

6. Atmospheric Railroads. The many accidents which occurred when railroads were first introduced, and the great expense of running locomotives, made it very desirable that the latter should be dispensed with, and that a cheaper and safer motive power should be found to take their place. Compressed air was thought of, and experiments were made to render this available, but without success. Rarefied air was then thought of; and Vallance, an Englishman, suggested a large hollow cylinder of sufficient capacity to contain the whole train of cars within its interior; in advance of the train, and attached thereto, there was to be a piston sufficiently large to fill the cylinder, from one side of which the air was to be exhausted, and the pressure of the air upon the other was to drive it along, together with the train attached to it. The proposition carried upon its face entire impracticability, and was never acted upon.

The same idea was however afterwards carried out with considerable modification, and an experimental tube was laid near London, 1200 feet long and 9 inches in diameter; a 16-horse steam-engine was used to pump out the air from the tube. The result of this experiment being entirely satisfactory, the system was put into practical operation in Ireland upon a branch of the Dublin and Kingstown Railroad. This branch, with the Croydon and South Devon Railroads in England, and a few minor trials in France, are the holy ones ever constructed npon this plan. The branch of the Dublin road to Dalkey was full of curves and inclinations which rendered the use of a locomotive perfectly impracticable; it was opened in December, 1843, and still continues in operation.

In *pl.* 6, we have represented the Kingstown and Dalkey railroad, and shall explain its construction sufficiently in detail to manifest the principle upon which it acts. In the centre of the track is laid a hollow cast-iron cylinder, which is secured to the sleeper by bolts and screws (*figs.* 2 and 4). The joints of the cylinder, where the separate pieces come together, are made air-tight, and are firmly secured by screws. Within the cylinder, which is 15 inches in diameter, moves a solid piston B (*figs.* 3 and 4), with an exceedingly elastic packing, that it may adapt itself as nearly as possible to the small inequalities of the interior of the cylinder. The piston is provided with an advancing head, which serves to open the valves, and has attached to it a piston-rod 18 feet long, the central portion of which is a plate, C, balanced by the weight, W, so that the piston always lies horizontal.

The plate C has four rollers, E (*figs.* 3 and 4), the object of which we shall learn hereafter. The driving-piston is connected to the carriage above by the plate D (*figs.* 3, 4, 5, and 6), which, however, must pass through the cylinder, which has a slit running its whole length for the purpose. This it is necessary should be closed air-tight in advance of the piston, and open only at the moment of the passage of the plate D, that the pressure of the air may operate upon the back of the piston. *Fig.* 8 shows the arrangement adopted for this purpose. A is the cylinder, K L the valve, which consists of a strip of stout sole leather covered with a thin plate of steel, surmounted by a cast-iron plate, K, which prevents the valve from being forced into the opening by the pressure of the atmosphere; beneath the valve there is also an iron plate, not shaded in *fig.* 8, but seen in *fig.* 6, which entirely closes the opening in the tube; this latter plate is curved upon the same radius as the cylinder, that the piston may fit air-tight all round. At *l* the leather valve is held firmly, and at L is a trough into which a composition of wax and tallow is poured, which assists to pack the valve air-tight. In order to protect this apparatus from the weather, plates of sheet-iron, H, 5 feet long and hinged at *h*, are made to hang over the whole. To understand the operation of this apparatus, we must turn to *figs.* 3, 5, and 6. The roller, E, upon the piston, projects into the longitudinal slit, and raises the valve, K, breaking the wax cement which holds it to the cylinder; at the same time the roller, M, upon the bottom of the driving-car (*figs.* 5 and 6) comes under the plates, H, and raises them, so that the atmosphere is free to press upon the after-surface of the piston, which is thus driven along the cylinder, and with it the driving car, the two being connected together by the plate, D, as seen in *figs.* 1 and 5. That the valve may be returned to its place after the passage of the plate, D, the driving-car carries a roller, F, (*figs.* 3 and 7), which runs upon the surface of the plate, K, and presses the leather, L, again down upon the valve-seat. At the same time, immediately over the trough, L, there passes a tube, G, heated by a small furnace upon the driving-car, which melts the mixture of wax and tallow, and again packs the valve air-tight. This heating arrangement was subsequently found to be ineffectual and unnecessary, and has since been discarded.

It was doubted at first whether the trains, once started, could be stopped, but it was found that they were perfectly manageable with powerful brakes. In order that the conductor may be informed of the extent of the rarefaction in front of the piston a tube passes through it up into the piston-car, near his seat, where it communicates with a barometer, and he is thus informed of the amount of atmospheric pressure which he at any moment has on; he has also the means within his reach of regulating the speed of the train, and when it becomes too high of admitting air through another tube, which also passes through the piston and comes up near his seat, where it is furnished with a cock; by the admission of air through this tube the speed is soon checked, but the air-pump continuing uninterruptedly at work the vacuum is soon re-established.

The whole length of the line is 3050 yards or nearly 1¾ miles, with a rise of 71½ ft. from the commencement at Kingstown to the termination at Dalkey, the average rise being 1 in 140, but the last 365 yards have a rise of 1 in 57. The line is worked only one way by the atmospheric apparatus, the return being effected by the force of gravity.

As stated above the length of the line is 3050 yards, but the atmospheric main is only 2400 yards long, the remainder of the way, 650 yards, being run by the momentum previously acquired. The diameter of the main is 15 inches, and near its extremity branches out a pipe, C (*pl.* 6, *fig.* 2), which leads to the exhausting apparatus, distant 500 yds. The air-pump, which is double acting, is 66½ inches in diameter, with a stroke of 66 inches. It is worked by a high pressure condensing engine with 34½ inch piston and 66 inches stoke, working expansively, the cut-off valve being regulated by a governor, so as to vary the speed of the engine from ⅓ at the lowest to ⅕ at the quickest.

At the entrance end, and some thirty feet from it, is a kind of balance-valve, B (*fig.* 2), very ingeniously contrived to open by the compressed air in front of the piston; and at the other or exit end is another valve, opening outwards by means of the compression of the rarefied air, after the piston has passed the tube leading from the main to the air-pump.

2. Bridge-Building.

Bridge-building may, strictly speaking, be considered a branch of road-building, for a bridge is merely a road over a river or a ravine; still it appears to be of sufficient importance to merit a chapter by itself.

The oldest bridge of which we have any information is that over the Euphrates at Babylon, and described by Diodorus, Herodotus, and Philostratus. According to Diodorus it was built by Semiramis, but Herodotus ascribes the building of it to Nitocris, about five generations later, and the probability is that it was repaired or completed by him. The length of the bridge was near 3000 ft.; the piers stood 12 ft. apart in the clear, were of cut stone and built upon deep-laid foundations, the river having been turned from its bed for the purpose. The stones were bound together with iron clamps set with melted lead. The starlings formed an acute angle; down-stream the pillars were semicircular; the roadway was 30 ft. wide, and consisted of cedar and cypress timbers overlaid with palm wood. A draw-bridge was raised every night to break the communication. Without doubt all the bridges of antiquity differ but little in their construction from this.

The Romans are the first the remains of whose bridges have come down to the present time. So great was the importance which they attached to these structures that the supervision of them was intrusted to a priest who received his title therefrom, PONTIFEX MAXIMUS.

Before we enter upon the details of the subject, we will lay down certain well established principles respecting the position and construction of bridges, which principles must rest upon the four conditions which should govern all architectural structures: suitableness or convenience, durability, beauty, and economy.

The situation of the bridge should be such at the confluence of streets or highways, as to shorten the journeys of the greatest number of individuals without uselessly increasing the number of bridges. The bridge should be located upon a good foundation, and where it is in no danger of being undermined by the water.

The direction of the bridge should correspond with that of the streets leading to it, or nearly so, that the entrance of vehicles may be unobstructed and easy; and its axis should be perpendicular to the direction of the stream, that the bridge may be as short as possible and the piers present their shortest face to the current.

There should not be any considerable ascent or descent from the street to the bridge, while at the same time the bridge must be so high as not to obstruct the water-way.

The width should be such that vehicles may pass each other, while upon each side there must be sufficient room for foot passengers, except in bridges of short span where there is but little travel; in such cases, if two carriages chance to meet at opposite ends of the bridge, one of them may wait, and the roadway may be sufficiently wide only to accommodate one at a time.

The foundations must be well laid and broad, particularly where the ground beneath is not solid, and in such cases they may be carried up in steps, as seen in *pl.* 7, *fig* 14 *a*.

The form of the bridge must be decided with relation to the material employed and other attendant circumstances, whilst its beauty will result from the proper application of architectural principles.

There are three distinctly different constructions of bridges, according as they are built of stone, wood, or iron.

A. *Stone Bridges.*

We turn now to the construction of stone bridges, which, from the rudest form of rustic bridge seen in *pl.* 7, *fig.* 1, to the noble structure represented in *fig.* 23, are characterized by a feature common in some shape to them all, the *arch*, the various forms of which exert an important influence upon the whole arrangement and appearance.

It is the fortune of but few architects to be intrusted with the building of large bridges, and consequently to have experience on this subject.

Perronet in France is among the most celebrated of modern bridge-builders, and has planned and erected a great number of important bridges, amongst others that of Neuilly, which will be referred to hereafter, and which has already been mentioned under Architecture, and represented in Plates, Div. VII., *pl.* 60, *fig.* 9. The first step towards the erection of a bridge is to build the piers and abutments; for this purpose, when possible, the bed of the river where the pier is to rest must be laid bare, and we will here exhibit some of the usual methods of accomplishing this and of laying the foundations beneath the surface of the water.

The space which the pier is to occupy is first inclosed with a *coffer-dam.* For this purpose piles are driven into the ground below, inclosing a rectangular space, and four to six feet within these another series is driven; the two walls thus formed are well stayed and strengthened with timbers, and the space between the two is rammed full of puddled clay. Much depends upon the careful preparation of the coffer-dam, as a slight blunder may lead to disastrous consequences, even the entire destruction of the dam.

Under certain circumstances, the dam may be built cylindrical. *Fig.* 5 shows the disposition of the piles and timbers, and *fig.* 6 is a vertical section of the same; *a* is the outer wall of piles, *f* the interior piling, and c c' c'' braces for the greater security of the dam. The dam being completed, the next operation must be to empty the inclosed space (*fig.* 4), for which pumping arrangements of some kind are necessary, which are driven by a water-wheel placed in the stream at the side of the dam, or by a steam-engine. It is very seldom possible to lay the bottom dry; so great is the pressure of the water from without, that it is constantly forced up through the bottom of the dam, which obliges the pumps to be kept in operation until the masonry of the pier is completed to a level with the surface of the water. So soon as the bottom of the dam is dry, or as nearly so as possible, the foundation of the pier is commenced, preliminary trials having been made to ascertain the nature of the ground below. If rock be found, the intermediate layer of earth is removed, and the pier is placed immediately upon the rock.

In most cases, however, sand, gravel, or clay is found, and then a framing of timber becomes necessary, which, if the ground below be firm, is laid upon the surface, and covered with a plank floor, upon which the masonry is commenced; generally, however, it becomes necessary to pile the whole area to be covered by the foundation. To this end large piles are driven, at a distance of 2 feet from each other, to such a depth that they can no longer be sunk deeper by repeated blows of the monkey. When the piles are driven, they are all cut off upon the same level, and upon the surface thus produced the floor is laid, which is to receive the masonry, the space between the piles and lower timbers of the frame being rammed with clay, stones, &c.; the pier is then raised of cut stone, or, if of rubble, the stone for the exterior only is cut. So soon as the pier has reached the level of the spring of the arch, the coffer-dam is destroyed, and the water allowed to come to the pier.

It often happens that the stream where the bridge is to be built is so deep or so rapid that no coffer-dam can be built, or that the ground below is of such a nature that timber framing is not necessary; in such cases another method of laying the foundations is adopted, the pier being built in large water-tight boxes, or chambers, called *caissons*, which are afterwards sunk upon the spot where the pier is to stand.

These caissons must be sufficiently large not only to build the pier, but also to accommodate all the workmen who may be employed upon it at a time. *Pl.* 7, *fig.* 11, is the plan of the bottom of the caisson, which shows the grating or framework on which the masonry is laid. Around the edge of this bottom double water-tight plank walls are built, between which tenacious clay is rammed, and so arranged, that on the completion of the work the sides may be separated from the bottom. *Fig.* 9 is a front view of the caisson, *fig.* 8 is a vertical section. In this caisson, as seen in *fig.* 12, the pier is built, the caisson sinking as the work proceeds until it reaches the ground below. *Fig.* 10 shows a caisson grounded upon the bottom, already prepared for it by divers; here is also seen the manner in which the caisson is stayed to the pier as it sinks into the water. *Fig.* 7 shows the manner in which the piers of Westminster Bridge, London, were built in caissons. When the pier has reached the springing line of the arch, or at least is above the surface of the water, the sides of the caisson are loosed from the bottom, to be used again in the same manner. The arch of the bridge is now to be commenced, but previously the centring, which is to support the *voussoirs* or separate stones of the arch, must be built. The centring must be sufficiently strong to sustain the weight of the whole structure without sinking, until the key-stone is put in, which binds the whole together, and for large bridges must be constructed with extreme care and of great strength; otherwise, as the two ends of the arch are built, the weight of the materials depresses the centring at these points, causing it to rise in consequence in the centre, and the arch of the bridge to become higher or more pointed than was intended. To prevent this, even with the best constructed timbering, the top of the centre should be loaded with stones as the work proceeds at the ends, and the tendency of this part to rise thus counteracted.

Centrings are either supported from below, or are self-sustaining, as seen at *figs.* 16 and 13. Piles may be driven, or small stone pillars may be raised for the purpose, upon which the centring is built; *fig.* 14 shows an arch of London bridge, with one of the centrings resting upon the piles, *a*, upon which are placed the tie-beams, *b*, suspended by the trusses, *d*, *e*; the other struts of the centring, *f*, also rest upon the piles, which thus carry the whole weight of the centring and bridge until the key-stone is in. *Figs.* 19 and 20 represent a supported centring of a bridge built in Berne in 1842; here the support is afforded partly by stone pillars, partly by piles, which carry the temporary bridge for the support of the laborers and materials; the construction of the centring itself is apparent from the drawings. When it is not possible to support the centring from below, it must be made self-supporting, and can only rest upon the pillars at its ends. This problem is one of importance and difficulty, and in large bridges requires an architect of great experience. *Pl.* 7, *fig.* 13, is the centring contrived by Perronet for the very flat arches of the Neuilly bridge. *Fig.* 16 is the centring constructed by Rennie for the new Waterloo bridge in London; the bearing points of the ties and struts are all in iron shoes, to enable them to resist the great strain put upon them. *Fig.* 23 represents Westminster bridge in process of building, together with its centrings. The latter are supported upon a great number of wedges, that any particular portion requiring it may be tightened, and ultimately to facilitate the removing of the centrings when the work is completed.

As the wedges are very easily lost or misplaced, Elmes contrived for London bridge a species of screw wedge, of which a representation is given in *fig.* 15: the wedges *m* and *n* were moved by the screws *l*, and by this means the whole centring was capable of being raised, and ultimately of being lowered; *d* are the shores or supports resting upon the heads of the piles.

In *fig.* 20 are seen the derricks used in laying the stone, also the trucks which bring them to the work upon the temporary working frame; in *fig.* 20 the stones are seen slung in can hooks; *figs.* 21 and 22 represent the ordinary lewis, used where the stone is hung from the centre. A hole, *c*, enlarged at the bottom is cut in the stone, and the wedge, *a*, is inserted; the two cheek pieces, *b*, are then put in, and as the wedge, *a*, cannot be withdrawn by a straight pull, the stone is raised by the book, *e*. To withdraw the lewis it is requisite only to take out the pieces, *b*, and the whole is loosened.

Formerly the voussoirs of bridges were all of the same height (*pl.* 7, *figs.* 2, 19, and 17, a side view of the Nydeck bridge in Berne), the *extrados* or outer surface of the arch being parallel with the *intrados* or inner surface, as in the Pons Senatorius at Rome. More recently the surfaces of the stones in the vicinity of the key-stone were made horizontal, as in the Pont Royal in Paris, the Neuilly bridge, and many others of recent times. At present the voussoirs are made to increase from the key-stone gradually to the springing line (*figs.* 3, 16, and 18), for the purpose of enlarging the bearing surface of the arch upon the pier. For lightness the bridge is sometimes filled in with minor arches as seen in *pl.* 7, *fig.* 18.

B. Wooden Bridges.

Wooden bridges are characterized by the arrangement of the timbers which support the roadway over the openings to be bridged.

In the simplest form of wooden bridges the roadway is supported upon piles driven into the bed of the river, or upon stone piers, either with or without trussing or framing.

In all wooden bridges of large span the roadway is suspended from trussed frames or wooden arches.

In *pl.* 8, *figs.* 1–8, is represented the bridge over the Rhine at Schaffhausen; this was one of the most celebrated wooden bridges ever built. It was planned and constructed in 1757 by a common carpenter, Ulric Grubenmann, and was burned by the French in the campaign of 1799. It consisted of two spans of 171 and 193 feet, resting upon an old stone pier which belonged to a former stone bridge upon the same site, and which had been swept away. *Fig.* 1 is a side view with one half of the covering removed: *fig.* 2 a plan of the road timbers; *fig.* 3 a plan of the roof; *fig.* 4 a cross-section; *fig.* 5 a view of one of the hollow suspension frames; *fig.* 6 a section of the roof; *fig.*7 a portion of the notched girders; *fig.* 8 a perspective view of the joints used for uniting the separate pieces of the above. From these figures the construction of the bridge and the arrangement of the timbers are apparent. Originally it was intended that the bridge should stand without the pier; this was suffered to remain, however, and some years later Grubenmann, fearing that it might also be carried away, added the braces, *b*, *f*, seen in *fig.* 1, for the purpose of making the bridge independent of its central support.

A bridge over the Limmat, near the Abbey of Wittengen, was also erected by the same carpenter, assisted by his brother, John Grubenmann, and burnt soon after that of Schaffhausen; it consisted of one opening of 390 feet span, with a rise of 43 feet, and was a more solid and even a superior piece of carpentry to that at Schaffhausen. This was the greatest span ever executed with timber. Its radius of curvature or curve of equilibrium was about 600 feet.

Fig. 9 shows an arch of peculiar construction of the viaduct over the valley of the Ouse, on the North Shields and Newcastle railroad; *fig.* 10 is a cross-section of the same; *fig.* 11 a view from above of one of the piers, showing the arch upon one side and the road timbers upon the other; *fig.* 12 is a side view of a portion of the pier A, with the foot of the arch B; *fig.* 13 a vertical section showing the manner of uniting the planks; *fig.* 14 is a cross-section showing the connexion between the arch and the braces; *fig.* 15 is a front view of a pier A, with the cast-iron shoe in which the arches B rest; *fig.* 16 is a view of the said shoe, C; *fig.* 17 a longitudinal section of the same; *fig.* 18 transverse section of the same, with the clamps which secure it to the pier A; *fig.* 19 is a section of the top of a pier, showing the road timbers and railing; *fig.* 20 shows the manner of bolting the ribs beneath the roadway F and E to the crown of the arch; *fig.* 21 shows the connexion of the roadway H with the railing D at a point immediately over the crown of the arch B, over which the timbers E and F meet; *fig.* 22, cross-section of this joining on a larger scale; *fig.* 23, side view of the same; *fig.* 24 section of joinings of these timbers; *fig.* 25, the joint between the timbers F and E and the cross-ribs; *fig.* 26, joint between the rib G and the flooring; *fig.* 27, detail of the connexion between the timbers E and the pier A, and by means of the cross-ribs L with the arch B, also through the carriers O with the longitudinal timbers of the roadway; *fig.* 28, section of the foundation piles, with the platform and grillage.

Another bridge with a notched timbered arch deserves to be mentioned in this place. This is a bridge over the Schuylkill at Philadelphia, covering an opening from one abutment to the other of 340 feet 3¾ inches. *Pl.* 8, *fig.* 29, is a view of the bridge, with the covering removed from the left half to show the arrangement of the timbers. The boldness and simplicity of this bridge are equally to be admired. The greatest part of the thrust and the whole weight of the covering are thrown by the framework *a b* upon the abutment *e* and the timbers *d c c'*, whilst the arch has only its own weight and that of the movable load to support. In 1838 this bridge was burned, and its place is now supplied by a wire bridge of single span.

A new system of bridge-building recently come much into use should be here mentioned; it was invented by Laves, chief architect to the court of Hanover. Laves had already invented a peculiar method of building beams, by which he had attained great strength at comparatively small cost. The girders were sawed longitudinally each way from the centre to within two feet from the ends, as seen in *fig.* 35. At each end where the cut commences the girder is bound with iron rings, *a*, two inches wide and half an inch thick, to prevent the entire splitting of the timber. The two portions of the bridge were then driven apart by wedges, *b*, and a girder was obtained, having all the strength of a flat arch without the thrust, only wall-plates A B being required to give the ends an even bearing. Shortly afterwards the inventor carried the idea further and constructed his girders of two timbers notched together at the ends, *fig.* 36; as in the former case no abutments were required and no thrust was exerted.

Subsequently this method of construction was extended to bridge-building by the inventor. The principles of the application will be made apparent by an inspection of *pl.* 8, *fig.* 30, the cord below being united with the bridge by the braces *a c* and *b c*, whilst the diagonal braces serve to render the structure self-sustaining and stiff.

The same system, carried out with rather more attempt at beauty and ornament, is seen in *figs.* 31 and 32; *fig.* 33 is a cross-section, and *fig.* 34 a plan showing the arrangement of the braces. This system would be very limited in its capabilities of extension were it confined to a single beam; this is not the case, however. Any number of beams may be scarfed together, as seen in *figs.* 37 and 38, to form either the roadway or the tie-beam beneath. In *fig.* 39 is seen the method of giving the ends of the bridge-frames a solid bearing upon the abutments. *b* and *a* are the upper and lower timbers bound together by iron rings, *d d*, and *c* are wedges also notched to the lower beam and which serve to give it a firm bearing upon the head of the pier. *Fig.* 40 is a section through an arch of this description; *a* and *b* are the timbers, and *g* the blocks which serve to keep them in their places. A large bridge built entirely upon this principle is seen in *fig.* 41; *fig.* 42 is a plan showing the diagonal braces, and a portion of the road covering; *fig.* 43 a cross-section of the bridge; *fig.* 44 the scarfing of the timbers of the tie-beam; *fig.* 45 the joint at the end where the girders rest upon the abutment.

C. Iron Bridges.

When the arch of a bridge is constructed of iron it is called an iron bridge, although the piers and abutments may be of stone, and the floor or roadway of wood. These bridges are variously constructed; in very short spans the arch may be cast in a single piece, in larger spans it may be cast in many pieces and united by bolts, or voussoirs may be cast and set after the manner pursued with stone bridges, or the roadway may be hung upon chains or even wire cables. Desaguiliers and Garrin, in the commencement of the 18th century, proposed the building of iron bridges, but the idea was first carried out in England. The first iron bridge was that over the Severn near Colebrookdale, erected in 1779. *Pl.* 9, *fig.* 1, is a view of one half of the arch; *fig.* 2, a cross-section; *fig.* 3 is a plan with the roadway removed; *fig.* 4, a plan of the springing plates on which the arch rests; *fig.* 5 shows the fastenings of the diagonal braces, E, of *fig.* 3 with the main arches; *fig.* 6, the connexion between the cross-braces and the arch ribs. These figures are so clear that they require no further explanation. The bridge is one arch of 100 ft. 6 inches span and 45 ft. high from the level of the springing-plates to the middle of the soffit. The height from ordinary low water to the springing-plates is 10 ft., making the whole height from low water to the soffit 55 ft.

The bridge was designed and executed by Abraham Darby, and formed a new era in bridge building. The form of the intrados is nearly a semicircle and consists of five ribs, upon each of which rests one of the longitudinal stringers which support the roadway. Upon these stringers are placed iron plates 2½ inches thick, which support the road-covering, consisting of clay with broken iron cinders.

Soon after the completion of the above bridge the second iron bridge was built, three miles higher up the Severn. The engineer, Thomas Telford, a county surveyor, introduced the principle of suspending the bridge upon two large ribs, one on each side of the bridge. The span is 130 ft., the versed sine of the ribs which bear the covering plates is 17 ft. and the breadth across the soffit is 18 ft.; the height from ordinary low water to the soffit is 34 ft. *Fig.* 14 is a side view of this bridge; *fig.* 15 is a cross-section of the same: *fig.* 16, a plan of the springing-plates; *fig.* 17 shows the connexion and bracing between the main arch B and the intersecting arch C, by the upright braces *a* and diagonal braces *b*; *fig.* 18 shows the connexion of the railing with the bridge road, and *fig.* 19 shows the connexion of the two arches at the crown. It will be perceived that the auxiliary arch is for the purpose of supporting the main arch at its weakest point, the latter being suspended by iron straps to the auxiliary arch. The cost of the bridge, including the abutments, was £6000 sterling.

The third bridge in regard to time and progressive increase of magnitude was that over the Wear at Sunderland, in the county of Durham. The arch is the segment of a circle, the chord being 236 ft. and the versed sine or height of the crown of the intrados above the level of the springing line 34 ft., so that the largest ships may pass beneath it.

It is of the boldest construction, and is put together very differently from those already described, the arches being composed of open-work boxes or gratings, which take the place of the voussoirs in a stone arch. *Fig.* 7 is a side view of the bridge, and *fig.* 8 a perspective view of one end; *figs.* 9 and

10 show the open work of arches upon a larger scale; *fig.* 11, the vertical bars uniting the three ribs of the arches, whilst the latter are firmly stayed together by the transverse rods (*fig.* 12). In the sunken panels of the ribs, *a* (*fig.* 10), over the vertical joints, between the voussoirs, lie wrought-iron plates (*fig.* 13), which are screwed to the ribs and bind the voussoirs firmly together.

A peculiar construction of iron bridges was introduced in 1837, by a French architect, Polonceau, who built upon this plan the Carrousel bridge in Paris. In this construction the strength of iron is united to the elasticity of wood. The arches of the bridge consist of hollow cast-iron tubes filled with wood and imbedded in asphaltum. *Fig.* 20 is a view of this bridge, which consists of three arches, with stone abutments and piers. Upon each askew-back are five cylindrical boxes or springing-plates, into which the arch ribs are set (*fig.* 32). These ribs consist of elliptical tubes, composed of two pieces, one of which is seen in *fig.* 26 in various views and sections. The two halves united are shown upon a large scale in *fig.* 25, in which the plank filling is seen. Between each layer of wood is a thick layer of asphaltum. The semi-cylinders are united together by screws (*pl.* 9, *fig.* 25); *fig.* 21 shows the foot of the arch upon a large scale. The large rings between the arch and roadway are seen in section in *fig.* 29 and in elevation in *fig.* 30, from which the connexion between the rings is apparent; *fig.* 31 is a horizontal section of one of these rings; *fig.* 23 is a view from above of the ribs of the arch, the roadway being removed, and showing the diagonal braces, K, and the transverse braces L; *fig.* 22 is a vertical section of the arch of the bridge; *fig.* 28 shows the connexion between the diagonal and transverse braces with the ribs of the arch. The stringers *b* (*fig.* 24) are borne in iron shoes (*fig.* 27) by the five arch ribs and the supporting-rings D; the stringers are made in two parts screwed together, and the two outside stringers are covered with iron plates, *o* (*fig.* 24). Above these stringers come the transverse sleepers of the roadway *a*, carrying the console plate G, the elevated foot-walk being supported by the tringle K, the support *l*, and the bearer *h*. The sleepers also carry the iron plates *e*, which support the foundations, F and G, with the road-covering above. *Fig.* 22 shows the whole roadway in section.

For laying the arch ribs, C, a peculiar centring was constructed (*fig.* 33), resting upon two temporary piers; the ribs were supported upon this centring, on blocks and wedges, where they were filled with the wooden plates, screwed together, and secured in place.

Of an entirely different character from the bridges described above are those in which the roadway is suspended from chains or wire cables, stretched from the top of towers or tall piers. The suspension system, though new in Europe, has been long known in India and America; to the English, however, is due the credit of having perfected the system, which rests upon the properties of the so called *catenary*, that is the curve which a thread takes when suspended at both ends and left to itself. If now, in lieu of the thread, two chains or wire cables be imagined, suspended at a distance from each other equal to the width of the bridge, with the roadway suspended horizontally by rods of different lengths from these cables, we shall have the rough idea of a suspension bridge.

At first chains were used for this purpose, made something after the manner of watch chains with links 10 to 15 feet in length, but it was found that cables made of a great number of iron wires bound together were preferable on many accounts to chains, which they have almost entirely replaced in the construction of suspension bridges.

By means of bridges upon this principle distances are now spanned, and ravines and gorges bridged, which before their introduction were never attempted.

The difficulties of constructing a bridge across the Danube have long been considered insurmountable; the current is very rapid, and the least depth of water is 20 feet, while at times the water rises 36 feet above low-water mark, bringing with it immense masses of ice which break down embankments and carry away whatever impedes its progress. Suspension bridges have, however, been found to be perfectly practicable; and one constructed at Pesth by an English engineer is said to be the first permanent bridge erected over the Danube below Vienna for upwards of seventeen centuries It was opened for the first time on the 5th January, 1849, and the same day was put to the severest test to which the stability of a bridge can be subjected, by the retreat of the Hungarian army over it, followed by the Austrians. The passage over the bridge is thus described in a letter written from the spot. "First came the Hungarians in full retreat, and in the greatest disorder, hotly pursued by the victorious Imperialists; squadrons of cavalry and artillery in full gallop, backed by thousands of infantry; in fact the whole platform was one mass of moving soldiers; and during the two first days 60,000 imperial troops, with 270 pieces of cannon, passed over the bridge." This fact is of the first importance, as it proves that suspension bridges, when properly constructed, may be erected on the most exposed situations, while their cost is small in comparison with that of stone bridges. It should be mentioned in connexion with the above, that the marching of a close column of infantry is considered to be the severest test to which a bridge can be subjected. The distance between the points of suspension of this bridge is 665 feet, and the platform is 42 feet wide. This is the first bridge with stone piers built between Ratisbon and the Black Sea since the time of Trajan, A. D. 103, when a bridge was built across the Danube near the confines of Hungary and Servia, the ruins of which are still pointed out.

At Vienna a steel suspension bridge has been erected over the Danube, the span of which is 234 feet. It is calculated that the weight of the steel in the bridge is only one half that of the iron required to build a bridge of equal strength.

The first suspension bridge in England appears to have been erected over the Tees, for the use of the miners in 1741. The most noted of this description in England is the chain bridge over the Menai straits, which separate the island of Anglesea from the county of Caernarvon.

The main opening is 560 feet between the points of suspension; in addition there are four arches on the western side and three on the eastern side of the principal opening, each of 50 feet span. The under side of the roadway is 100 feet above the high-water line.

In France wire suspension bridges have been extensively introduced. In the United States also suspension bridges have been erected to a limited extent. At Philadelphia there is a wire suspension bridge over the Schuylkill upon the site of Wernway's wooden bridge, burned in 1838. At Wheeling, over the Ohio, one of the finest structures of this kind in the world has been erected by Mr. Charles Ellet, Jr., with a span of 1,010 feet, which is 152 feet longer than the celebrated bridge at Freyburg, which has the greatest span heretofore constructed.

The flooring of the Wheeling bridge is 24 feet wide, and is suspended from twelve cables of iron wire 4 inches in diameter, and 1,380 feet long.

The same architect has also constructed a suspension bridge over the Niagara river, between the falls and the whirlpool, and in sight of both; the span is 800 feet, and the roadway 230 feet above the surface of the river.

Thus it will be seen that distances have been spanned by suspension bridges far exceeding anything even attained by any other species of construction, while the experiments made by Vicat during an examination of the state of the suspension bridges over the Rhone lead to the conclusion, that with proper care they will prove as durable as the most solid stone structures. It is to be regretted, however, that they do not afford that stability which is necessary to enable them to be used as railroad bridges.

A few years ago it became necessary to construct a bridge over the Menai straits for the passage of the Chester and Holyhead Railway. It was impossible to make use of the chain suspension bridge, as was at first intended, its flexibility rendering it unsuitable to the passage of trains of cars. It was also necessary that no centring or scaffolding should be used, as this would interrupt navigation; a stone bridge was therefore out of the question.

Mr. Stephenson offered a design of an iron tube, a proposition which was received at the time with general incredulity; the company, however, having confidence in their engineer, after some preliminary experiments, decided to adopt the plan, and it has since been built. The tube is not cylindrical, but rectangular; it is constructed of thick plates of boiler-iron, and is made of several sections resting upon piers. The distance spanned by the longest section is 460 feet clear, the greatest distance ever yet attempted except in suspension bridges. One of the longest sections is estimated to weigh 1600 tons. These tubes were floated upon pontoons to near the position they were to occupy, and raised to their place by huge hydraulic presses. The trains pass through the interior of the tubes.

3. Inland Navigation.

Hitherto we have treated of communication by land only; but streams also form an important means of communication wherever they are capable of bearing shipping. All streams, however, are not adapted to this purpose, some being either too shallow, or having many small crooked windings, which retard the current and cause bars; and in others the current is so swift as to render navigation dangerous. In all such cases certain works are necessary to render the streams navigable. By cutting off the small windings, and giving a river a straight course, the current will be increased and the formation of bars prevented. When the channel of a river is obstructed by rocks they may be removed by blasting; where it is generally too shallow to bear vessels, successive portions of it are dammed up in order to obtain sufficient depth, the vessels entering the successive *reaches* by means of locks. Canals are constructed for the purpose of inland navigation, where no natural means are available, or to connect one stream with another. Some of these structures we will now proceed to consider in detail.

A. Dams.

When shallow streams are to be made navigable by means of dams, the latter are built of a height sufficient to maintain the depth of water required for navigation, and allowing the surplus water to run over the top, on which account they are called *overfall-dams.* They are built of wood or stone. In building wooden overfall-dams, large beams of timber are first laid in several contiguous rows across the bottom of the stream, and are firmly settled into its bed. Upon these sills are laid successive rows of beams, breaking joints, and planed throughout on the horizontal faces so as to prevent leakage; they are pinned together with treenails both vertically and horizontally, and the interstices between the vertical faces are closely packed with clay and sod. The sides of the dam are sloped towards the top, the pressure sustained at the bottom being much greater than at top; that face which slopes against the current is called the *breast;* the downward slope is called the *apron.* To protect the breast from being undermined, a double row of thick plank is driven into the bed of the river above the breast. For the protection of the apron, piles are driven, on which a hearth of thick plank is laid to receive the fall of water, or else a bed is made of rocks firmly packed between the piles.

On *pl.* 11, *figs.* 16, 17, and 18, is represented a wooden overfall-dam across the river Witogra in Russia. This river being large and rapid, a very wide base has been given to the dam. The mode of construction is different in some respects from that above described, as is seen in the cross-section (*fig.* 17). The base consists of piles and grillage; the breast, F, is made by driving piles of different lengths so as to form the required slope, across which the breast-sills are laid, on which are spiked heavy oak planks closely fitted. A bulkhead of timber is built into the bank on each side of the dam, to prevent the water from passing through. Below the dam strong piles are driven into the bed of the stream, and between them large stones are packed to receive the shock of the falling water, and prevent the undermining of the dam.

The upper surface of the dam is sloped in the direction of the current; thick planks are spiked upon the dam-sills, and their joints caulked and covered with laths. In order to have the means of regulating the height of water, frames with flood-gates A A′ A″ (*figs.* 17 and 18), are built on top, and between these frames and the sides bulkheads are built to the height which the water is to assume when the gates are closed.

Stone overfall-dams are built massively of heavy dressed stone, on a foundation of piles and grillage, unless the bed of the river is rocky. The stones are clamped together by brass clamps, to prevent their being displaced separately. A stone dam, built by Smeaton, is represented on *pl.* 10, *fig.* 15 being a top view, *fig.* 16 one half of a longitudinal section, and *fig.* 17 a cross-section.

Between the two slopes of stone dams an open space is sometimes left, which is lined with two rows of closely fitted planks, and then filled up with rammed clay, in order to oppose an impermeable barrier to the water which may pass through the joints of the walls. Stone dams are protected against the undermining action of the water in the same manner as described in speaking of wooden dams. The form of an arch, with the convexity up stream, is often given to stone dams (*pl.* 10, *fig.* 15), by which they are enabled better to resist the action of the current.

B. Canals.

Canals are open trenches filled with water from lakes, streams, or springs, to a sufficient depth to bear loaded vessels, thus affording a means of inland navigation. They are formed either by excavations in the solid earth, or by embankments upon it. In some cases aqueducts are built, of which we shall treat separately.

For the invention of canals we scarcely know to whom or to what age we are indebted, such is their antiquity. The most ancient vestiges seem to exist in Egypt, where a canal was once undertaken to connect the Red Sea with the Mediterranean. Other canals of antiquity still remain; for instance the Yussuff Canal, and others in Persia and Afghanistan, where they had reached great perfection, and where canals had been constructed under ground for miles in length. We also find ancient canals on the Tigris and Euphrates. The Greeks and Romans did very little in the construction of canals. Charlemagne was the first to plan the connexion of the Danube with the Rhine, which work was commenced under him, but completed only in modern times. Within the last three hundred years canals have been constructed in all civilized countries, the Dutch, English, and French leading the way in improvements in the system of construction.

Excavation is the simplest and cheapest method of forming canals, and is resorted to wherever existing conditions make it possible; but few cases occur where any great length is obtained without embankments, which become necessary when a shallow stream is formed into a canal, and when a canal is carried along the side of a hill or across low or marshy land.

Embankments are mostly formed of rammed clay, and when they attain a considerable height the outside slope at least is protected from washing and caving by a stone wall of dry masonry. In cases of great height both slopes of the embankment are formed of stone walls, while the space between them is filled with clay, which is wetted and worked into a mass of the consistency of potter's clay, and well rammed down, an operation termed *puddling*.

The two sides or banks of the water-way are sloped; in hard and clay soils the slope need not exceed 1½ base to 1 rise; but in softer soils a greater slope must be given, and in loose soil the banks must be well protected by fascines, piles, or stone walls, from the washing caused by the fluctuation of the water attending the passage of the boats. The depth and width of the canal depend of course on the size and capacity of the boats intended to be put upon it. The width at bottom should be sufficient to permit the passage of two boats abreast without their rubbing against the side slopes.

If a canal is to be navigated by steam, both the slope of the banks and the depth should be increased, and the protection of the banks made more permanent, as the washing caused by the wheels and the rapid passage of the boats is very great. Most canals, however, are navigated by means of horses or mules, for which purpose the top of one bank is formed into a road called the *tow-path*, which continues uninterruptedly, occasionally changing sides by means of bridges. The surface of the tow-path is formed either of hard sandy clay or of small broken stones; it should be from eight to twelve feet wide, to admit readily of the passage of two horses and riders abreast, and should have a lateral slope from the canal to shed off the rain-water. At suitable intervals drains are constructed to carry off the water either into the canal or away from it, as opportunity may serve.

It is seldom practicable to continue a line of canal on the same level for a great distance. The points to be joined by the canal are frequently on different levels, and hills or valleys intervene on the route, which it is impossible or too expensive to cross on the same level by means of excavation or embankment. In such cases successive portions of the canal are built on different levels, the boats passing from one level or *reach* into the other by means of *locks*, of which we shall treat fully below.

A longitudinal slope should be given to the bottom of the canal sufficient to cause a moderate current of water, not exceeding three feet per second. If the current is too slow the water is liable to become stagnant in places, and to accumulate mire and rubbish to a great degree; if too fast, the expenditure of water and the resistance to the boat is too great. In long reaches and on hill sides, openings are left at intervals in one of the banks, in which dams are built even with the water-line of the canal, for the purpose of discharging the surplus water occasioned by rains and lockage. These dams are called *waste weirs*, and are constructed either of wood or stone; they retain the water at the required height, but allow it to flow over in case of a rise. They are also provided with draw gates to act as drains for the purpose of carrying off mire and rubbish, and of emptying a reach in the canal when necessary for repairs.

Among the most important canals in the world is that of Languedoc, in France, which connects the Mediterranean Sea with the Atlantic Ocean, and thus avoids the dangerous passage of the Straits of Gibraltar It was projected in the year 1660 by François Andreossy, and commenced in 1666 by Peter Paul Riquet, on the upper Garonne.

This canal runs across the isthmus which connects the peninsula of Spain with France, and which is inclosed between the Pyrenees and the mountains of the Rhone. It commences in the river Garonne, on the west side of the city of Toulouse, and after rising through eight locks reaches the river Lers, along which it ascends through thirteen locks to Villefranche. From this point, after crossing the Lers by an aqueduct, it reaches the summit level by means of five additional locks. These 26 locks make a rise of about 220 feet above the level of the Garonne, in a distance of 22 miles.

From the summit level, after crossing six streams, the canal descends through 37 locks to the river Aube; continuing northwards from the city of Trebes, it arrives at the main level near Olangac, by another descent through 22 locks, after having crossed five other streams, which have their sources in the Montagne Noire. The main level continues along the sides of the mountains, in many places with aqueducts, crosses two streams, and after considerable winding around the Ecurene mountain cuts through a ridge of the Malpas hills with a tunnel 575 feet long, which ends with a chain of eight locks. Here the canal descends to the plateau of Fonseranne, whence continuing southwards, it crosses the rivers Orbe, Libron, and Agde, and makes its final descent into the Mediterranean. In its approach to the latter it crosses a small lake, through which for about four miles it is carried between two embankments, the level of the canal being higher than that of the lake.

From the summit level to the Mediterranean the distance is about 114 miles and the descent 658 feet. The canal has in all 102 locks (one of which is circular, with 95 feet diameter, *pl.* 10, *fig.* 18), 55 aqueducts, numerous dams and dykes, one tunnel, and 92 bridges, in a distance of about 136 miles. The lift of the locks is from five to twelve feet. The width of the canal is generally 36 feet at bottom and 68 feet at the waterline; the depth is seven feet. The boats used upon it are 90 feet long, from 18 to 20 feet wide, draw 5 feet 6 inches of water, and carry 100 tons. The first trip was made in June, 1681.

For the supply of water at the summit level feeders were constructed, which deserve some attention. Eight small streams of the Black Mountain (*Montagne Noire*) were brought together by means of ditches and excavations in the rocks into one channel, which was blasted out of the rock for a distance of five miles along the mountain, and then carried through it by a tunnel 420 feet long and 9½ feet wide. At this point it is joined by another feeder, the two forming a larger one, which, continuing its course along the mountains, enters the great reservoir of St. Ferreol. From here it takes the direction to the river Gorge, and entering the basin of this river, the combined waters are carried by the great feeder to the reservoir of the summit level which supplies the whole chain of locks. The whole length of these feeders is about 37 miles, although in a direct line the distance is not over 16 miles.

The most important structure on this canal is undoubtedly the great reservoir of St. Ferreol, of which *pl.* 11, *fig.* 1, is a section, and *fig.* 2 a part of the ground plan. The inner or principal wall of this reservoir is 110 feet high, and contains about sixteen hundred thousand cubic feet of masonry. To about 40 feet from the bottom this wall is 40 feet in thickness; then suddenly contracting to 18 feet, it tapers to the top, where it is about six feet thick. At a distance of 200 feet from the inner wall, the outer wall is built 64 feet high, and the space between the two walls is filled with binding clay, which is well rammed. Through an arched aqueduct which commences about the middle of the reservoir (D, *figs.* 1 and 2) the water is let into the feeder-canal through guard-gates, at a rate insuring safety to the works. The reservoir is 530 feet long and 265 feet wide.

Another important reservoir of this canal is that at Lampy: *pl.* 11, *fig.* 3, represents a side elevation of it; *fig.* 4, a section through A, and *fig.* 5, a section through B. The water can be let off at different heights, as seen at A and B.

C. Locks.

A lock is a small basin which connects different levels of a canal, and through which boats ascend or descend from one level to the other. The bottom of the lock is even with that of the lower level, and the top is even with that of the upper level of the canal. Both ends are closed by gates provided with valves, through which the water can be let into the lock from the upper level, or lowered to the height of the lower level, the lock forming thus at pleasure a continuation of either portion of the canal. When a boat is to descend through the lock, the water is let in from above, the upper gates are opened, and the boat is drawn into the lock; the upper gates are then closed, and the valve in the lower gate is opened, when the boat will descend with the water to the lower level, and on the lower gates being opened it can continue its course. The inverse operation will be pursued when the boat is to ascend to the higher level.

From this it is apparent that locks form the most important feature in the construction of a canal. By means of them navigation is made practicable and easy where otherwise it would be impossible. Their use is not confined to canals proper, but they are also used where shallow streams have been made navigable by means of damming up successive portions, as mentioned in the introduction to this subject.

The construction of locks demands the greatest attention on the part of the engineer, as the pressure which they sustain and the action of the water upon them are greater than at any other point in the canal. The size and proportions of a lock are dependent upon the size of the boats to be used, the frequency of navigation, and the supply of water. The form is usually rectangular, unless a special object dictates a different form; *pl.* 11, *fig.* 12, is a top view of a lock, which stands by the side of a wooden dam in one of the canals in Russia; *figs.* 13 and 14 are the two side views, and *fig.* 15 a section. *Pl.* 10, *figs.* 6, 18, and 21, give the top views of different locks in the Languedoc Canal in France; *figs.* 2 and 4 show cross-sections, and *figs.* 19 and 20 longitudinal sections of various other locks, and *fig.* 29 is a perspective view of a chain of locks on the Rideau Canal, near Bytown in Canada.

A lock consists of three divisions, viz. the upper entrance, called the *head-bay;* the middle, called the *chamber;* and the lower entrance, called the *tail-bay.* The difference in elevation between the bottom of the head-bay and the top of the tail-bay is called the *lift*, which varies according to circumstances from 5 to 15 feet. The highest single lift is in a lock at Bouzingen, near Ypern, in the Netherlands, amounting to 22 feet. The chamber is the narrowest part of the canal; it is made just large enough to admit of an easy entrance of the boat, and to leave some space for play during the commotion of the water while being lifted. It is formed by two solid walls of cut masonry, slightly battered towards the top; or if of wood the walls are built of heavy beams and planks fitted water-tight. Any excess in the size of the chamber above that required for the easy passage of the boat would only occasion loss of water and time. The head-bay as well as the tail-bay, being continuations of the main water-way, have of course the general depth of the canal; their form is usually that which we give in *pl.* 10, *figs.* 1, 3 *a*, and 3 *b*. The side-walls of the bays are called *wing-walls,* which are also battered, the batter or slope increasing from that of the chamber to that of the bank of the canal, where the wing-wall joins it.

The *lock gates* are large and heavy gates consisting of two parts or *leaves*, each leaf turning upon its own hinges, and the two abutting against each other in the middle of the water-way, where they form an angle projecting against the head of water. There are always two gates to a lock, one at each end. They are usually made of wood, but latterly cast iron gates have come into use and are greatly preferred. Those made of wood are carefully put together of heavy timber; the frame is usually composed of two upright and from four to eight horizontal pieces, which vary in thickness and depth according to the size of the gate and the head of water; these are mortised together, and covered on the side next to the head of water with durable two-inch planks, which are rabbet-jointed and caulked. The upright posts upon which the gate hinges are called *heel-posts* or *quoins;* and the other uprights forming the edges of the two leaves of the gate are called the *mitre posts.* *Pl.* 10, *figs.* 22 and 23 *a*, are representations of different lock gates. Single leaves are also seen at A and B in *fig.* 20. The heel-post (*fig.* 26) is made to turn upon an iron gudgeon which fits into an iron plate below (*figs.* 24 and 25); it is kept in its vertical position by means of two iron collars, which are fastened into the wall of the lock, and in which it turns. The mitre-posts are so bevelled that when the gate is closed they abut against each other along the whole edge, and form a water-tight seam. The bottom of the gate is also bevelled and fits closely against the *mitre sill*, which forms the head of the head-wall and tail-wall running across each end of the chamber (*a* and *b*, *fig.* 21). The water by its pressure produces a close contact of the bevelled faces, and is thus prevented from leaking through.

The gates are opened in various ways: when they are very large, a chain attached to the mitre-post is wound upon a drum by means of cranks and cog-wheels, and the gate thus drawn into its open position. At each end and upon each side of the chamber a recess is left in the wall for the reception of the gate when opened (*pl.* 10, *fig.* 21), allowing it to form an uninterrupted line with the wall, leaving no projection against which the boat may strike in passing. The most common method of opening the gate is by means of a heavy beam, termed the *balance beam*, because it assists in balancing the weight of the leaf upon the gudgeon and keeping the quoin in an unstrained position. A lock-gate with a balance beam is represented in *pl.* 10, *fig.* 2. The balance beam is mortised upon the mitre-post and quoin, and extends some distance out upon the bank; in many cases an additional weight is put upon the end of the beam when it is not sufficiently heavy. When the gate is to be opened it is backed through the water into the recess by a steady push against the end of the balance-beam.

A lock-gate of a different construction from that above described is represented on *pl.* 10, *figs.* 3 *b* and 4. The gate here consists of a single leaf, *a*, and instead of turning on a pivot, it slides into a lateral recess, being moved by means of the windlass *d*, and ropes which pass over the pulleys *b* and *c*. This method of construction is not to be recommended, and is rarely met with.

Pl. 10, *fig.* 5, shows a kind of drop-gate, which may be used in small canals; on the left is a side view with open gates, on the right a front view with closed gates; the drop-gate may describe a quadrant, and be opened and closed without trouble. These doors have not been found very practicable.

The *valves* through which the water enters and leaves the chamber are small doors, made either in the side of the chamber-wall, the top of the end-walls, or in the lock-gate. In the former case a conduit must be built by the side of the lock for the discharge of the water, as seen in *pl.* 10, *figs.* 27 and 28. It is usual to have the valves in the gates. They must be so constructed as to be readily opened and closed, and to be water-tight when closed. Those generally employed are either *slide-valves* or *paddle valves.* The slide-valves may move vertically or horizontally; the vertical slide-valve is the simplest in its arrangement, and is therefore most frequently used. It moves in grooves, and is opened and closed by means of a rod which passes up to the top of the gate, and is raised or lowered by a screw, or a rack and pinion. *Pl.* 10, *fig.* 22, shows a vertical slide-valve in the gate, and *fig.* 28 a similar one in the side wall of the chamber. The horizontal slide-valve is moved in a similar manner, but slides horizontally, which may be effected by means of a rack on the side of the valve, driven by a pinion on a vertical axis projecting above the water, and turned by a crank. The paddle-valve is one which turns about its middle, or at one side on a vertical axis which reaches up to the top of the gate, and is turned by means of a crank. The paddle-valve is neither as safe nor as easily worked as the slide-valve. The size of the valves is dependent upon the quantity of water to be discharged in a given time, and upon the head of water; they vary from 20 inches to four feet square, and are generally made of cast-iron.

We have thus far confined our remarks to locks of a single water-way which pass only one boat at a time. Where navigation is frequent, double locks are built, consisting of two separate chambers side by side, by which arrangement two boats can be locked through at the same time, either in the same or in the opposite directions. Double locks of the best and most durable construction have been built on the Erie Canal in the State of New York.

D. Aqueducts.

When a canal meets in its course with a river or ravine, it must be carried across on a bridge, which differs from ordinary bridges only in the superstructure, which embraces the canal and tow-path. As a specimen of a stone aqueduct, we give on *pl.* 11, *figs.* 6, 7, and 8, a side-view, cross-section, and top-view of the Cesse Aqueduct, designed by Vauban for the Languedoc Canal. The water-way is frequently carried across the bridges in wooden trunks; of this there are many examples in the United States, where wooden aqueducts have been more extensively constructed than elsewhere.

The first aqueduct of cast-iron was the Chirk Aqueduct on the Ellesmere Canal, built in 1795, by Thomas Telford, who, encouraged by its success, constructed immediately afterwards, on the same canal, the Dee Aqueduct, in the valley of Llangollyn, 127 feet above the bed of the Dee, and 1000 feet in length. It consists of 19 arches of cast-iron, abutting on stone piers (*pl.* 10, *fig.* 10). Each arch consists of four ribs, as shown in the cross-section (*fig.* 11), secured against lateral motion by connecting-plates (*fig.* 13). An abutting plate or skew-back is shown in *fig.* 12. The bottom plates (*fig.* 14), as well as the side-plates, are firmly connected by flanges, and are made water-tight by iron cement. The position of the tow-path is seen in *fig.* 11. The canal is 12 feet wide.

The carrying of canals across rivers is not the only object of aqueducts. They have been built since the remotest times for the purpose of conveying water into cities. The Egyptians, Greeks, and Romans had large structures of that kind, and they continue to be built in modern times. The Croton Aqueduct, by which the city of New York is supplied with water, completed in 1842, under the direction of J. B. Jervis, is the most gigantic modern work of the kind, of which we will here give a description.

It was constructed at the expense of the city of New York, and cost about twelve millions of dollars. The conduit commences at the Croton river, in Westchester county, where a dam has been constructed which raises the water of that stream 40 feet above its natural level, and 116 feet above mean tide, setting back the water of the river about 5 miles, and forming a reservoir of about 400 acres surface. The aqueduct runs down the valley of the Croton to the shore of the Hudson, which it leaves again at the village of Yonkers, and, crossing the valley of the Sawmill river and Tibbitt's Brook, gains the summit between the Hudson and East Rivers, and continues on it to the Harlem River, a distance of 33 miles of continuous masonry. Iron pipes are then laid 1450 feet on an arched bridge across the valley of the Harlem River, after which the aqueduct of masonry is resumed, and continues two miles to the Manhattan valley, which is passed with four iron pipes, descending 102 feet to the bottom of the valley, and rising again to its opposite side, forming a syphon of 4100 feet in length. The masonry conduit is again resumed, and crossing the Asylum ridge and Clendenning valley, is continued two miles to the receiving reservoir at Yorkville, whence iron pipes laid beneath the surface of the ground conduct the water a distance of two miles to the distributing reservoir at Murray Hill, three miles from the City Hall.

The length of the aqueduct from the Crotom dam to the receiving reservoir is 45½ miles. Its general declivity is 13¼ inches to the mile. The form of the masonry conduit is seen in *pl.* 11, *fig.* 11; the bottom is an inverted arch, the chord of which is 6 feet 9 inches, and the versed sine 9 inches; the side-walls rise 4 feet from the springing line of the bottom arch, with a batter of 1 inch to a foot rise, making the width at the top of the side-walls 7 feet 5 inches. The roof-arch is a semicircle, making the area of the interior 53.59 feet. The supply of water furnished daily is about fifty millions of gallons, which is more than the aggregate of all the London water-works, and more by ten millions of gallons than the quantity furnished by the fourteen aqueducts which supplied Rome in the days of her greatest splendor.

There are on the line sixteen tunnels, driven chiefly through gneiss and marble, the aggregate length of which is 6841 feet. The streams encountered are crossed by 114 culverts with spans from 12 to 25 feet, at depths varying from 12 to 70 feet below the grade. There are also five road crossings of from 14 to 20 feet span. The aqueduct is covered with earth to a sufficient depth to protect the water from frost. There are thirty-three ventilators placed at a distance of one mile from each other, to give free circulation of air through the aqueduct; they rise 14 feet above the surface of the ground, and have a circular aperture of 15 inches diameter; eleven of them are provided with doors by which the aqueduct may be entered. There are also six waste-weirs to allow the water to run off when it reaches a certain height, and to allow the aqueduct to be emptied should it become necessary. They are constructed of well dressed stone, with cast-iron gates and frames.

The Croton reservoir, which has received the name of Croton Lake, is available for 500 millions of gallons above the level that would allow the aqueduct to discharge thirty-five millions per day. The greatest height of the weir of the dam above the bed of the river is 55 feet. The width of masonry at low-water line of the river is 61 feet; the form on the lower face is a curve described by a radius of 55 feet, which continues to within 10 feet of the top, when a reversed curve of 10 feet radius carries the face over to meet the back line of the wall. The back line is carried up vertically with occasional projections. The waste-weir is 270 feet in width. At 300 feet below the main dam is a second dam 9 feet high, which sets the water back over the apron of the main dam, and thus forms a pool to check the water as it falls over the weir. The gateway which guards the entrance to the aqueduct is placed on a solid gneiss rock, through which the aqueduct passes by a tunnel of 108 feet in length. The gate chamber is provided with a double set of gates, one set of guard-gates of iron, the other a set of regulating gates made of gun metal. The gates are all 18 by 40 inches, and there are nine in each set; they are operated by means of wrought iron screw rods.

The Harlem bridge is represented on *pl.* 11, *fig.* 9; it crosses the valley of the Harlem river with eight arches of 80 feet span, and seven of 50 feet span; they are semicircular, and the height to the top of the parapets is 114 feet above ordinary high water; the width on top of the parapets is 21 feet. The material of the bridge is dressed granite. The water is conveyed across the bridge in three iron pipes of 3 feet diameter, having an extra fall of 2 feet in order to make their capacity for conveying water equal to that of the aqueduct.

The greatest depression of the Clendenning valley is 50 feet below the top of the aqueduct, and the valley is 1,900 feet across. Streets cross the line of the aqueduct in this valley at right angles, and archways are constructed over them. *Pl.* 11, *fig.* 10, represents the aqueduct, and *fig.* 11 is a section of the same.

The receiving reservoir is 1,826 feet long and 836 wide, and covers with its embankments an area of thirty-five acres. It is divided into two parts, having respectively the depths of 20 and 30 feet; its present capacity is 150 millions of gallons. It is formed by earth-banks, the interior having regular rubble walls; the outside is protected by a stone wall on a slope of one horizontal to three vertical, the face laid in cement mortar, and the inside dry.

The distributing reservoir at Murray hill is 420 feet square, and covers four acres; it is 36 feet deep, and holds twenty millions of gallons. The walls are of hydraulic stone masonry, constructed with openings made by an interior and exterior wall, connected every 10 feet by cross walls, in order to give an enlarged base and reduce the quantity of masonry. At 17 feet from the top the cross-walls are connected by brick arches; the exterior wall, 4 feet thick, is then carried up single to the top, where it has an Egyptian cornice surmounted by an iron railing. On each corner of the reservoir pilasters 40 feet in width are raised, projecting 4 feet from the main wall, and in the centre of the street-façades are pilasters 60 feet wide; they have doors and stairways leading to the top of the walls and to the pipe chambers, in which the supply of water can be regulated by stop-cocks. The reservoir is divided by a wall of hydraulic masonry into two divisions, from both of which the city is supplied, and in each there is a waste-cock to draw the water from the bottom. The level of the reservoir is 45 feet above that of the adjoining streets, and higher than any part of the city of New York.

E. Canal Bridges.

On canals which are not navigated by vessels carrying masts, the foot and road bridges crossing them are built like other structures of the kind; care should be taken to give them sufficient height to allow persons to stand upright on the deck of boats passing under them. When on the contrary sailing vessels are used on a canal, drawbridges of various kinds are constructed, which may be opened to allow the passage of the boats. The common drawbridge is raised vertically on hinges, by means of a windlass or other machinery. *Rolling bridges* are those which are drawn back horizontally on rollers, and *turning bridges* move aside by revolving on a vertical axis or hinge. *Pl.* 10, *fig.* 7, is a side view of an iron turning bridge of 40 feet span; *fig.* 8 is a top view of one wing with the roadway partially removed; *fig.* 9 is one of the inner ribs or semi-arches which support the roadway. Both wings turn about an axis at *c*, *c*, and when they meet they are rounded off in such a manner as to slide past each other when turned. This bridge is preferable to a drawbridge, being more readily moved and more durable.

II. WINDLASSES AND CRANES.

Of the great variety of machines which have been invented to facilitate the labor of raising weights which manual labor alone could never move, we propose to describe and illustrate only the most important and interesting.

WINDLASSES and JACKS are simple machines designed for raising heavy weights. The simplest forms of these are too well known to require illustration. A windlass of more elaborate construction is represented on *pl.* 12, where *fig.* 10 is an end view, *fig.* 11 a front view, and *fig.* 12 the bottom frame. The wooden drum *a* is mounted on an iron axle, which also carries the spur-wheel *b*, which is driven by the pinion *c*, the axle of which is turned by the two winches *d d'*; the frame B rests on the rollers *f f*, which may be made to run on a railway. The windlass is used in building and in manufactories, where heavy loads require to be moved from one place to another. In France they are employed, as shown in *fig.* 10, to lift the bodies of mail coaches, D, off the ordinary wheels, E, and place them upon the railroad trucks, C. The ropes or chains pass down over the pulleys, *q q*.

CRANES have a two-fold motion; that by which the load is raised, and a rotary motion by means of which it may be deposited in another place. The frame of a crane consists of a post or upright beam, from the upper end of which projects horizontally or obliquely upwards a beam called the jib, at the end of which the load is raised, and which is supported by a brace or stay. The post turns on pivots at both ends, or sometimes on the lower end only. At the end of the jib is a pulley, over which, in cranes of a simple construction, passes a rope from the load to a drum which is turned by winches, or, when heavy loads are to be raised, by a spur-wheel and pinion, as in the machine last described. Cranes are generally erected on wharves for the unloading of vessels, and they are universally employed in foundries and machine shops, where enormous loads are lifted and moved by means of them.

Pl. 12, *fig.* 6, is a side view of a crane generally used in foundries; *fig.* 7 is a top view of the same. It is entirely of iron; the frame consists of two plates separated by cross-pieces, and held together by screw-bolts, *h h*; B is the post, C the stay, D the jib; the gudgeons, *p p′*, of the post turn on friction rollers, as shown in *fig.* 8. The force is applied at the winches, O, on the axle of the pinion, N, which drives the spur-wheel, M, on the axle of which is another pinion driving the spur-wheel, K, which carries round the drum, L. On the axle of the pinion N is a ratchet-wheel, into which a catch or detent falls to prevent the load from descending when the power ceases to act. The chain passes from the drum over the pulleys, Q and H, to the load. Besides the circular motion about the gudgeons, a rectilinear motion towards or from the centre can be given to the load in this crane by means of the following construction. The pulley, H, is attached to a small truck, G, which can be drawn along the track, T, by means of the rack F; the latter is driven by the pinion, P, which is turned by means of the rope, *n n*, wound several times around the drum, J, on the axle of P.

Another crane, of French construction, composed of wood and cast iron, and intended for raising very heavy loads, is represented on *pl.* 12, *fig.* 1, being a view from behind, and *fig.* 2 a side view; *fig.* 3 shows the arrangement of the wheels on a larger scale. It is supported entirely at the lower end on the axis A, which is a hollow cast iron cone (a section being partly shown in *fig.* 2) turning on a gudgeon, B, at the lower end, and at the top in an iron collar, C, which are fastened in a pier of solid masonry. The jib, E, and stay, F, are of wood; the drum, Q, on which the chain, *r*, is wound, and the wheelwork arms, G G, attached to the posts are of iron. The operation of the machinery is readily understood from the figure. In order to sustain the load when raised, and to allow it to descend slowly when desired, a small drum, *n*, is attached to the spur-wheel, J, having a ratchet-wheel and brake, as shown on a larger scale in *figs.* 4 and 5.

Pl. 12, *fig.* 9, is a drawing of a very ingenious crane in the machine-shop of Maudslay, in London, which is mounted on wheels in a room used for setting up large engines, and which serves for raising and transporting the heavier parts of the engines, and for adjusting them in their positions. It has two arms, Q Q, which are movable about the bolts, *a a*, and may be raised or lowered by means of the chains attached at *b b* and wound around the drum, A, when it is desired to bring the load nearer to or further from the centre of the crane. The drum, A, turns with the cog-wheel, B, which is driven by an endless screw on the spindle, E, which also carries the wheel, D; the latter is driven by the pinion, F, when the spoke-wheel, G, is turned by hand. The load is raised at one arm only, while at the other a counterpoise is suspended, which descends as the load is raised, and vice versa, and serves to establish the equilibrium of the crane. The chains by which the load and counterpoise are suspended are attached to the arms at *c c*, and passing over the pulleys, H and J, are wound over the drum, K, the axle of which rests in bearings at *d*, which are set into the post, T. The force is applied at the crank, O, and turns the drum by means of the pinions, *e* and M, and the spur-wheels, N and L; if lighter weights are to be raised the crank is applied at *f* to the axle of the pinions, M, and *e* is thrown out of gear by releasing the detent, *g*. The frame, P, turns on a centre pin, *i*, and is supported on six rollers, *h*, which run in a circular track on the truck, R. The latter is mounted on four wheels, *t*, which can be set in any direction by means of bolts, *k*. When the whole crane is to be moved, it is done by means of blocks and tackle, as the application of levers under the truck would disturb the equilibrium of the machine.

III. HYDRAULIC MACHINES.

Hydraulic machines, by the aid of which water is raised or thrown from a lower to a higher point, are very various in their character and construction, and will be considered under their appropriate subdivisions.

1. Pumps.

We have in general three classes of pumps, viz. *suction* or *lift pumps*, *forcing pumps*, and *double action pumps*, which combine the principles of the two former.

A *lift-pump* (*pl.* 13, *fig.* 1) consists of a straight or bent pipe AB, the *suction-pipe*, extending below the surface *cd* of the water, enlarged at the lower end, and generally provided with a strainer or perforated cap, *ab*, to exclude impurities; joined to the upper end of the suction-pipe is a pipe CD, which is generally larger than the former, and must be bored truly cylindrical, in order to allow the box G to fit perfectly water-tight and move with as little friction as possible. At the junction of the two pipes is placed the valve A, the *suction-valve*, which in its simplest form moves on a leather hinge, opening upwards. The box G is perforated and provided with a similar valve F, also opening upwards. HJK is the pitman, which is moved up and down by means of the bent lever or pump-handle KLM. Frequently there is a contrivance to insure the rectilinear motion of the piston-rod, or at least there is a joint at J, which allows the portion JH to remain nearly perpendicular during the reciprocating motion. The action of this machine is quite simple: at the commencement the suction-pipe is filled with water to *ei* (the level of the surrounding water), and the space between *ei* and the bucket G is filled with atmospheric air. As the bucket rises the air between it and the suction-valve A will expand, and the latter will be opened by the greater pressure from below; when the bucket has reached its highest position, *kl*, the water will have risen to a height, *mn*, at which its pressure added to that of the rarefied air in the space *klmn* equals that of the exterior air; the suction-valve will now be closed by its own weight. By the descent of the bucket the air between it and the valve A is condensed again until its pressure begins to exceed that of the exterior air, when the bucket-valve F will open and allow the air to escape. By repeating the motion the water will be caused to rise successively in the suction-pipe, and will reach the valve A, open it, and arrive at the bucket. In descending through the water the bucket-valve will be opened, and the water will ascend through it, while the pressure will keep the suction-valve closed: on rising, the bucket-valve will close, the bucket lifting up the water in its ascent, while the pressure of the atmospheric air will force the water in the suction-pipe to follow the bucket to its highest position. By the continued play of the bucket the water will thus finally be raised to a reservoir, EE, at the top of the pump, whence it is discharged by spouts or cocks.

In this pump the water is raised entirely by the ascent of the bucket and the pressure of the atmospheric air. When the height, *qe*, of the bucket in its lowest position above the level of the water, *cd*, exceeds that of a column of water the pressure of which equals that of the atmosphere, then the water will not follow the bucket in its ascent, and cannot, therefore, be raised above it. The greatest height at which the bucket may therefore be placed above the level of the water to be raised is 32 feet, the height of the above column. In practice this height will be diminished by 2 or 3 feet, as the development of air contained in the water and the want of a perfectly air-tight fit of the piston will not allow a perfect vacuum to be formed.

A *forcing pump* in its simplest form is represented in *fig.* 2. The cylinder AB, immersed in the water, is closed at the bottom by the valve *f*, and communicates by the valve D with the pipe DE, through which the water is forced to the required height. The solid piston or *plunger*, C, has no valve, and is here moved by means of a lever of the second kind. When the plunger rises, the water will ascend into the cylinder by its own pressure and that of the air; as the plunger begins to descend, the pressure will close the valve *f* and open D, through which the water will be forced into the pipe DE. As the plunger ascends again the valve D will be closed by the pressure of the water in DE, which is thus prevented from returning into the cylinder. If the plunger in its highest position is below the surface of the exterior water, the pump will act independent of the pressure of the air, and is then a forcing-pump, properly so called.

A *double action pump* is one in which the cylinder is elevated above the level of the water, communicating with it by a suction pipe. This is a kind of pump very frequently employed to raise water to great elevations. A simple lift-pump, however, may also be employed to raise water to a considerable height.

As an example of this kind *fig.* 3 represents Stephenson's pump for wells. A is the surface of the ground; BB the wall of the well in which the water-level is below C. D is the pump-handle by which the pitman *a* is worked: the latter consists of wooden rods, joined together by iron fastenings, as shown in *fig.* 6. All the pipes are of wood; the cylinder E has a brass lining, intended to diminish the friction of the bucket *d*; *f′* is the suction-valve. The upper end of the cylinder is closed by a metal cover, *g* (*figs.* 4 and 5), which has a stuffing-box in the centre for the iron piston-rod, *h*; *k* (*fig.* 3) is a guide which keeps the piston-rod in a vertical position. The lift-pipe F consists of as many pieces as are required to carry the water to the desired elevation: the conical joints of the pieces are seen in the figure. It would be preferable to have a valve at the inclined junction-pipe *e*, in order to relieve the valve *f'* from the pressure of the water in F. The water is discharged at the spout *i*. N is a second spout provided with a screw, on which a hose may be screwed to convey the water to a distant point.

Pl. 13, *fig.* 7, represents a pump of superior construction in the mine Huelgoat, in Normandy. The plunger P in its upward motion lifts the water through S T', and L, and the lift-valve S' into the lift-pipe B; during its downward motion the water is forced up from the reservoir B', through the suction-pipe A, by the pressure of the air, raising the valve S. The cylinder C is of bronze, open below, and provided at the top with a stuffing-box for the piston-rod X. The packing of the plunger P is shown in *figs.* 8 and 9, consisting of a leather ring pressed outwards by the eight sectors, *l*, and the springs, *l'*. The valve-box consists of the two portions L and L', the upper one of which is fitted to the lift-pipe at *vv'* and has a vent at *r'*; and the lower one connects with the cylinder by the pipe T, and has a vent at *r*. The valves *s* and *s'* are conical or *puppet valves*.

When the pump is to be put in operation the lift-pipe is brought into communication with the suction-pipe by opening the cocks *u u' u''* of the bent tube D, and water is poured into the pump, the valves Z Z' at the bottom of the suction-pipe preventing its escape. The confined air is allowed to escape by the vent W, the cocks *u u' u''* are closed, and the pump is ready for action.

A pump by Letestu of Paris, which differs from those heretofore described in the construction of the valves and piston, is represented in *figs.* 10, 11, and 12. The latter shows the construction of the suction-valve, which consists of the disk, G, perforated by a great many holes, and covered by a leather disk, *a*, which is fastened by the screw, *b*. During the ascent of the bucket the leather disk is raised up by the pressure of the water admitting it into the cylinder, while during the downward stroke it is pressed firmly upon the disk, G, closing the openings. The bucket (*fig.* 11) consists of a perforated funnel with a loose conical leather-cap, *d*, which in the upward stroke is pressed against the sides of the funnel and of the cylinder, and thus makes a perfect packing. The lift-valve, J, is of the same construction as G, and the packing of the piston-rod, D, is also effected by a leather funnel, *e*.

2. The Hydraulic Ram.

The *hydraulic ram* is a machine designed to make use of water-power when with a considerable elevation or *head* of water the supply is so small as not to suffice for the turning of wheels. The mechanical effect is produced by the pressure of a high column of water confined in a pipe upon a piston, and the momentum it accumulates in descending a certain distance. The essential parts of the machine are, besides the main-pipe, a cylinder with the driving piston, and an arrangement of self-acting alternating valves.

by means of which a reciprocating motion is given to the piston. This machine is generally employed for the purpose of raising water, the driving piston being connected with the plunger of a pump. The construction and play of it are best illustrated by reference to *pl.* 13, *fig.* 15, which represents a section of a machine of this kind constructed by Reichenbach in the salt-works at Illfang in Bavaria, which forces the saline water to an elevation of 1,218 feet. *Figs.* 16, 17, 18, 19, 20, and 21, represent details of the same.

The column of water which acts as the motive power enters by the main-pipe, A (*fig.* 15), the supply being regulated by the throttle-valve, *a*, and after having performed its work it is discharged by the pipe, N. The whole mechanism is in the four verticals, A′, C′, F′, O′; in A′ is the pipe B branching off from the main-pipe, and communicating with the horizontal pipe, B′, when the stop-cock, *b*, is opened. In the vertical C′ is the pipe, C, which is seen on a larger scale in *fig.* 21; it communicates with the pipes, B′, and contains two small pistons, *d* and *d′*, both on the same rod, D, and drawn in *fig.* 15 in their lowest position. In the vertical, F′, is the distributing box, consisting of two cylinders, F and G H, the lower one having a larger diameter; in the former moves the piston K, in the latter the pistons, L and M, all fixed in the same vertical axis. In the vertical, O′, are the three cylinders, P, Q, and R, the first of which contains the counter-piston, S, the second the main driving piston, T, and the third the plunger, U, which forces the saline water to the required elevation. The cylinders P and R have equal diameters, and are both open at top, while Q is open at the bottom. The cylinder, R, of the forcing pump, the suction pipe, X, the chamber for the puppet valves, *x* and *x′*, and the pipe, Y, are supported by a strong wall.

We will now suppose all the parts of the mechanism to be in the positions represented in *fig.* 15; the stop-cock *a′* is closed, *b* is open, and there is no air in any of the pipes. The water from the main-pipe fills the cylinders, G, F, P, and the pipes, B, B′, Q′, and P′. The small pistons, *d* and *d′*, are at rest, having equal diameters and suffering equal upward and downward pressures. The pressure on the unequal pistons, K and L, is greatest in the downward direction, but their descent is prevented by the rod, *m*. The water therefore passes through Q′ to the main piston, T, which is driven downwards by a pressure equal to the weight of a column of water having the diameter of the piston, T, and the height of the main pipe. In its descent, T carries with it the counter-piston, S, and the plunger, U; the action of the latter is to force the saline water into the conduit pipe, Y, while the former expels the water contained in P through the spout, *j*. As the main piston arrives at its lowest point, a small pin, *e′*, on the rod *t* (*figs.* 15 and 19), pushes down the end, E′, of the lever, E′E, and thereby raises the opposite end, E, and the rod, D, with the piston, *d* and *d′*. The water will now enter below the piston, M, through *c*, and will neutralize the pressure from above upon L; the pressure upon K will therefore carry all three alternating pistons rapidly upwards, cutting off the communication of Q′ with A, and establishing that between A and P′, which will immediately produce an ascent of the counter-piston, S, and consequently of T and U, the water in Q passing through Q′ and I into the discharge pipe, N. When T reaches again its highest position the pin *e* will push the lever, E', E, into its former position, carrying with it the pistons *d* and *d'*, and cutting off the communication of the water below M with the main pipe. The downward pressure on L exceeding the upward pressure on K, they will descend again to the position of *fig.* 15, the water below M being expelled though *c*, C, and *c'*, into N, when everything is again in the position first assumed.

The two small cut-off pistons, *d* and *d'*, are of block tin. The alternating pistons, K, L, and M, consist each of brass cylinders with a ring of block tin, which, being soft and elastic, serves as packing. The counter-piston, S, has the same construction. The main piston, T (*figs.* 15, 18, and 19), consists of a cylindrical piece of brass (shaded in *fig.* 19) encircled by two rings, *s*, *s*, of block tin, which are sufficiently elastic to expand a little when a pressure is exerted from within, and to contract again when the pressure ceases. This property is made use of by means of the small tubes, Z', Z', which communicate with circular grooves in the brass body under the middle of the rings. During the descent of the piston the water entering the grooves will press the rings outwards and produce a perfect packing, while during the ascent the pressure is in a great measure relieved, allowing the wings to contract and experience very little friction. The plunger, U, consists of disks of leather saturated with oil; the manner of putting them together is seen in *fig.* 19. A better construction is shown in *fig.* 20, where it consists of two different layers of leather disks, the upper set forming the plunger, and the lower set, of less diameter, receiving the blow of the piston on the plate, *y*. The piston-rod, S', has a ball and socket-joint, as is seen in *fig.* 19, which also shows the connexion of T and U. The piston-rod, *kf*, also has a ball and socket-joint at L. *Fig.* 17 represents a horizontal section along the line, 3,4, in *fig.* 15, of the forcing pump and valve chamber; *fig.* 16 a similar section along the line, 1,2, in *fig.* 15.

A second hydraulic engine of this kind is represented in *pl.* 13, *fig.* 13. It was built by Jordan in the mine of Clausthal, in the Hartz, and was completed in 1835, together with another similar one, which works in the same shaft. The main piston has a diameter of 17 inches, and is driven by the hydrostatic pressure of a column of water 688 feet in height. The operation of this machine is similar to that just described, and will be readily understood. E is the main pipe, 6 inches in diameter; O M U are the alternating pistons by which the driving-column is cut off and let on; T is the main cylinder in which the piston is driven upwards by the pressure of the water; H is the back-water pipe through which the spent water is carried off; *h* is a double stop-cock, which opens or cuts off the communication of the pipes E and H with the cylinder U, by means of the tubes L, L', and L'', which have a diameter of $\frac{7}{8}$ of an inch. The figure represents the machine just after the completion of the upward stroke; the communication of the main pipe with the cylinder T is cut off by the piston-valve M, and the main piston-rod D will descend, and by its own weight and that of the long piston-rod G, which descends to the bottom of the shaft, will force the spent water in T up the back-water pipe H to an elevation of 80 feet, where it flows off. In descending, the projection B operating against the angular arm *a'*, causes the axle W to turn through a certain arc, which, by means of the rod *g* and the lever *z*, turns the cock *h* so as to shut off the main water from the cylinder U. The pressure upon M exceeding that upon O, will cause M to descend, and admit the water from the main into T, when the main piston will commence its upward or working stroke. As it reaches the top, the projection B will, by acting on the arm *a*, turn the cock *h*, so as to admit the main water through L into U, and to close L′; when the piston-valve M will ascend and close the communication between the main pipe and cylinder, leaving the piston to descend as before. The couplings of the pitman-rods are shown in *fig.* 14.

3. Fire-Engines.

A further application of the suction and forcing-pumps are *fire-engines*, which serve to throw water or other fire-extinguishing fluids to a considerable distance or elevation. The chief requisites of a fire-engine are, that it should be as compact and portable as is consistent with the power of furnishing a large quantity of water, and that the stream of water thrown by it should not be intermittent but continuous, and that any desired direction may be given to it. All fire-engines consist of a single or double forcing-pump, provided with an air-chamber, the effect of which is to make the discharge of water continuous. The essential features of the machine are the following: one or two cylinders, at the bottom of which is the bottom or suction-valve, opening into the cylinder; each cylinder is connected with the air-chamber by a pipe, at the junction of which with the air-chamber is a valve which admits the water into the latter, but prevents its return. In the lower part of the air-chamber is the pipe through which the water is expelled, and which consists of several portions so joined together as to allow the mouth or *branch-pipe* to be turned in every direction, or else a leather pipe or *hose* ending in a brass nozzle is screwed to the first piece. The plungers in the cylinders are moved by levers on which the firemen operate. The cylinders and air-chamber generally are mounted in a water-box, which is supplied with water from a reservoir by means of a hose; when this reservoir is below the level of the fire-engine, the water is drawn from it by suction, and the suction-hose is stiffened out by spiral coils of wire (*pl.* 14, *fig.* 20 *b*) to prevent its being compressed by the atmospheric pressure.

The operation of fire-engines differs from that of ordinary pumps only by the action of the air-chamber. At the beginning of the play of the engine the chamber contains a quantity of air corresponding to its volume; as water is forced into it while the nozzle remains closed, the air will be compressed in the chamber to a great degree, and will, on the nozzle being opened, expel the water with great velocity in a copious stream, which retains its force without much variation while the pump continues to be worked. The suction-valves are either conical, spherical, or plane-valves. The spherical or ball-valves (*pl.* 14, *fig.* 19) are the most usual, and deserve the preference over conical valves, as they close perfectly, even when coming down a little inclined, which is not the case with the latter. Plane or hinge-valves consist of square or round plates of brass, well polished, and moving on hinges; or else a disk of leather is screwed between two plates of metal, one of which is a little smaller, the other a little larger than the opening to be closed, the leather disk thus closing the opening, while a prolongation of it serves as a hinge. The valves in the pipe connecting the cylinders and air-chamber are always hinge-valves in an oblique position.

We will now proceed to explain the construction of different kinds of fire-engines, with the aid of plate 14. *Fig.* 1 is an elevation, *fig.* 2 a section of the simplest machine of the kind, which is readily worked and carried about by one person, and, having no air-chamber, throws an intermittent stream. A is the cylinder, B the suction-valve, C the perforated suction-pipe; when the plunger, I, is raised, the water enters the cylinder through B, and in descending the plunger drives the water through the pipe, D, and the valve, F, into the hose, G, and expels it in a stream from the nozzle, H. The crutch, L, serves to manage and support the machine.

A portable fire-engine with a single cylinder, which acts far more powerfully than the above, but requires several persons for its management, is represented in *figs.* 3 and 4, the former being a cross-section in front of the air-chamber, the latter a longitudinal section. In the trough, *a*, is the sill, *b*, to which the main parts of the engine are screwed; *c* is the plunger, *d* the air-chamber, with the orifice, *f*, opening into the branch-pipe, *i k*, which is movable in every direction by means of the joints at *g*, *h*, and *i*, and the construction of which is shown in detail in *fig.* 18. The pump is worked by the lever, *n*; the levers, *p p*, which turn about the bolts, *q q*, serve for transporting the engine, when they bear against the projections, *r r*.

A double-acting portable fire-engine of very simple construction is that by Letestu, having pistons and valves on the principle explained above in speaking of his pump. *Fig.* 11 is a longitudinal section, *fig.* 12 a top view, *fig.* 13 a cross-section through the air-chamber, *fig.* 14 a horizontal section along the lower dotted line in *fig.* 11, and *fig.* 15 a front view of the engine. On a strong support, A B, provided with the rings, C, through which poles may be passed for transportation, rests the trough or water-box, D; in its centre is the air-chamber, E. The piston, K, in ascending admits water into the cylinders, H, and in descending forces it through the valve, G, into the air-chamber, whence it is expelled through the pipe, O, to which the hose and branch-pipe are screwed. At L the piston-rods are attached to the lever or balance-beam, M, which moves about the centre-bolt, P, and is worked by means of the arms, N N.

A more complex fire-engine is that by Pontifex, of London, which is frequently used on board ships, on account of its requiring but little space. *Fig.* 5 represents a longitudinal and *fig.* 6 a cross-section. It is inclosed in a box, A, which has at the bottom the projecting leaves, *e* (the one on the left hand is omitted), that fold up about a hinge, *f*; when the engine is in use they are turned down and a part of the men stand on them, giving stability to the engine. The upper part of the box consists of two pieces which turn on the hinges, *a*, and when closed are held together by the hook, *b*, *fig.* 6. Four ring-bolts, T, are attached to the box by which it is carried, the brake-bars, M, being put through them. The working parts of the engine are now readily understood by inspection of the figure. *t* is a guide-rod which passes through a packing-box at *l'*, and insures the rectilinear motion of the plunger. Two uprights, *x x* (*fig.* 6), support the axis, R, of the balance-beam, K H K L. The pipe, *p q*, leads from the air-chamber to the hose. Two cross-pieces, N, limit the extent of the stroke. The volume of the air-chamber is nearly four times that of one cylinder. Six or eight persons can work this engine, and water may be thrown with it to a height of 60 feet.

A fire-engine constructed on an entirely different principle is that invented by Repsold, in Hamburg, in 1843. It works by revolving pistons, and is represented in *fig.* 7 in a side elevation; *fig.* 8 is a top view of the active machinery, *fig.* 9 a front view, and *fig.* 10 a section. On a light hand-cart, A, is placed a sliding frame, B, which can be fixed in any position by the set-screw at B. The engine, E, rests on the platform, C D; the hose, cranks, and other apparatus are carried in the box, J. The body of the engine, E, consists of a metal box formed by two cylinders partly inserted into each other, and closed at the ends with two plates. In this box play the two pistons, L and M, which are mounted on the axles of the wheels, *a* and *b*, and are turned by the cranks, F F. The pistons are of an epicycloidal form, and so arranged that their surfaces are always in close contact at a line between the centres. The larger segment of the epicycloid is in close contact with the surrounding cylinder, which is effected by a packing on the latter of lamina of metal covered with leather, *e* and *f*. G and H are the orifices by which the water enters and is discharged. The action of the engine is as follows. Whenever by turning the cranks the pistons, L and M, are set in motion, revolving in opposite directions, a vacuum will be formed before the smaller segment of one piston, and will be filled with water from the supply-pipe; the piston in continuing its revolution carries the water before it, and throws it out at the opposite orifice. In this way both pistons operate alternately, and the pressure of one will have commenced before that of the other ceases to act, thus furnishing a continuous stream of water without the aid of an air-chamber. An engine of this kind worked by four men will do as much work as an ordinary one when worked by six or eight men.

Pl. 14, *fig.* 16, represents a fire-engine mounted on carriage-wheels, as it is in general use by the firemen in cities. It differs in nothing but the larger dimensions from the portable double-acting fire-engine described above, and its operation will be readily understood by inspection of the figure. The connexion of the several sections of pipe or hose is shown in *fig.* 17. *Fig.* 21 represents a stop-cock as it frequently occurs in different parts of the engine. It will be seen that the cock, G, is so perforated as to admit the water in the position in which it is drawn; when turned at right angles to that position it will cut it off completely.

Pl. 14, *fig.* 22, is a longitudinal section, and *fig.* 23 a transverse section, of a fire-engine constructed by Bramah, which differs essentially from those already described. Upon a strong four-wheeled truck rest the saddles *a*, cut out circularly on top to receive the cylindrical chamber B, made of staves or boards and hooped with iron: it is divided into three divisions, A, B, C. A contains the pump-cylinder; the middle portion, B, is the water-box; and C receives one of the gudgeons of the centre shaft and the levers or arms by which it is worked.

At *a′* is an opening with a closely-fitting cover, through which the interior of the water-chest is cleansed. Above the engine is a box, D, for carrying tools, at one end of which, in a separate division, is the air-chamber E; beneath the engine is a cock, *c*, to let off the water. At *d* is seen the brass pump-cylinder, 10 inches in diameter and 7½ inches long for an engine to be worked by 10 men. Above this cylinder communicates with the air-chamber, and below with the water-chamber through the pipe *i*; *k* is a cock which establishes a communication between the pump-cylinder and either the water-chamber or with the external air, according as it is turned in one direction or the other. When water is to be drawn from a well, the cock is turned, as seen in *fig.* 22, so that the pump-cylinder *d* is opened to the tube on the left, to which is attached a suction-hose reaching to the bottom of the well.

When water is to be drawn from the water-chamber B, the cock *k* is turned in the opposite direction, opening a communication between the pump-cylinder and the pipe *i*. Beneath the central axle the pump-chamber *d* is divided by a vertical partition, reaching from the axle to the bottom of the chamber, and upon each side of the division-wall are valves in the bottom of the chamber opening inwards. The axle is packed water-tight where it enters the pump cylinder, and also at the joint between it and the vertical partition. Attached to the axle within the cylinder are two plates or pistons, one upon each side of the partition, which are packed tight by rings or disks of leather. In these plates are valves opening upwards. A reciprocating rotary motion is communicated through the brakes o to the centre axle, and the plates or pistons attached to it are thus alternately made to approach and recede from the stationary partition. The water is thus drawn through the valves in the bottom of the cylinder, and forced through the valves in the reciprocating pistons into the upper portion of the cylinder *d*, which communicates with the air-chamber E, from which the pipe passes which receives the hose.

Steam-power has also been applied to the working of fire-engines, Braithwaite in London being the first who made the attempt. *Pl.* 14, *fig.* 24, represents a side view of a fire-engine driven by steam; it works on the high-pressure principle, and has six horse-power. It has two horizontal cylinders, one of which is the steam-cylinder and the other that of the forcing-pump; the pistons of both are on one rod and act at the same time, the alternating motion of the steam-piston producing that of the plunger immediately. *a a* is a wooden frame which rests on springs that are supported on the axles of the wheels; on this wooden frame is an iron one, which supports the cylinders and other main parts of the engine; *b* is the boiler; *c*, the cinder-box: in order to produce a rapid combustion, a blowing apparatus is contained in the box *n*, which may be worked either by the engine or by hand; *m* is the boiler-pump; *w*, the mercurial gauge; *u*, the escape-pipe; *v* is the coke-box, serving also as a platform for the fireman. The steam-cylinder has 7 inches diameter, the length of stroke is 16 inches, and the number of strokes 35 to 45 per minute. The parts belonging to the fire-engine proper are the air-chamber *r*, connected by the pipe *s* with the cylinder of the pump *p*, of 6½ inches diameter: *q* is a suction-pipe or hose which supplies water from a reservoir; or if water cannot be procured in that way, it is supplied by other engines to the water-box. This engine can throw four streams at once, if required. In Berlin there is one of the kind described, with 10-inch double-acting cylinders and 15 horse-power.

Having treated at length of fire-engines, this may be the proper place to add a few words on other means and apparatus employed to save persons and property in case of fire.

In all large cities there are regularly organized fire-companies, who are always ready to act when the alarm is given. In France the corps of firemen have a military organization under the name of *Sappeurs Pompiers*. One third of each company is always on duty, while another third is in reserve, and only the remaining third is off duty. Those on duty are engaged in patrolling through their districts, to give the alarm in case of fire. Their dress uniform is very tasteful; I, L, M, and N (*pl.* 14, *fig.* 28) are parts of the accoutrement of a pompier; K is the hat of an officer. The working-dress of course is very different; one of the main pieces is the casque, H (*fig.* 29), which protects the head against falling bodies. *Fig.* 27 represents a fireman in a safety-dress of leather, with a thick glass-plate before the face, by which he is enabled to enter burning rooms, the dress being well wetted before.

Among the apparatus used by firemen we notice the hook-ladders, A (*figs.* 28 and 29), by means of which the upper stories of buildings can be reached when the stairs are already on fire, the ladders being hooked successively on the window-sills of the several stories. It requires some art and practice to scale these ladders, which of course are nearly in a vertical position, and persons who are to be saved from the higher stories cannot be expected to descend by them; for such the fireman carries with him a long bag of leather or strong twill, B, which reaches to the ground and is held away from the house at the lower end by several persons; through this persons are sent down, sliding rapidly down the inclined bag, and are caught up below in a horizontal position. The hose, D, accompanies the fireman everywhere; a short folding ladder, E, an axe, G, and a bucket, F, also belong to his equipment. Among the larger apparatus designed for rescuing persons and property from burning houses one of the best is that represented in *pl.* 14, *fig.* 25 being a side view, and *fig.* 26 a front view; the former represents the machine when entirely raised, the latter while it is partially elevated. Like all other machines of the kind, it can only be used in cases where time and room admit of it, as it can be raised but slowly and requires much space. A square frame, *b*, is mounted on the truck A, and supports the posts CC, which are united by ties and braces to form a square tower, the stability of which is secured by the stays HH when mounted for use. In front and in the rear is a ladder, G, which moves on a hinge at top, and when in use is braced out by the strut G′. In the interior of this tower are two more of the same kind, sliding out like the tubes of a spy-glass, the second within the first, the third within the second. The third story has on top a platform provided with a railing, from which communication with the building is established by means of planks or ladders thrown across. The several stories are raised by means of the machinery seen at the bottom, which winds the ropes *f* and *i* on a drum.

IV. MILLS.

Before entering upon the subject of MILLS, it may not be out of place to say a few words upon the power by which they may be set in motion, and the improvements made in modern times in this branch of industry.

Whatever power may be made use of, it should be so arranged as to produce a rotary motion. Man-power, horse-power, steam, wind, and water, may be used, or in fact any agent capable of being employed to drive machinery. The simplest mode of driving machinery is by *horse*-power. The horse in this case is harnessed to a long horizontal lever, mortised into a vertical shaft, and is forced to travel round in a circular path, and thus the shaft is made to revolve and to give off the power to the machinery to be driven. There are a great variety of methods of making use of the power of horses for driving machinery, which are too special to be discussed in this place.

Another common motive power for mills is *wind*. This power is obtained by the pressure exerted by the wind upon the inclined arms or sails of the wind-wheel, and is thence communicated to the mill. In some cases the whole mill is made to revolve, in order to bring the wheel in a proper position to be acted upon by the wind; in others, as in the case of the Dutch mills, only the upper portions or hood are made to revolve.

Steam is also frequently employed for this purpose, but more commonly *water*, as this agent is more generally at hand to meet the primitive wants of man, before an advanced stage of the arts introduces the use of steam-mills, and the costly machinery necessary in the application of this power.

1. VERTICAL WATER-WHEELS.

Vertical water-wheels are those in which the shaft of the wheel is horizontal. Those wheels in which the force of the moving water is communicated to the buckets beneath the wheel are called *under-shot wheels;* and those which are driven only by the weight of the water which is poured upon the top of the wheel, *over-shot wheels*. In *breast wheels* the water strikes the wheel upon a level with its axis.

Formerly water-wheels were built of wood; more recently, however, cast-iron has been used, not only for the disks which support the buckets, but also for the buckets themselves, the whole being put together by screws upon the spot where it is to be put up.

An important part of the water-wheel is the bucket, an idea of the form and position of which may be gathered from *pl.* 15, *fig.* 1. It will readily be seen that one desideratum with over-shot wheels is to keep the buckets filled with water until they reach the lowest point of their revolution; this in practice it is impossible absolutely to accomplish. At first, the buckets were placed in the prolongation of the diameter of the wheel (*fig.* 3), but in this position their power to retain the water ceased when the bucket became horizontal. Then the buckets were inclined, as seen in *gf*, *fig.* 6; but this arrangement was liable to the objection that the capacity of the buckets was much diminished, while the wheel itself was made very heavy. Subsequently the buckets were formed with two inclinations, as seen at M *o* F, *fig.* 6, which insured the advantages without the disadvantages of the inclined bucket.

Under-shot wheels, as already remarked, are those in which the water acts only by impulsion or concussion. There are many varieties of the same. *Pl.* 15, *fig.* 5, is a form often used in small but rapid streams. Where a stronger wheel and larger bucket is required, the wheel seen in *figs.* 3 and 4 is used; in this case, it will be seen that the buckets do not project beyond the sides of the wheel as in the former case.

Pl. 15, *figs.* 1 and 2, are a side and front view of an iron over-shot wheel; E is the flume which conveys the water to the wheel; *f* is the gate which regulates the flow of the water, and is worked by the screw *e*; C is the bevel-wheel which transmits the power to the machinery. *Figs.* 3 and 4 are vertical sections and plan of iron breast-wheel; A is the gate, raised and lowered by the pinion *d*, worked by crank; C is the cog-wheel which drives the machinery. In *fig.* 5 the gate E is raised by the pinion *b*, and guided by the roller *c*. *Figs.* 7 to 18 show the details of an under-shot wheel of approved modern construction, the principal parts of which are of cast-iron; *fig.* 7 is a side-view, showing the driving circles and the wheel which transmits the power; *fig.* 8 is a vertical section of one half of the whole; *fig.* 9 is a plan showing the apparatus for raising the gate and the driving-wheel L; *fig.* 10 is a vertical section through the axis; *fig.* 11 a portion of the annular disks which support the ends of the buckets, showing the grooves which receive the same; *fig.* 12 shows the construction of the buckets on a large scale; *fig.* 13, section through one of the buckets; *fig.* 14 is a section of the apron or gate, furnished with shelves forming shutes at different heights, that the water may be delivered horizontally upon the wheel, whatever may be the height of the water in the flume; *fig.* 15, pillow boxes of main shaft; *fig.* 16, the same seen from above; *fig.* 17, the box for the shaft which raises the apron; *fig.* 18, front-view of the same. The same letters indicate corresponding parts in all the drawings. A is the hollow iron shaft, running in boxes, B, upon the masonry of the mill; C, arms of the wheel; D, sockets of cast-iron upon the axle which receive the iron arms C, and the wooden ones E; F, circles or annular plates of cast-iron made in segments, bolted or screwed together, and also secured to the iron arms C; G, an interior ring of wood which received the arms E; H, grooves for the reception of the ends of the buckets; K is the driving gear, with teeth on its interior periphery, made fast to one of the annular plates; M is the gearing for raising and depressing the gates; *n*, crank for driving the same; *o*, pinion driving cog-wheel P, on shaft *q* (*fig.* 9), which carries another pinion, engaging with the rack R of the apron or gate, which is thereby raised and lowered in the grooves in the side-walls of the flume.

2. Horizontal Water-Wheels.

Horizontal water-wheels differ essentially in their construction and operation from those already described. *Pl.* 15, *fig.* 19, is a vertical section of a *turbine* as improved by Fourneyron. F is the vertical axle which carries the horizontal water-wheel, from which the power is communicated in any known way to the machinery to be driven.

This shaft is stepped into the lever, K, having its fulcrum at P, and adjustable by means of the screw, M, upon the rod, L, so that the wheel with its shaft may be raised or lowered at pleasure; at the foot of the axle is secure the concave disk which terminates in the annular plate, A, upon which are fixed the vertical curved buckets, *a*. These buckets perform a duty analogous to that fulfilled by the buckets of the vertical wheels, receiving the impulse of the water and transmitting it to the machinery to be driven: *nn* is a tube by which the step, *m*, is oiled. The water flows from the flume above into a cylinder, DD, and thence into the cylinder containing the curved guides, *b*, *b* (*pl.* 15, *figs.* 19 and 20), which serve to guide the water upon the wheel, that it may strike the buckets perpendicularly. This cylinder rests upon a flange, *i*, of the tube, G, which surrounds the shaft of the wheel, the latter turning freely whilst the guide cylinder remains stationary. In order to regulate the force of water upon the wheel, the cylindrical gates, C, are so arranged as to be raised or lowered by the rods, E, attached to the ring, *d*, to which the gates, C, are secured.

At the bottom of the gate, C, are wooden wedges, so formed as to fit into the guide curves, and close the openings to the water-wheel in proportion as the gate is depressed.

Pl. 15, *fig.* 21, is a section; *fig.* 22 a front view, and *fig.* 23 a plan of a turbine of a little different construction, which will be easily understood from what has gone before; *f* is the water way; *h* the gate. The backwater passes off through the channel, A, and above is seen, at *b*, *m*, *n*, the machinery for transmitting the power.

In order to lessen the friction upon the step of the vertical shaft in wheels of this description, Nagel in Hamburg conceived the idea of admitting the water to the wheel from below, instead of above, which he did with the happiest effects, increasing the power of the wheel from 55 per cent. to 80 per cent. of the power applied. *Pl.* 15, *fig.* 24, is an elevation of a wheel arranged in this manner; *fig.* 25 a plan; *fig.* 26 a section of the wheel upon a larger scale; *fig.* 27 shows the bearing of the main shaft; *fig.* 28 a vertical section of the water passage; *fig.* 29 a view of the small gate; A is the flume; B the wheel secured to the shaft, C; D, the stationary curves which conduct the water to the wheel, and are secured to a nave made fast to the vertical post, F, in such a manner as to be easily raised or lowered; G is a gudgeon made fast by the wedge, X, to the vertical post, E, to which the wheel, B, is hung. The oiling of the gudgeon is accomplished by means of the canal, *y*, bored through the shaft, C, of the wheel (*fig.* 26). The guide-curves serve also the purpose of a gate to admit the water, and are raised and lowered for that purpose in the following manner (*fig.* 24). The rods, *n*, passing into the opening, *m*, of the nave carry the guide-curves; these rods, by means of the joint, *op*, and levers, *pq*, are connected with the rod, *s*, passing through a stuffing-box, and moved by the lever, *r*, and vertical rod, *t*.

3. Grinding Mills.

With mills as commonly constructed and arranged every one is supposed to be familiar; having therefore already noticed the power by which they are driven, we will turn our attention only to some important improvements which have been made in the United States during the last fifteen years, and which are now generally introduced into Germany and other parts of Europe. Amongst the advantages which these improvements possess are the following: 1st. A much larger proportion of superfine flour is obtained from the grain. 2d. The flour is better adapted to keeping and to transportation to hot climates, being in a great degree deprived of its moisture, and this without kiln-drying the grain, which has not been found fully to answer the purpose. 3d. The compactness and general arrangements of the machinery, together with the use of cast-iron for the mill-shafts and gearing, materially lessens the friction of the running parts, the frequent recurrence of breakages, and the consequent cost of repairs.

In *pl.* 16 is a system of mills upon the American plan for six run of stone; *fig.* 1 is an elevation, *fig.* 2 a vertical section through the main driving-shaft, *fig.* 3 a vertical section perpendicular to the latter, *fig.* 4 a section showing the disposition of the stones, *fig.* 5 a portion of the ring supporting the vertical shafts of the stones, *fig.* 6 a view from above, *fig.* 7 a view from above of the ring upon which the separate shafts are supported, *fig.* 8 a vertical section of the mill-bush in the stationary stone, through which the vertical shaft which drives the upper stone passes, *fig.* 9 the horizontal section of the same; *fig.* 10 vertical section of the upper portion of the boxes in which the mill-shafts run, with the apparatus for raising the same; *fig.* 11, plan of the same; *fig.* 12, horizontal section immediately above the mill-spindle, *fig.* 13, horizontal section immediately above the base of the column; *fig.* 14, horizontal section immediately over one of the driving-wheels, T; *fig.* 15, box in which the spindle of the main driving-shaft rests. The same letters indicate corresponding parts in all the figures. The base, A, carries the pedestal, B, and the columns, C, which support the flooring, D, carrying the ring E, which supports the different bed-stones. Upon the bed, D, are the triangular frames, F, regulated by set-screws, and upon which the bed-stones, F′, rest, while the runner-stones, F″, hang upon the top of the upright shafts, G. Within the bed-stone is the mill-bush, H, through which the shaft, G, passes. In the eye of the runner-stone is the rind, *f*, and the tube, *l*, which feeds the grain to the stones, from the receptacles, *v*, to which it is brought by the tubes, *s*, from the room above. The runner, F″, is raised and lowered by a suitable arrangement. The shaft, G, which carries it, is supported in a box, *j″*, on the top of the hollow column, J, within which is a rod, I, on which the above named box rests; this rod rests upon a lever, K, which is raised or lowered by a rod, L, passing up through one of the columns, C (*fig.* 4), by which means the box, *j″* and with it the shaft which carries the runner-stone, is raised and lowered.

The whole system is driven by the main-wheel, M, upon the horizontal shaft, N, which is in gear with the driving power (*fig.* 7). Upon the other end of this shaft is a bevel wheel, O, which engages with another wheel, P, upon the upright shaft, Q, carrying the large cog-wheel, S, which drives the smaller wheels, T, upon the shafts of the mill-stones. The stones are inclosed in cases, U, which prevent the waste of the flour; from these cases the flour is delivered into a circular trough X (*fig.* 3), in which are made to revolve the arms or scrapers, *x′* (*fig.* 2), which sweep the flour round into another trough, through which it is carried by the screw-formed *conveyor*, Z, to the elevators, Z′, seen at the right hand upper corner of the machine in *fig.* 3.

Upon the main shaft is a small pulley, *c′*, from which a band passes to the governor, A′, which regulates the velocity of the steam-engine, and consequently of all the machinery driven by it.

In all well arranged mills the grain, before being ground, is freed from foreign substances; this is sometimes accomplisned by passing the grain through a cylindrical riddle, furnished with screw-formed divisions on the inside, so that as the riddle revolves the grain passes over a great extent of surface, and is measurably freed from dust and other extraneous substances. Very perfect machines have been invented and put into use for the purpose of cleaning grain, which is accomplished in most of them by subjecting it first to friction and then to a current of air which carries off the impurities. By one process recently invented in the United States the grain is not only freed from the impurities which it may contain, but entirely deprived of its hull or skin. This process is briefly as follows: the grain is moistened for a few seconds in either steam or water, and is then passed through rubbers, which take off the outer skin entirely, leaving the useful portion of the grain clean and white; from the rubbers it passes through a kiln, in which it is again dried, and then it is run through a fan which blows off all the impurities with the skin, leaving the grain ready for the mill; it is then ground, and may be packed at once in barrels, as it requires no bolting or any further preparation. The seeds of garlic and other weeds, which have heretofore proved so troublesome to the miller, are by this process entirely removed. The preliminary soaking, which is just sufficient to moisten the skin of the wheat, entirely penetrates other seeds, so that they are subsequently ground or crushed in the rubbers, and after being dried are blown off with the hull of the grain. It is said that by this process fifteen per cent. more flour is obtained from wheat, and at a less expense, than by the usual process of grinding and bolting.

The mill-stones in use in the United States and Europe are mostly made of a porous silicious stone obtained from France. As this stone is not obtainable in masses sufficiently large to make the mill-stones in a single piece, they are put together in smaller pieces with cement and secured by iron bands. After being accurately balanced, the stones are cut upon their grinding surfaces, as seen in *pl.* 16, *fig.* 6. The bed-stone must not only be adjusted level, but concentric with the axis of the spindle. To accomplish the first, the bed-stone rests upon a frame, F, which is adjusted by three screws, one under each corner. The centring of the stone is accomplished by means of screws working against the sides of the stone (*pl.* 16, *fig.* 6).

The operation of the mill-bush is seen in *figs.* 8 and 9. This bush is of cast-iron, and is secured in the centre of the bed-stone. Three pieces of brass or wood rest against the mill-shaft, and are pressed against it by screws, in order to perfectly adjust the main shaft in the centre of the bush; the interstices not occupied by the brass or wooden blocks are filled with oakum or tow saturated with oil, in order to lubricate the bearing. After the grain is ground, it is necessary that the flour be thoroughly cooled before it is bolted; where there are no arrangements for effecting this, the flour has to remain twenty-four hours before being bolted. In most mills, however, this is accomplished by a machine, also an American invention, called the *hopper-boy*. The flour is run into a circular room, where it is stirred by revolving arms until it is completely cooled, when it passes immediately to the bolts, where the preparation of the flour is finished.

V. COTTON MANUFACTURE.

Cotton is the production of a genus of tropical plants of which there are many species; these again run easily into varieties, so that there have been enumerated over one hundred different sorts. The dwarf varieties found in America, India, and China grow to a height of eighteen inches to two feet; the blossoms are a pale yellow and are succeeded by triangular three-celled seed-vessels, which gradually turn brown as they ripen, and ultimately burst open, exposing the cotton fibres wrapt round the seed. The shrub and tree cotton grow in America, the West Indies, East India, Egypt, &c., the latter reaching a height of from 12 to 20 feet.

When cotton is to be spun, it is first subjected to the operation of *ginning*, to separate it from the seeds. This is performed upon the plantation where it is grown, as when packed with the seeds it becomes oily and soiled, and is unfit for manufacturing purposes. The close adherence of the fibres to the seed renders this a tedious operation, which is now entirely performed by machines called *gins*. That most commonly used in the United States is the *saw gin*, of which *pl.* 17, *fig.* 1, is a section, *fig.* 2 a plan showing the saws and brush cylinder. The prominent parts of the machine are two cylinders of different diameters, F and H, which lie in a strong wooden frame, and are set in motion by crank, bands and pulleys, or other means.

Upon a horizontal axle *ff*, circular steel plates or saws are secured, the circumference of which is filled with sharp-pointed inclined teeth. These plates, which are 10 to 12 inches in diameter, and half a line thick, are separated a distance of 9 lines from each other by small washers. In front of this saw-cylinder, and secured to the main frame of the machine, is a grating of bent iron bars, placed so near each other that the saws can just pass between them without rubbing. This grating forms a portion of the forward side of the hopper L, which receives the cotton to be operated upon. Connected with the back wall of the hopper is a strip hung upon hinges, and adjusted by a set of screws, by which means the opening through which the seeds pass when cleaned is regulated. Behind the saws, and parallel with their axis of rotation, is the drum H, carrying six horse-hair brushes, *cc*. The saws and brushes move in contrary directions, the former making about 100 and the latter 150 revolutions per minute. The teeth of the saws, which project more or less between the rods of the grating into the hopper, seize the fibres of cotton and draw them through, whilst the seeds, being too large to follow, fall through the opening at the bottom of the hopper into the box N below; the cotton is then swept off the teeth of the saws by the revolving brushes. The brush-cylinder also acts as a ventilator, which partially cleans the wool. The ginned cotton falls upon the inclined table O, and thence into the box P; such a machine requires two-horse power to move it, and turns out 5000 lbs. of cotton per day.

1. Picking, Scutching, and Lapping Machines.

The first operation in cotton-spinning is to pick open the closely packed mass, and separate the sand and other foreign substances which it may contain. The finest cotton, as the Sea Island, is first opened by hand, spread upon a table of coarse netting called a *flake*, and beaten with rods by women and children. The shaking of the net-work loosens the cotton and frees it from sand, whilst the larger extraneous substances are picked out by hand. This labor was tedious and expensive, and machines have been invented to perform it. One of the best and most common for this purpose is the *wolf* or *willow*, originally a cylindrical willow basket, but as now constructed, a most powerful and effective machine. *Pl.* 17, *fig.* 3, represents an exterior view of a conical willow, showing the side which receives and delivers the cotton; *fig.* 4 is an end-view, and *fig.* 5 a plan, a portion of the covering and frame being removed to show the interior mechanism. *Fig.* 5 *a* shows the perforated plates on the grating which forms a portion of the bottom casing round the cone. The cone A consists of a strong shaft, *a a*, carrying three cast-iron rings, one at each end and one in the middle, on which the sheet-iron is secured which forms the surface of the cone.

Longitudinally upon this surface are four iron rods, in which are secured rows of strong iron pins, *b b*; upon each side of the framework is a row of pins, *d d*, corresponding to the spaces between the pins upon the cones. The cone is surrounded by a concentric covering, the bottom of which consists of a grating or perforated plate; at the small end of the covering is a rectangular opening, *e*, connected with the frame D, in which travels the endless feeding apron E, which consists of parallel stripes of thin sheet-iron, ¾ inch wide, and secured half an inch apart, upon endless bands of leather running upon rollers.

At the larger end of the machine is a chamber, F, into which the cotton is thrown by the revolving cone, whence it is received by an endless apron similar to the feeding apron, and shown by dotted lines at G G. About an inch above the apron, and upon an axis parallel thereto, revolves a wire cylinder, H, having a sheet-iron covering which communicates with the chamber F by the openings *f f*. Above the wire cylinder is a ventilator, which draws the dust of the cotton through the wire cylinder from the chamber F, and blows it out at the opening *g*. The wire cylinder seems not only to prevent the cotton from being blown away with the dust, but lays it upon the delivering apron, and is connected with the ventilator by means of a covering of sheet-tin, which embraces the openings at the ends of both these cylinders, the dust passing through the meshes of the wire cylinders being blown out by the ventilator.

The motions of this effective machine are as follows: Upon one end of the shaft *a* of the cone A, are the usual fast and loose pulleys K, and upon the other end the two pulleys *i* and *k*, of which the former communicates motion to the ventilator, by a band upon the pulley *l*. From the pulley *k* an endless band drives the pulley *m*, upon the axis of the roller carrying the delivering apron. Upon the axle of the latter roller is a pulley, *n*, which gives motion by another band to the pulley *o* of the wire cylinder H. Upon the other end of the last-named axle is a pinion, *p*, which drives the wheel *q*, and the small pulley *r* attached to it. From the latter a band runs to the pulley *s*, upon an axle *t*, having a universal joint, which permits the deflection of the direction of its motion to one parallel with the exterior surface of the cylinder. The universal-jointed axle *t* runs in boxes in the frame D, and carried a cog-wheel, *u*, which engages another cog-wheel, *v*, upon one of the rollers of the feed apron, by which means the latter is driven.

The operation of the willow is as follows: The cotton, which is gradually carried to the machine by the feeding apron, is torn open at the smaller end of the cone, and its heavier impurities, dust, stones, &c., fall out; the cotton being carried by centrifugal force to the other end of the machine, the lighter particles of dust are thrown through the cylindrical revolving sieve. This is a powerful and safe machine, and capable of cleaning 7200 lbs., or 24 bales of cotton per day.

The next operation to which the cotton is subjected is performed by what are called *batting* (*beating*), *scutching*, and *blowing* machines, by means of which the fibres of the cotton, which have been loosened by the willows, are more perfectly opened, and by the use of sieves and ventilation entirely freed from dust. The beating is accomplished by flat rods, which strike the cotton whilst it is slowly carried through the machine upon endless cloths.

In each machine there are generally two beating arrangements, from the second of which it is taken to a new machine, called a *lap* machine, which, after again blowing and scutching the cotton, coils it upon a wooden roller, in the form of a lap or sheet.

The first blowing machine serves to prepare the cotton for the second, and is sometimes called a *spreading* machine; it is shown in *pl.* 17, *fig.* 6. The frame is of cast-iron and is covered in with boards, only the necessary openings being left for the introduction and extraction of the cotton and the separation of the dust. The feeding takes place through an endless apron, *a*, which runs over two wooden rollers, *b* and *c*, by the revolution of which it is moved. A table, *d*, between the rollers *b* and *c*, on the surface of which the feeding apron travels, serves as a support for the latter, and keeps it always flat. The cotton is spread by hand upon this apron, which feeds it with the utmost regularity to the fluted rollers, *e*, by which it is drawn in and subjected to the operation of the beater or scutcher, *f*, which consists of an axle and two arms, which carry thin iron beaters with rounded edges.

Beneath the beater is a curved grating of iron wire, *n*, which permits the dirt and seeds to fall through, whilst the filaments of cotton are blown upon a second apron, *a'*, which conducts the cotton to the second scutcher, *f'*, arranged precisely like the first. In order that the cotton may be delivered regularly to the feeding rollers *e'*, it is pressed down upon the apron by a wire-gauze squirrel-cage, *h*, which bears with its whole weight upon the feeding apron, *a'*, and transfers to it, in the form of a sheet, the cotton which is blown against its circumference. The dust and short fibres of cotton are blown through the meshes of the sieve, from which they are again drawn off by a sucking fan-ventilator above.

The second beater drives the cotton through a long wooden canal, *xx*, a portion of the floor of which consists of a grating of inclined slats. The progress of the cotton through this canal is assisted by a ventilator, *m*, placed beneath the beater.

The second blowing-machine, called a lap-machine, because it converts the cotton into a lap or sheet, resembles in its elements the before described machine, and is represented in *pl.* 17, *fig.* 7. The cotton, which, by the pressure of the wire-gauze drum *h*, is already measurably compressed, passes from the endless apron *op*, between the two smooth rollers *r*,*s*, which are pressed together by heavy weights, and serve to give the sheet of cotton an additional degree of firmness. As it leaves these rollers the lap is rolled upon a wooden roller, *v*, whose gudgeons run in vertical grooves, which permit it to rise as the size of the roll of cotton increases. This roller rests upon the revolving rollers *t*,*u*, covered with leather, by friction upon which the lap-roller is turned; and thus the winding of the lap takes place with entire regularity. A weight is hung upon each end of the roller *v*, for the purpose of giving firmness to the lap.

With this machine first commences the determining of the fineness of the thread to be spun. As this fineness depends upon the weight of a given length of thread, the manufacturer must keep himself informed in the whole course of his operations of the length produced in each step of the process by a certain quantity of cotton. This comparison must commence with the lap-machine.

The cotton is spread upon the feeding apron, *a*, not only with great regularity, but care must be taken that a specified weight of cotton be distributed upon a certain length of cloth. To the accomplishment of this end the cloth is divided into equal lengths by red and black lines, and the cotton is weighed in small portions as it comes from the first blowing-machine, so that an equal quantity of cotton is always distributed upon an equal distance of the apron. When a number of such portions of the apron requisite to fill the lap-roll have passed a division is left empty, that the laps may be separated from each other as they come out of the machine.

Carding is the next operation to which the cotton is subjected; its object is to draw out the imperfectly opened fibres, to lay them parallel with each other, and to cleanse the cotton more perfectly. The operation consists in the mutual action of two contiguous surfaces, both furnished with hook-formed elastic teeth of hardened iron wire, of the form seen on *pl.* 17, *figs.* 8 and 9. These wires are bent and placed in the card-plates by machinery, the utmost regularity being requisite in both operations, otherwise an uneven fabric would be the result. American ingenuity has given birth to the most beautiful automatic machines for making these cards. Mr. Ellis's machine has been justly characterized by an English writer on the subject as "one of the most elegant automatons ever applied to productive industry." The leather and wire are furnished to the machine in rolls; the former is shaved to a uniform thickness and pierced with the requisite holes to receive the wire, which is cut into proper lengths, bent, and passed through the leather, and the strips of *card cloth* leave the machine completed. Suppose *a* and *b* (*pl.* 17, *fig.* 11) to be two cards whose teeth are set in opposite directions, and whose surfaces are parallel and at a short distance from each other; suppose a bunch of cotton to lie between them; let *a* move in the direction of its arrow, whilst *b* remains stationary or is moved in the opposite direction; the teeth of *a* tend to carry the cotton with them, whilst those of *b* retain it, or carry it in the opposite direction. Each of the cards takes a portion of the cotton, the small bunches are all drawn apart, and the fibres laid in a parallel direction. If the cards are placed as in *pl.* 17, *fig.* 10, the teeth pointing in the same direction, and *a* be moved in a direction contrary to that indicated by its arrow, whilst *b* remains stationary or moves slower than *a*, then *a* will comb the wool out of the teeth of *b*, since the hooks of *b* have in this position no power of retaining it. By considering these two relative positions of the cards, which take place in hand cards simply by reversing one of them, any person will be able to under stand the play of a cylinder card against its flat top, or against another cylinder card, the respective teeth being in what we may call the teasing position (*fig.* 11), and also the play of a cylinder card against the doffer cylinder, in what may be called the stripping position (*fig.* 10). Generally one carding is not sufficient for long-stapled wool. In order to produce the requisite lightness and parallelism of fibre, the cotton is twice carded; first in what is technically called a *breaker*, and afterwards through the *finisher*. The card cloth is placed upon cylinders or plane surfaces, the latter being at rest and the former revolving in contact with them. Sometimes large cylinders work against the surfaces of small ones moving with less velocity than the large ones. *Figs.* 12, 13, and 14, represent a carding machine combining both the above systems in one; *fig.* 12 is a longitudinal section; *fig.* 13, a view of the end from which the carded cotton leaves the machine; and *fig.* 14, an end view in which the principal wheelwork for the motion of the machine is shown.

A is the main card drum, consisting of parallel segments of mahogany secured by screws to iron rings made fast to the axle. Upon each of these segments is nailed a strip of card cloth, the length of which is equal to the width of the drum. The direction of the card teeth is apparent from the figures. B B are parallel segments of mahogany, resting at their ends upon the heads of screws, *b b*, upon the frame, C, of the machine, and maintained in their places by pins passing through their ends. The interior surface of these segments is covered with stripes of card cloth, and they are then called *top flat cards;* their distance from the drum, A, is regulated at each end by the set screws, *b b*, which arrangement is seen in *fig.* 14. D, E, F, G, are rollers covered with narrow strips of card cloth running spirally from end to end. These small cylinders, called *runners*, *urchins*, or *workers*, revolve in supports, *d*, *e*, *f*, *g*, which are furnished with set screws for the purpose of adjusting the distance of these small cylinders from the main card cylinder. At H are two fluted cast-iron feeding rollers pressed together by a screw; *h* is a feeding table which conducts the fleece to the feeding rollers as it is given off from the lap roller by the friction of the revolving roller, K. The first cylinder card or runner, D, moves slower than the main card drum, takes the fibres from the feeding rollers, and is therefore called the *licker-in;* these fibres are immediately stripped off by the main drum to be again drawn out by the second roller, E, which revolves slower than D, and serves to take the knots of uncarded fibres off the main cylinder, and carry them round and transfer them to the licker-in, D, with which it is almost in contact, which again transfers them to the main cylinder with the fresh cotton from the feeding rollers. The knots or bunches which escape the two first rollers, D and E, are seized by the fourth roller, G, which lies nearer to the main cylinder, and revolves with the same velocity as the runner E. The knots caught by G are drawn out again by the roller F, also called a *stripper* from the office its performs, which travels faster than G, but not so fast as the main cylinder. From F the fibres are again transferred to the main drum, which carries them forward and draws them again a second time over the runner. Should any uncarded knots still remain they are stopped by the first flat top card, on the surface of which they remain until entirely carded out by the revolutions of the drum. On this account the first top cards require cleaning oftener than the others. The fibres of cotton are now, after being subjected to the operation of the top cards, taken off by the small cylinder, L, called the *doffer*, which is clothed with spiral strips of card cloth, and revolves in contact with the main cylinder. By its slow motion, in a direction contrary to that of the main cylinder, the doffer strips the cotton from the main cylinder drum, and clothes itself with an exceedingly thin fleece, which is taken off upon the opposite side of the doffer by the *doffing knife*, M. This apparatus consists of a steel plate, the lower edge of which is finely toothed, and which has a rapid up and down motion imparted to it tangentially in contact with the surface of the cylinder. The cotton is thus *combed* off in a thin bat of the width of the doffer cylinder, but it is immediately condensed into a small riband or *card end* by passing through a funnel, *i* (*fig.* 12). This card end, called also a *sliver*, is drawn forwards by the rollers seen at N. This apparatus consist of three pairs of cast-iron rollers, *k*, *l*, *m*. The underneath rollers, *k* and *l*, are finely fluted, and the upper ones are covered first with flannel, then with leather, to give them a smooth elastic surface.

The upper rollers are pressed firmly against the lower ones by uprights. As the rollers *l* revolve with greater velocity than the rollers *k*, the card end is drawn and extended between them. After the fleece has been converted by the action of the rollers into a flat riband, it again receives an elliptical form by passing through a vertical slot in a metallic plate, through which it is drawn by the rollers, *m*, which are pressed together with but little force. The card end now has a very open, spongy texture, and scarcely sufficient tenacity to hold itself together. From the last pair of rollers it falls into tin cans, *o*. In many manufactories the card ends from several machines are wound immediately upon a lap roller or large bobbin, ready to be taken immediately to the drawing-frames. In other factories the card ends as they run from a number of machines are united together and conducted through wooden troughs, and at last are wound upon a large bobbin into a fleece of parallel ribands ready to be taken to the drawing-frame.

Motion is communicated to the different parts of the machine in the following manner. Upon the axle of the main drum, without the frame of the machine, are the ordinary fast and loose pulleys, and a smaller pulley (*fig.* 14), giving motion by a crossed band to the stripper, F; also a pulley, R, seen in dotted lines in *fig.* 12, communicates motion through a crossed band to the licker-in, D. There is also another pulley, S (*figs.* 12 and 13), upon the axle of the main cylinder which drives the pulley, T, on the axle of which are two cranks (*fig.* 13) which communicate a rapid up and down motion through the rods, *p*, to the toothed knife, M. The rods, *p*, are guided by the horizontal arms, *o*, which are so adjusted that the knife vibrates in contact with the surface of the doffer cylinder, L. Upon the opposite end of the main cylinder shaft is a pinion, *m*, which engages with a wheel, 2, on whose axle is another pinion, 3, which meshes with a wheel, 4, producing a slow motion which the latter wheel transfers to the doffer cylinder, L, through the wheel, 5. A band from the axle of this cylinder drives the workers E and G as shown by the dotted lines in *fig.* 12. Upon the other end of the axle of the doffer is a bevel pinion, 6, which by means of the oblique axle, U, and the bevel gearing, 7 and 8, drives the lower feeding roller. From this feeding roller, by means of an intermediate wheel, 9, motion is communicated to the roller K, which unwinds the lap roller I. The wheel, 2, already mentioned, drives another wheel below it, 11, and a pulley upon the same axle; from which pulley motion is communicated to the drawing rollers at N (*fig.* 14).

The axle *g* has upon one end two wheels, one of which drives both pairs of drawing-rollers, *l* and *m*; the other drives a larger wheel upon one of the rollers, *k*, so that this pair has a slower motion than the others; *l* and *m* move with nearly the same velocity; *m*, being slightly larger than *l*, has a somewhat greater surface motion. That the two rollers *m* may run together, they are connected together by small wheels, *t*.

As before mentioned, in most manufactories the cotton passes successively through two carding-machines, the breaker and the finisher; this is particularly the case with that destined for fine work. *Fig.* 15 is an end view, *fig.* 16 a plan of a fine carder or finisher.

2. The Drawing-Frame.

We turn now to another operation, the principles of which differ essentially from those of the former. It has for its object to draw out and lengthen the loose ribands of cotton furnished by the carding-machine, and also to complete, as far as possible, the parallelism of the fibres. This operation, the *drawing and doubling*, is performed by rotary drawing rollers, and is a very important step in the process of spinning. Upon this principally depends the uniformity of the cotton, as many ends are united in one and the faults of each are lost in the crowd. The drawing, when properly executed, completely does away with all these faults.

Pl. 17, *figs.* 17–20, represent a drawing-frame of the most approved construction; *fig.* 17 is an end and *fig.* 18 a front view; *fig.* 19 a section of the working parts of the machine upon a larger scale, and *fig.* 20 shows the manner in which the upper rollers press upon the lower ones.

A is the frame, upon the strong cross-timbers, B, of which the drawing-rollers are placed, as seen in *fig.* 18; C is a horizontal axle furnished with pulleys, D, which drive the drawing-rollers. In *fig.* 19, *a b c* are the lower, *a′ b′ c′* the upper drawing-rollers. The former run in composition-boxes in an iron frame, *d*.

The bearer of the first roller, F, is stationary, but the two others are adjustable, and can be brought more or less near to each other and the forward rollers, according to the length or *staple* of the cotton to be operated upon. The length of the upper rollers is equal to that of two fluted portions of the under rollers, as seen in *fig.* 18, and the upper rollers run with their necks in boxes, which are adjustable like the bearings of the under rollers.

In the middle of each of the top rollers, *a′ b′ c′*, are smooth necks supporting composition-boxes, *e* and *f*, upon which are suspended weights, *g* and *g′*, by means of wires, *h* and *h′* (*figs.* 19, 20). Generally the two back rollers, which move the slowest, are pressed down by a common weight, whilst the front roller has a separate weight.

The three other rollers are covered with a bar of mahogany, *i*, which is covered underneath with flannel, and wipes off any fibres left remaining upon the surface of the roller. A corresponding bar, *b*, about one inch thick, and covered upon its upper surface with flannel, of the length of the drawing-roller, is pressed against the under side of the two forward rollers, *b* and *c*, by means of the small weight *m*. This bar also serves to keep the forward rollers free of fibres. The cord or wire upon which *m* hangs goes over the roller *e*, and then down again, in order to support the wiper bar *l*.

In *figs.* 17 and 19, G represents a smooth curved plate of brass, with curved channels upon its surface, which conduct the slivers *nn* from their respective *cans*, H, at the back of the machine to the drawing-rollers. The slivers are kept apart by the pins *o* in the brass rod *p*. In this manner three to six slivers are united upon each division of the fluted rollers, and are extended by the drawing-rollers, particularly the front pair, into one thin, uniform, and much elongated sliver. Generally two such slivers are conducted through a funnel, I, and pass off through the smooth rollers K into the cans L.

The motions of the machine are as follows: N is the usual fast-and-loose pulley on the prolongation of the shaft of the lower forward drawing-roller; this pulley is driven by a band from the pulley D upon the shaft C; upon the same front roller shaft is also a pinion, which, by means of the intermediate wheel 2, drives the wheel 3 upon the end of the smooth roller K (*pl.* 17, *fig.* 18). Upon the other end of the forward fluted roller *c* is a pinion, which drives the shaft *o* by means of the wheel 5. By the side of the latter wheel and upon the same shaft is another small wheel, 6, which drives a larger wheel, 7, upon the prolongation of the lower middle roller *b*. Upon the other end of the shaft *o* is the wheel 8, which engages with a wheel, 9, upon the back lower roller *a*.

Having examined the operation of the drawing-frame, we will notice more closely the changes brought about upon the fibres of the cotton. Were the surface velocities of the three rollers *a b c* equal, the slivers *nn* would pass through the machine unaltered. As, however, the velocity of *b* and *c* is greater than that of *a*, the former will deliver a greater length of riband than they receive from the latter, or than this receives from the cans H, and there results, in consequence, an extension of the riband between the rollers *a*, *b*, and *c*, and a proportional approach to parallelism in the fibres during the process. The distances between the drawing-rollers, *a*, *b*, and *c*, are so adjusted to the staple of the cotton that no disruption of the fibres will take place, which must inevitably occur if the length of the individual fibres were less than the distance between the rollers.

It would be impossible to continue the drawing upon a single sliver until the requisite parallelism of fibre were attained, on account of the excessive attenuation of the riband; this inconvenience is obviated by the simple expedient of uniting together several of the formerly drawn slivers at each repeated drawing. This operation is called doubling, and insures this advantage, that the uneven portions of the slivers mutually correct each other, and finally a uniform riband results.

3. The Roving Frame.

The next operation after the above-described process of drawing is the preparation of the roving, which is a thin sliver with a slight twist. In the tube-roving frame this twist is only momentary. In this stage of the cotton manufacture the greatest care is necessary to preserve the uniformity of the spongy cord, upon which the evenness of the yarn depends. Since the first can-roving frame, invented by Arkwright, numberless machines have been contrived for performing this operation with exactness. In Arkwright's machine the slivers, after passing through the ordinary drawing-rollers, received a slight twist by the revolution of the tin cans into which the roving fell, and around the interior surface of which they were regularly coiled by the centrifugal force. This machine is in fact the ordinary drawing-frame (*pl.* 17, *fig.* 17), with the receiving-can revolving on a pivot. This frame, though effective in the hands of its inventor, was still defective; the torsion was unequal upon different portions of the yarn, and even when the twist was put in it was liable to be deranged as it was drawn from the cans.

A machine constructed upon the principle of the common spinning-wheel is in very common use for the preparation of the rovings. The difficulty with these machines arises from the soft and delicate nature of the roving and the care necessary to regulate the winding-on, that it be neither slower nor faster than the delivery from the front rollers. The care required was increased by the constantly varying size of the bobbin within the flyer, as successive layers of roving were wound upon it, as well as by the changes occasionally required in the degree of twist to be given to the roving for particular purposes.

The operation of this machine, called the *bobbin-and-fly frame*, is twofold, twisting and winding. The twisting is accomplished by the revolution of the spindle, F (*figs.* 21 *a* and 21 *b*), to which the fly-fork is united, whilst the sliver, A, in its progress from the rollers to the bobbin, passes through the hollow arm, H, which being made in one piece with the spindle, revolves with it.

The amount of twist given to the roving depends upon the relative surface velocities of the drawing-rollers and the bobbin.

The winding-on is accomplished by giving such a velocity to the bobbin that the difference between the motion of the surface of the bobbin and the motion of the delivering end of the flyer-arm is equal to the surface motion of the roller supplying the sliver.

The first on the list of machines of this class is the tube-roving frame of

Danforth, an American invention, introduced, however, soon after its invention into the factories of England and other countries. The twisting of the roving, as it comes from the front drawing-rollers, is here performed by revolving tubes, through which it is made to pass on its way to the bobbins. The latter consist of simple hollow wooden tubes without ends, which rest upon iron axles, and are moved by friction upon horizontal iron drums or rollers, upon which the bobbins bear by their own weight, whilst the feeding tube has a transverse motion for the purpose of distributing the roving upon the bobbin. This transverse motion is diminished gradually as the spool increases in size, for the purpose of producing conical ends. This machine contains a drawing arrangement similar to that already described.

Pl. 17, *fig.* 22, shows one end, and *fig.* 23 the other of the machine. In the latter the three pairs of drawing-rollers are seen in section at A, and in the former an outside view of the front rollers, B, is given, to show their arrangement upon the roller beam, C. The position of the usual fast and loose pulleys upon the main shaft, *a*, is indicated by dotted lines, as also the large pulley, *c c'*, which communicates motion to the revolving tubes. *Pl.* 18, *fig.* 1, is a portion of the forward view of the machine, to show the working gear and the manner in which the bobbins are filled; *fig.* 2 shows the principal spinning parts of the machine on a large scale; *fig.* 4, a forward view, showing some details subservient to the traverse motion of the tubes; *fig.* 6, a side view of the same. A' B', *pl.* 17, *fig.* 22, are the two rows of drawing-rollers, which receive the rovings as they come from the cans behind the machine. After the rovings have passed the front rollers of the first set, they enter the back pair of the front set, both sets revolving with equal velocity, and are delivered by the front roller of the second set to the bobbins in slender *slubbings*. The bobbins are arranged in a line in front of the machine and rest upon fluted rollers, D, the common axle of which passes longitudinally through the machine. These rollers are fluted for the purpose of creating friction upon the surface of the cotton-covered bobbins, one of which is seen at E (*pl.* 18, *fig.* 1), filled and in its place, and revolving in slots in the upright pieces *d*, by which arrangement the bobbin is enabled to rise as it increases in diameter. *e e* (*pl.* 17, *fig.* 23) are several arms secured to the roller-beam, C, upon the inclined surface of which the bearings, *f*, receive an up and down motion by means of the pinions, *g*, engaging in the racks, *h*. The part *f* of these bearings serves to slide a small iron frame, *i*, best seen in the section *fig.* 3. Upon its surface are secured the bearings *l l*, in which the carriers of the revolving tubes may vibrate or swing on an axis, as seen at one point in *pl.* 18, *fig.* 1. *m m* (*fig.* 3) are the tubes revolving with their ends in the carriers, *k k*; *n* is a guide plate for conducting the roving after it has received a momentary twist in the tubes; *o* is a catch attached to the carrier, *k*, to hang it upon an iron rod running the whole length of the machine, when the bobbins are to be changed; at other times it presses with the plate, *n*, upon the roving of the bobbin, E.

As the roving is being wound upon the bobbin, the frame, *i*, with the carriers, *k k*, gradually rises by means of the pinions, *g*, engaging in the racks, *h*, of the bearings, *f*, thus producing a constant pressure of the delivering ends of the tubes, *m m*, in the same direction upon the bobbins, E, which being turned by the roller, D, wind up the roving as it passes from the opening in the plate, *n*. At the same time the frame, *i*, is sliding to and fro in a direction parallel with the axis of the bobbins, for the purpose of distributing the roving evenly upon their barrels. The extent of this sliding motion is shortened a little each time for the purpose of forming the ends of the bobbins into a conical shape. When the bobbins are full the machine is adjusted to stop itself by throwing the driving band from the fast to the loose pulley. The motions of the machine are produced as follows:

The dotted circle *b b* (*pl.* 17, *fig.* 23) indicates the position of the driving-pulley, and *c c'* a larger pulley, from which a strap runs over the pulleys *r*, *s*, and *t*. The strap then passes the whole length of the machine and over the pulleys *u* and *v* at its other end (*fig.* 22). This strap, in its progress from the pulley *s* to the pulley *u*, passes round the tubes *m m*, in such a manner as to go over one of the tubes and under the next, which are thereby made to revolve without interrupting their sliding or traverse motion.

Upon the axle *a* is the wheel 1, which drives the front roller of the series B by means of the wheel 2. A small wheel upon this roller drives through the intervention of two intermediate wheels, 4, a wheel, 3, upon the back roller. From this back roller the front roller of the other series, A, is driven with equal velocity, by means of intermediate wheels (not represented); motion is communicated to the back roller A in the same manner as at B. The middle rollers of both sets are moved by wheels 5 and 6, attached to them and their respective front rollers, at the other end of the frame, and intermediate wheels 7 and 8 (*pl.* 17, *fig.* 22).

Upon the front roller shaft of the set B, behind the wheel 2 (*fig.* 23), is a bevel pinion, which engages a bevel wheel, 9, upon an inclined shaft, which, by means of other bevel gearing seen at 10, drives the bobbin-roller D. Upon the other end of this shaft is a roller, *x*, from which a band passes to the pulley *y* and drives the axle *z*.

This axle operates by means of a bevel wheel, *a'*, upon two bevel wheels, *b'* and *c'*, which drive the axle *d* in one direction or the other, according as *a'* is shifted in gear with *b'* or *c'*.

This shifting is effected by moving the bar *l'* (*pl.* 18, *fig.* 1), in which is the end-bearing of the shaft *z*, a little one way or the other, and locking it in that position by one of the catches, *m* or *n'*, which fall into notches in the bar *l'*; this bar is moved by one of two weights, *d* and *p*, hung upon a chain running upon rollers, seen in dotted lines (*pl.* 17, *fig.* 23). This chain is attached at its centre and midway between the two weights to a pin secured to the bar *l'*, in such a manner that when one of the weights is raised, the other by its weight moves the bar *l'*.

The two ends of the chain pass down through holes in a balance lever, *v'*, over each of which holes there is a small ball upon the chain, against one of which the balance lever *v'* presses alternately to raise that particular weight, whilst one of the catch-hooks, *m* or *n'* (*pl.* 18, *fig.* 1), is lifted from the notch in the bar *l'*, permitting the other weight to move the rod in the opposite direction, and the bevel gear *a'* to engage with the other of the two wheels *b'* or *c'*.

Upon the shaft is an endless screw, *c'*, which works in a horizontal wheel, *f'*, by means of which and a small pinion upon the upper end of the shaft carrying *f'*, the rack, *h'*, is moved (*pl.* 17, *fig.* 23, and *pl.* 18, *fig.* 1). This rack is connected by means of the rod *i'* with the apparatus H, for the purpose of shortening the traverse motion of the beam *i*, and thus forming the tapering ends of the bobbins; the rack *h'* is also connected with the bell crank lever *t'*, which has at the sides of its upright branch two screws, for the purpose of alternately raising the catch-hooks *m* and *n'* whenever the lever *t'* arrives at one end of its traverse motion. In *fig.* 1 is seen the manner in which this is effected. The other end of the bent lever *t'* raises or depresses one end of the balance-beam *v'* at the end of each traverse motion, and thus stops the action of one of the weights *d* and *p*, whilst the other is drawing the bar *l'*, so that the catch *m* or *n'* not previously raised by the screw *u'*, falls into the notch in the bar *l'*, holding the wheel *a'* in gear, until the bent lever *t'* at the other end of the traverse motion raises this catch and suspends the other weight. We can thus perceive how the rod *i'* is regularly moved to the right and left, and have only now to show how this motion is constantly shortened, and communicated to the beam *i*; *a''* is a curved arm, vibrating upon a centre *b''*, its other end being attached to the rod *i'* (*pl.* 18, *fig.* 1). During the working of the machine, a toothed plate *c''* slides downwards, in the teeth of which and upon opposite sides two clicks engage, *d'' d''*, which are connected together and kept in contact with the rack-plate *c''* by a spiral spring. When the arm *a''*, moved by the rod *i'*, has reached the end of its traverse motion, it presses one of the clicks against the head of the set screw *e''*, which raises the click out of the tooth of the sliding piece *c''*, and permits it to fall the distance of half a foot, the other click *e''* immediately catching it. Thus as the extremity of the lever *g''* constantly approaches the centre of oscillation *b''*, the traverse motion communicated by the rod *g''* to the beam *i* becomes shorter, the arm *a''* vibrating always through equal spaces. The teeth upon the sliding-rod *c''* are cut at alternate intervals on either side, so that its motion at each time is limited to half a tooth. *h''* is a guide screwed to one of the posts G to guide the rod *i''* connected with the rod *g''*; *i''* is joined to a slotted arm *k''* upon the beam *i*, on which the tube-carriers, *k*, stand, as explained above. At each traverse motion of the arm *a''* a pin, *b''*, projecting from the bent piece, strikes against a lever, *m''*, the end of which is seen in *pl.* 17, *fig.* 22, and which, through the lever *n''* and click *o''*, moves the ratchet-wheel I upon the same shaft as the pinion *g* (*pl.* 18, *fig.* 3) one tooth, whilst another click, *p''*, prevents the ratchet-wheel from being forced back by the weight of the beam, *i*, which gradually rises as the spools enlarge. When the toothed rack *c''* has reached its lowest point, a projection upon its side, not seen in the drawings, strikes against the end of the lever *m''*, which sets free a catch at its other end, which makes the upright lever *t''* move the horizontal lever u''. The latter extends the whole length of the machine, and carries a fork, which shifts the driving-band from the fast to the loose pulley, and thus the machine is stopped. By pushing this rod the attendant is enabled to stop the machine at whichever end he may happen to be.

4. Completion of the Rovings.

After the cotton has passed through one or two bobbin-and-fly frames, or through the tube frame, the rovings are handed over to the *mule* or *throstle*, and spun into yarn. In the finer qualities of yarn the roving is subjected to a process called stretching, in order still further to attenuate it; this is done upon the bobbin-and-fly frame. The machine heretofore employed for this purpose is called a stretching-frame, and differs but little from a mule-jenny. Its operation is briefly as follows: The bobbins filled by the foregoing operations are placed in the frame, and the ends passed through the back drawing rollers, and thence to the front ones, from which they pass out in a lengthened and fine-drawn state, proportional to the amount of drawing which they receive. The rovings thus attenuated are severally attached to the spindles of the carriage; the machine is set in motion; the rovings pass from the front rollers, and the carriage recedes from the stationary part of the machine with a velocity equal to that with which the roving is given out by the drawing rollers. Thus the roving is kept extended between the spindles and the forward drawing rollers. Whilst the carriage is drawn back, the rovings are twisted by the rotation of the spindles, and when it has receded about 54 inches it stops, together with the drawing rollers. The twist is produced without the help of the flyer (of the fly-frame), by the rovings being coiled diagonally up to the point of the spindle, where, from the inclined position of the latter towards the rollers, one end of the roving remains during the revolution of the spindle, and thus receives its twist. The carriage and spindles stop together; it then becomes the business of the attendant to wind up the 54 inches, which she accomplishes by depressing the faller wire with her left hand, so as to bring the rovings at right angles with their respective spindles. At this juncture she turns the spindles by means of a crank with her right hand, whilst she pushes the carriage back to the drawing rollers with a velocity corresponding to that with which she winds up the roving. As the carriage approaches the drawing rollers she raises slowly the faller wire, during the last turn of the spindles; and then the rovings, in consequence of the relative position of the spindles and rollers, coil themselves again to the point of the spindle, and the twisting commences again with another length of roving.

The roving is wound in an oval form upon the spindle, and when the *cop* is sufficiently large it is taken off, *skewered*, and placed in the *creel* of the spinning machine.

The product of the stretching frame is a very soft and delicate roving, and must be handled with great care.

Besides the mule frame, the throstle frame is also used in the preparation of rovings. It differs from the former in this, that it spins and winds simultaneously: it is, however, used only for the coarser kinds of yarn. The yarn spun upon the two machines is very different; that from the throstle frame is hard and wiry, while that from the mule frame is soft and woolly. The former is used for the warp of heavy goods, for the filling of coarse goods, and also for both warp and filling of fine goods. The object of the throstle frame is to extend the rovings into slender threads, and at the same time to twist them. It consists of two roller beams, each provided with the usual three-fold set of drawing rollers. The fluted rollers receive the roving from the spools, which are placed upon vertical *skewers* fixed in shelves in the middle of the frames, called *creels.* A throstle frame has seldom less than 72 spindles.

Pl. 18, *fig.* 2, is a view of a portion of the front of Danforth's throstle frame; *fig.* 7, an end view; *pl.* 17, *fig.* 24, is a section through the spinning parts of the machine, and *fig.* 22 *a* is a peculiar spindle for winding on cops. A B (*pl.* 18, *fig.* 2) are the usual fast and loose pulleys, the former making about 480 revolutions per minute. Next to the pulley, B, and upon the same shaft, is a pinion which drives the cog-wheel, C; and a pinion, D, upon the same shaft with the latter, drives the wheels, G G (*pl.* 18, *fig.* 7), through the intermediate wheels, E and F. The wheels, G G, drive the drawing rollers, H H, on both sides of the machine. These drawing rollers are arranged as in the other machines already described, the upper ones being pressed upon the lower by weights, K (*pl.* 17, *fig.* 24). The fluted rollers are set in motion by wheels and run with different velocities, the front rollers making about 120 revolutions in a minute, the middle ones about 17, and the back rollers 12. Their relative velocities are capable of regulation by the change of the intermediate wheels. In this manner the roving, I, is drawn out proportionally to the relative velocities of the front and back rollers.

The twisting is effected as follows: *a* (*pl.* 17, *fig.* 24) are the spindles secured to the rail, *m*, by a screw; *b* is a small pulley, with a hollow axle, running freely on the spindle, *a*. The pulley, *b*, is driven by a band from the drum, L (*pl.* 18, *fig.* 2). The band runs first round two spindles on one side of the machine, and then round two upon the other side, and lastly round the tightening pulley, M, back to the drum. In this manner four pulleys are driven and four threads are spun. Upon the pulley, *b*, and over the said tube, the bobbin is placed, on which the thread is wound after being twisted by the revolution of the pulley, *b*. The winding is effected by a hollow cylinder fast to the immovable spindle. The thread is forced to pass below the lower edge of this cylinder to the bobbin, which is revolved by friction upon the pulley, *b*, and winds up the thread as fast as it comes from the rollers. This winding up would be very imperfectly performed, were not an up and down motion imparted to either the bobbin or the cylinder, in order to fill the bobbin evenly. It has been found preferable to give this up and down motion to the bobbin. The small whorls which carry the bobbins slide freely up and down the spindles, and rest upon a bar, *f*, called the copping rail, which is raised and lowered by means of the levers, *o*, *o* (*fig.* 7). These levers receive their motion from the heart-formed cam, P, upon a shaft with the wheel, R, which is driven by a pinion upon the shaft, S, and a worm, T, on the shaft of the wheel, E. The whorls, *b b*, make about 6,000 revolutions in a minute. To prevent the interference of the threads with each other at this great speed, the bobbins are sometimes separated from each other by partitions of tin plate secured to a board back of them.

5. The Mule, and Mule Spinning.

The finer qualities of thread are spun upon the mule. The operation of the machine is in general similar to that of the stretching frame, and may be stated as follows:

The rovings coming from the bobbins in the creel pass between the rollers and the spindles, the carriage in this machine moving somewhat faster than the rollers, and not as in the stretching frame, where they move with equal velocities. This excess of velocity is called the *gain* of the carriage, and has the effect of rendering the thread uniform by drawing out the larger and less twisted portions. When the carriage has advanced 45 or 50 inches, according to the fineness of the work, a general change takes place in the operation of the mule; the drawing rollers stop, the velocity of the spindles is nearly doubled, and the carriage slackens its pace to about one sixth of its former velocity; this part of the operation is called *draw*. When the threads are sufficiently extended the carriage stops, but the spindles continue to revolve until the requisite twist is communicated. The thread is then wound upon the spindles, as the carriage returns to repeat the operation.

Pl. 18, *fig.* 8, is an end view of a self-acting mule, or mule jenny; *fig.* 9, a plan of the head-stock, showing a portion of the drawing-rollers, certain portions of the head-stock being removed, which are shown in *fig.* 10; *fig.* 11 is a cross-section, *fig.* 12 a front view of a portion of the carriage which moves beneath the head-stock; *fig.* 13, the frame opposite to the head-stock; and *figs.* 14 and 15 are detached portions, to which reference will be made.

A A A (*fig.* 8) is a cast-iron frame, to which, on each side of the head-stock, is fixed the roller-beam B, seen in section. C C′ C″ (*figs.* 8 and 10) are three pulleys upon a horizontal shaft, *a*. The pulley C, secured together with the wheel *l* upon a hollow axle, turns freely upon the shaft; C′, on the contrary, is secured to the shaft, and the narrow pulley C″ is the loose pulley.

Two bands, D and D′, drive these pulleys; the first moves the pulleys by covering one half of each, but it is moved at a certain stage of the process upon C alone. At the same time the band D′, running in a contrary direction and with a less velocity, runs for a few seconds on the pulley C′ and immediately returns to the loose pulley C″. The pulley C, which revolves constantly with a uniform velocity, drives the apparatus for changing the motions, and carries the carriage back to the head-stock when the other motions have all ceased. This apparatus consists of the cam-shaft, *b*, and a friction-pulley, *c*, which has four parallel grooved cavities at equal distances in its circumference, in any one of which the leather-covered pulley *d* (*fig.* 10) may slide, when revolving opposite to the groove; the pulley *d* is moved by a cog-wheel, 2, upon the same axis, which is driven by a cog-wheel, 1, connected with the pulley C. When an edge of any one of the grooves of the pulley *c* by the action of a spring is made to press against the leather-covered pulley *d*, the latter will turn the pulley *c* by friction through a quadrant, till the shaft *b* is arrested by a catch, which prevents the further action of the spring, and makes the pulley *d* run in the concavity of the next groove. By disengaging the catch, the grooved pulley *c* will turn through another quadrant, and so in succession, making four different motions in one complete stretch: 3 is a pinion upon the shaft *a*, which drives, by means of the intermediate wheel 4, the cog-wheel 5 (*fig.* 9), which gives motion by means of the bevel-wheels 6 and 7 to the shaft connecting the front rollers of both sides of the machine. Upon the shaft *f* is also a pinion, 8, which engages with the cog-wheel, 9, on the shaft *g*, carrying a drum, E, which draws the carriage out by means of a rope. The rollers are stopped by moving the bevel-wheel 7 out of gear with 6, uncoupling the wheel 8 with the shaft *f*, and at the same time bringing the small bevel-wheel 10 into gear with the wheel 11, from which the drum E now derives its motion. The wheel 10 is driven by a crossed band from a small pulley, on the shaft with the cog-wheels 5 and 6, to the pulley *l* on the shaft *i*; by which means a slower motion is communicated to the drum E and carriage. From the front roller shaft motion is communicated in the usual manner to the other rollers, the carrier-shaft *n* serving for the rollers on both sides of the machine.

F is a double spiral scroll upon a shaft running in the main frame A; to the smaller radii of the scrolls are attached ropes going round the spirals; these ropes, after making a few turns round the drums E and G, are severally attached thereto. Two other ropes are attached to the barrels E and G, the other ends of which are attached to two small drums of the carriage H (*fig.* 8); the ratchet-wheels seen upon the shafts of these rollers are for the purpose of tightening the ropes as required. The spiral scroll F has nothing to do with the outward motion of the carriage; this is effected by the revolving drum E. When the latter is disengaged by throwing the bevel-wheel 10 out of gear with 11, the carriage stops until it is to be returned, at which juncture the pinion 12 is engaged with the bevel-wheel 13, which thus drives the shaft bearing the scroll F. This now moves the carriage, first with an increasing, and then with a decreasing speed, as it nears the roller-beam; the drawing-out ropes remaining fully stretched, since the scroll gives off as much rope in one direction as it takes up in another. The pinion 12 upon the shaft *q*, which revolves uninterruptedly (although not in gear with 13), is driven by the wheel 14 (*fig.* 10), which receives motion from the intermediate wheel 15 upon the shaft *r*, which also carries the wheel 16 (*figs.* 8 and 10). The wheel 16 gets its motion from the wheel 1, which drives also the friction-pulley *d*.

We will now describe the driving parts of the carriage. S is an inclined shaft (*figs.* 8 and 12), parallel to the axis of rotation of the driving-drums (*fig.* 11), which give motion to the wharves of the spindles. Upon the shaft S is the double grooved pulley I, which gives motion by bands in the usual manner to the drawing-drums on each side of the carriage. On the lower end of the shaft S is a bevel-wheel, 17, which may be shifted to engage with either of the bevel-wheels 18 or 19 (*fig.* 12). The wheel 18 is placed upon a short shaft which carries a double-band pulley, L, driven by a band from the twist-pulley M, passing under guide-pulleys, *t* and *u* (*figs.* 8 and 9). One end of this band passes over the guide-pulley, N, of the carriage, round the driving-pulley L, for the purpose of increasing the friction between the band and pulley, and insuring the rotation of the spindles. The endless band then passes round the horizontal tightening-pulley, V (*fig.* 9), thence back under the other guide-pulley, *t*, and up to the twist-pulley M again.

After the backing off is performed, the shaft S is shifted, so that the bevel-wheel 17 engages the wheel 19 (*fig.* 12), on a short shaft carrying a wheel, 20, which gears into a wheel, 21, upon the shaft of the winding-on barrel *o*, on the periphery of which are grooves to carry the chain attached to it. The other end of this chain is fixed to the point 10 of the apparatus P (*fig.* 8).

As the carriage moves backwards to the roller-beam it causes the drum, *o*, to revolve as the chain pulls it round, the other end of the chain being fast at the point, 10. Thus the shaft S receives a slow motion on its axis through the wheels 21, 20, 19, 17, which, during the return of the carriage, causes the spindles to revolve and wind on the yarn by the depression of the faller. P (*fig.* 8) is a toothed quadrant revolving upon a centre, X, and having a grooved arm, *y*, in front of which is a screw, having on one end a small bevel wheel, 22, which gears with another, 23, turning with a pulley, *z*, on an axis. In the groove of the arm, *y*, slides a nut, 10, to which the end of the chain is attached, and which moves gradually to the end of the screw by the revolution of the pulley, *z*, and consequently the bevel wheels 23 and 22, the latter being fast to the screw, *y*. This quadrant moves through one fourth of a circle during the going out of the carriage, being in gear with the pinion, 24, on the shaft of the barrel, G, round which the rope passes which carries out the carriage. Therefore the scroll, F, moving back the carriage with a varying velocity, gives by the pinion, 24, a corresponding returning motion to the said quadrant, by which means the nut, 10, is caused to describe a quadrant of a circle of a diameter corresponding to the distance of the point, 10, from the centre of the quadrant. By this action the drum, *o*, does not turn in proportion to the advance of the carriage; the point, 10, to which the end of the chain of that drum is attached, following the motion of the carriage in the proportion of the cosines of the arcs through which the quadrant P has turned. The velocity of the drum, *o*, is consequently increased as the said cosines diminish, and therefore turns the spindles faster as the carriage approaches the roller beam, the faller guiding the threads upon the cop.

In the beginning of building the cop the nut, 10, is nearest the centre of the quadrant, P, and may then be considered as a fixed point for the chain, causing therefore the spindles to turn with the carriage during its going in.

During the making of the double cone foundation of the cop (*pl.* 18, *fig.* 16), the nut, 10, is moved gradually towards the extremity of the arm, *y*, thus describing increasing arcs, and thereby causing the spindles to turn at each stretch more slowly at the beginning, and more quickly towards the end of the winding-on; the faller beginning the winding-on each time at a higher point of the spindle.

When the double cone is made, the winding-on guided by the quadrant, P, remains constant, as the nut, 10, does not move any more, while the faller after each stretch continues to lay on the winding from a higher point of the spindle. The motion to the screw, *y*, is given at each stretch in the following manner. Over the small pulley, *z* (*fig.* 8), and over the guide-pulley *a'*, runs an endless band, a certain length of which is moved during the return of the carriage in forming the double cone foundation of the cop. *b* is a lever connected with the faller arm, *c'*, by a chain, and which, when the faller sinks, presses upon the said band and pinches it to the plate, *d'* (*fig.* 11), whereby it is fixed by the returning carriage and drawn along with it till the faller rises again and lifts the weight of the pinching lever, *b*, from the plate.

After the double cone is made, the faller no longer descends so low as to permit the lever, *b*, to press upon the band, and the nut, 10, is no further moved outwards; thenceforth the cop continues to be built by winding on uniform surfaces of yarn upon the top cone of the foundation (*fig.* 16); the faller at each stretch descending less and less, and consequently beginning the winding-on at successively higher points (*fig.* 16).

On the carriage (*figs.* 11 and 12) are two shafts, *e* and *f*, running its whole length, the former being the faller-shaft, and the latter the counter-faller-shaft, which latter is here put in front of the carriage.

On either side of the carriage both are moved by small arms attached to them, and by connecting-rods joined to arms, *t* and *k*, on the ends of horizontal shafts, *l' m'*. The faller-shaft, *e*, is always kept up by several spiral springs working on arms attached to it, unless when depressed during the winding-on action of the machine. On the counter-faller-shaft, *f*, are several segments from which by chains are suspended weights, *n'*, which are directly proportional to the number of the threads, and inversely proportional to the fineness of the yarn, and which serve to support the threads during their winding on the spindles. The faller-shafts on each side of the machine are depressed and raised in the following way. On the shaft belonging to the left side of the carriage is fixed a small pinion, *o'*, which is in gear with the toothed segment, *p'*, the shaft of which rests in bearings on the carriage (*figs.* 8, 14, and 15). The toothed segment, *p'*, has one portion smooth, at whose end is a notch, *q'*, into which by turning the segment, which is loose on its shaft, a catch, *r'*, may fall. This catch is fixed upon a curved arm, *s'*, which embraces the shaft of the segment, and is thus permitted to move up and down with the catch, *r'*. Another curved arm, r, turns loosely round the shaft of the segment, and is connected by a link to the arm, s', and has at its end a roller, u', which slides during the motions of the carriage on a long rail, Q, fixed to the frame of the head-stock (*fig.* 13) on the side opposite to that represented in *fig.* 8.

In *fig.* 13 this frame is shown with the rail, Q, in dotted lines behind; this rail has two pins, a'' and b'', going through the slots in the frame-piece, B, which rest upon two plates, c'' and d'', called the shaper plates, because they define the shape of the cops, and are connected with each other by the bar e''. The shaper plate, d'', has a nut, f'', in which a screw works, bearing on its end a ratchet-wheel, g'', one or two teeth of which are moved by a click from the carriage at the end of each of its comings-out. Thus the shaper plates c'' and d'' are gradually shifted, and the rail, Q, at the back of the frame-piece, B (*figs.* 14 and 15), is permitted to sink a little so as to make the roller u' (*fig.* 14) run lower upon its rail, Q, during the motions of the carriage. When the faller is depressed, which is at the time when the carriage begins its going-in, the segment, p', is turned, and the catch, r', falling into the notch, q', must now follow the action of the sliding roller, u', on the rail Q. The segment, p', now driving o', which is attached to the faller-shaft of the left side of the carriage, will give to that shaft a regular rising motion in proportion as the carriage approaches the roller beam, by being connected to the roller u', which runs over the inclined rail Q. The carriage having reached the end of its course, the arm s' goes over the bar v seen in section in *fig.* 15, by which means the catch r' is lifted from its notch q' (*fig.* 14), and the fallers are made to rise by the spiral springs attached to them: the same motion is transferred to the faller-shaft, e' (*fig.* 15), on the right hand side of the carriage by the horizontal shaft l', to which both are connected by arms and connecting-rods.

We have now to explain how all these motions are successively produced in the machine. b (*fig.* 8) is the shaft which by certain disengagements is permitted to revolve at each of four different periods through a fourth part of a circle. On this shaft are the following guides and eccentrics. In front of the pulleys, C, C', C'', is the guide, h'' (*fig.* 10), for the fork of the strap, D, which is attached to the top end of the lever; i'', the guide (l'' in *fig.* 10) for the other strap, D', which is shifted by the lever, k, working in the bar, l'', on the end of which is fixed the fork for the said strap. m'' (*fig.* 8) is an eccentric by which the bevel wheel, 7, and the coupling clutch on the shaft, f (*fig.* 9), is worked, whilst the wheel 10 is brought into gear with 11. The lever which carries the bearing of the shaft i and shift-wheel 10 into gear with 11 is connected with the lever n'' (*fig.* 8), working the coupling on the shaft f (*fig.* 9), and is moved by the eccentric m'' by a hook, which being subsequently lifted makes also the wheel 10 to fall out of gear with 11. o'' is a finger, seen best in *fig.* 10, by which the quantity of twist is regulated, and which keeps the shaft b from turning a fourth part of a revolution till a notch in the plate p allows that finger to strike through. The shaft is afterwards arrested in another way.

The plate p is fixed on a shaft with wheel 25 (*fig.* 8), which is driven by a worm on the principal shaft, a (*fig.* 10), and may be varied in diameter according to the quantity of twist the yarn is to have. *q''* is another eccentric, by which the wheel 12 is shifted into gear with 13 by means of the bell-crank lever *r''*, at the end of which is the bearing of the shaft *q*. *s''* is a plate on the shaft *b* (*fig.* 10), having on one end four pins, against which a spring presses so as to bring the friction-pulley, *c*, in contact with the pulley *d*, thus to make it turn through a quadrant. On the other side of the said plate *s''* are three square escapement pieces, against which presses the end of a rod, *u''*, connected with the end of the horizontal balance lever S. By either depressing or lifting this lever the rod, *u''*, is moved from one of the catches on the plate *s''*, by which it revolves through a quadrant, as has been said, and is then caught by the next escapement on the plate *s''*.

In the going-out of the carriage let us suppose the band D to be driving both the pulleys, C and C', and the strap D' to be on the loose pulley C''. The rollers are driven by the shaft *e'*, and the carriage moved by the drum E, getting motion by the wheels 8 and 9 (*fig.* 9). The twist is given from the pulley M driving the pulley L, and the bevel wheel 18, which engages with the wheel 17 upon the shaft S. The carriage coming near the end of its course lifts a catch from a latch (see dotted lines in *fig.* 8) of the lever S', which sinks a little and is caught by a second catch, which is connected by a rod, V'', to a lever, T, the latter resting on the boss of the curved arm *s'* (*figs.* 14 and 15). By the falling of the left hand end of the balance-lever, S', the rod *u''* has moved from one of the escapements of the plate *s''* (*fig.* 10), and after the shaft *b* has made a quadrantal motion, it is arrested by the finger *o''* striking against the plate *p*; by this means the eccentric *m''*, on the shaft *b*, has disconnected the coupling on the shaft *f* (*fig.* 9). The rollers are thus set at rest, while the carriage moves a little longer, but very slowly, being driven by the shaft *i* and the wheels 10 and 11 (*fig.* 9). The carriage, having arrived at the end of its course, strikes against a rod not seen in the figures, detaching the click, with which, by the lever *n''*, the wheel 10 was shifted into gear with 11, thus setting at rest those parts which gave motion to the carriage. The twisting motion, however, is continued till the principal shaft, *a*, has turned the wheel 25 so far round that the finger *o''* can strike through the notch in the plate *p* (*fig.* 8). The shaft *b* goes on to revolve through a second quadrant, and is now caught by the rod *u''* at one of the catches of the plate *s''*. By this quadrantal motion the straps are shifted, D moves to the pulley C, alone, and D', which moves much slower, and in an opposite direction, is shifted to the pulley C, which is fixed on the shaft of the twist-pulley M. The latter is therefore now turning in the contrary direction, and giving a like motion to the spindles, thus backing off the coils of the yarn from the noses of the spindles. At the same time, however, a ratchet-wheel, *w* (*fig.* 8), on the slant-shaft S of the carriage, turns by a click, *x''*, a plate connected with a spiral piece below, to which is attached the end of a chain which passes over two guide-pulleys, *z''* and R'', to an arm, *a'''*, at the top of the carriage, upon the same shaft with the pinion *b*.

By the reverse motion of the shaft S, therefore, the faller is depressed till the catch r' falls into the notch q' of the segment p', after which the faller follows the motion given to the roller u' by its sliding on the rail Q. At the time, however, that the catch falls into the notch, the lever T, which had been resting upon the boss of the curved arm s' (*figs.* 8 and 15), falls also, and takes away the catch which had suspended the latch of the left hand end of the balance-lever S′, and makes this end to fall a second time, after which the rod u'' lets another detent of plate s'' escape, and causes the shaft b to revolve through the third quadrant, by which the straps D and D′ are brought back to their former positions. Meanwhile the shaft S is shifted with its wheel 17 into gear with 19, as will presently be described, and the eccentric q'' (*fig.* 8) has shifted the wheel 12 into gear with 13, which is fixed on a shaft with the scroll F, by which the carriage is now returned towards the roller-beam, whilst the winding-on is performed by the drum o (*fig.* 12), turned by the chain attached to the nut 10 at the quadrant P (*fig.* 8). Round this drum there are a few coils of a rope, which passes over the two pulleys b''' and c''' (*fig.* 8), and suspends a weight, d''', in order to keep the chain tight upon the drum o.

When the carriage comes home to its place, near the roller-beam, it presses down the right hand end of the balance-beam S, and makes the rod u' to fall off from the third escapement of the plate s'', after which the shaft b turns through the fourth quadrant.

By this motion the eccentric q'' shifts the wheel 12 out of gear with 13, while the eccentric m'' sets the rollers in gear by the coupling upon the shaft f, and of course, also, the drum E which moves out the carriage by the wheels 8 and 9. The bar r (*fig.* 14) has now lifted the catch r', out of the notch q' in the segment p', and thus has disengaged the faller shaft; finally, the shaft S (*fig.* 12) is shifted together with its wheel, 17, to give twist again to the yarn spun during the next stretch of the carriage. It remains only to mention how this shifting of the shaft, S, is performed, at the moment of the carriage going in and out. The step-bearing of the said shaft is fixed on the end of a bell-crank lever, e''' (*fig.* 8), the other end of which is connected with an arm upon a shaft upon which is a kind of balance lever, h'' and i'', which passes, when the carriage arrives at each end of its course, under rollers attached to the large radial weights U at each end of the frame, which thus presses on that one of the arms h''' or i''', which is just arrested by a detent or click, and keeps the wheel 17 in gear with either 18 or 19. When the carriage is drawn out, and the wheel 17 is still in gear with 18, the arm h''' is suspended, and remains so, till by the falling of the lever T, the balance lever S′ makes its second fall, and disengages the click by which the arm, h''', is suspended; the latter is now depressed by the radial weight U, whilst the other arm, i''', is caught by another click. On the contrary, when the carriage arrives near the roller-beam at the same time that it depresses the balance-beam S, and changes the motion, the click which keeps the arm, i'', suspended is also disengaged, and the radial weight on the right hand of the machine (*fig.* 8) presses down the arm i''', whilst h''' is caught in its click, and keeps the wheel 17 in gear with wheel 18. k''' is a detent or click, in which an arm, connected with the counter-faller shaft, is caught when the carriage is going out. This arm has on its end a roller, which glides at the beginning of the course of the carriage over an inclined plane, X, fixed on the floor (*fig.* 11), and lifts the arm to be laid hold of by the catch k'''. When, however, the faller becomes depressed at the going-in of the carriage, the finger, t''', is attached to the arm t (*fig.* 11), near the left hand wheel, disengages the arm attached to the counter-faller from its catch k''', and causes the counter-faller to react against the tension of the threads.

The yarn is now reeled and bound in hanks. It is numbered according to its fineness, the number expressing the weight of a certain fixed length of thread. *Figs.* 22 and 23 represent the scales commonly made use of for weighing yarn; *fig.* 24 illustrates its operation. The assorted yarn is then packed for transportation in a press of simple construction, seen in *figs.* 27, 28, and 29.

6. The Singing or Gassing of Yarn.

The fine cotton yarn used in the manufacture of bobbin-net lace, and for hosiery, is generally subjected to a singing process, to free it from loose fibres, which operation gives it a more uniform, compact appearance. This singing is accomplished in a peculiar machine by passing the threads with great rapidity through the flame of gas. *Pl.* 19, *figs.* 16, 17, and 18, are different views of a gassing machine of simple construction, the general operation of which is apparent from inspection. *Fig.* 19 is the heart-cam serving to guide the thread upon the winding-on bobbin. The thread passes from the bobbins I round the glass pins *p* and the rollers *q* and *q'*, between which rollers it is subjected to the action of the flame; thence it passes through the guide-plate, *r*, to the winding-on bobbins, G, which are revolved by friction upon the rotating carrier pulleys, F. The bobbins make from 2500 to 3500 revolutions per minute.

7. Weaving.

The preparatory step to weaving is arranging the warp-yarn in parallel layers upon a wooden beam. This is effected by the aid of an ingenious machine called the warping-mill. *Pl.* 19, *fig.* 2, is an end view, and *fig.* 3 a plan of a warping-mill of approved construction. The threads pass from the bobbins A through guides *a* and *d* round rollers C C' C'', and are ultimately wound upon the warp beam G, which runs in vertical slots in the arms *f*, and is revolved by friction upon a cloth-covered roller, I.

For the purpose of showing the threads more plainly, the machine is painted black, and when the warper discovers a thread to be missing, she stops the machine, finds the ends and unites them, and the machine runs on again. *Pl.* 19, *fig.* 20, shows the arrangement of the spools in *fig* 3.

Pl. 19, *fig.* 1, shows the ordinary method of beaming for hand-weaving.

The spools are placed upon a frame, E, and the threads pass through the guide F, which descends as the reel is turned. This is effected by the attendant by means of a crank, pulleys, cord, &c.

Weaving proper is the art of making cloth by the rectangular decussation of flexible fibres, of which the longitudinal are called the *warp* or chain, and the traverse the *woof* or weft. The former extends through the whole length of the web, the latter only over its breadth. The outside thread on each side of the warp, round which the filling or woof thread returns, in the act of decussation, is called the *selvage* or list.

Pl. 19, *fig.* 4, exhibits the old European loom in its simplest form. The chain is wound upon the *warp-beam*, A, and passes thence through the *heddles*, C, which consist of twines looped in the middle, one half of the warp threads passing through the loops in each heddle. The yarns then pass through the reed beneath D at the bottom of the swinging frame E, called the *batten lay* or *lathe*. The weaver, seated upon the bench G, alternately raises and depresses the heddles C by pressing his foot upon one or other of the treddles, H, which are connected by cords to the bottom of the heddles. By this motion of the heddles, one half of the warp threads are carried up and the other half down, a few inches, thus *shedding* the warp, as it is technically termed, for the passage of the shuttle, which carries through the warp thread or filling. The shuttle is thrown through the shed by a sharp jerk given to the *picking-strings*, seen at I, by the hand of the operative, and leaves a *shoot* of weft behind it. The weaver then swings the batten E towards him, to *beat up* the thread thus laid in, and the heddles are changed again by the treddles, preparatory to passing the shuttle again through the shed. In more primitive looms the shuttle was passed through the shed by hand. The cloth is wound up as fast as woven, upon the *cloth beam* at I.

The power-loom has experienced many changes and improvements since its first introduction. In *pl.* 19, *figs.* 5, 6, and 7, is represented a power-loom of modern approved construction.

A is the frame of the loom, B fast and loose pulleys, upon the *crank shaft*. Upon the other end of the crank shaft is a cog-wheel D, driving a wheel D′, with double the number of teeth, upon the shaft E, which makes, therefore, only half as many revolutions as the crank shaft B. The shaft, E, is called the *wiper*, or *comb-shaft*; it throws the shuttle, and raises and lowers the heddles, while the shaft B by means of its crank F works the lay H, which drives home the weft towards the finished cloth. The cranks F are connected with the two levers G, called the *swords* of the lay, to which the batten H is made fast, which carries the reed in its middle, and the shuttle-boxes *h* at its ends. I is the warp-beam; the warp yarns pass from it, over the roller K, through the heddles L and reed *l*′, over the breast beam M (having now been woven into cloth), and are finally wound upon the roller N, or cloth beam. This roller bears at one end a toothed wheel *a*, moved slowly by a small pinion *u*, upon the axis of the ratchet-wheel *b* (*fig.* 7). This latter wheel is turned round a little after every *throw* of the shuttle, or shoot of the weft, by means of a stud projecting from one of the swords of the lay. The lifting of the heddles, L, is performed by two eccentric wipers O O′, upon the shaft E, which press the treddle levers P and P′, alternately up and down. These levers are connected by strings or wires with their respective heddles, which are in their turn placed in communication by straps, which play over rollers, *e*, at the top of the loom.

Pl. 19, *fig.* 21, shows these levers isolated. The shuttle is thrown by the two levers, Q Q, which are alternately moved with a jerk by the rollers, R, secured to the shaft, E, by means of arms, and working upon cams, S, connected with the shafts of the arms, Q Q. These arms are connected together at the bottom by a cord or strap, mounted with a spring of spiral wire.

The shuttle is lodged in one of the boxes, *f f*, of the batten, H, and is driven across along its *shed-way* by one of the pickers, *g g*, which run on the two parallel guide wires, *h h*, and are connected with the arms, Q, by strong cords.

If by any accident the shuttle should stick in the shed-way, the blows of the batten, H, against it would cause the warp to be torn to pieces. In order to guard against this, a contrivance has been introduced for stopping the loom immediately, in case the shuttle should not come home into its cell. Under the batten H (*pl.* 19, *figs.* 7 and 22) there is a small shaft, *i*, on each side of which a lever, *l* and *l′* (*fig.* 6), is fixed; these two levers are pressed by springs against other levers, *m m*, which enter partly into the shuttle-boxes. There they act as brakes to soften the impulse of the shuttle, and allow also the point of the lever *l* to fall downwards into a line with the prominence at *n*, provided the shuttles do not enter in and press the spring-point, *m*, backwards, together with the upright arm *l′*, and thus raise the horizontal arm *l* above *n*. When this does not take place, that is, when the shuttle has not gone fairly home, the lever *l* hangs down, strikes against the obstacle *n*, moves this piece forwards so as to press against the spring lever or trigger *o o*, which leaps from its catch or detent, shifts the fork *p p* with its strap from the fast to the loose pulley, and thus in an instant arrests every motion of the machine.

The shuttle is represented in *fig.* 8 in a top view and in *fig.* 9 in a side view. It is made of a piece of box-wood mortised out in the middle and tapered off at its ends, the tips being shod with iron points to protect them from injury by blows against the guides and the bottoms of the boxes.

In the hollow part, *a b*, there is a skewer or spindle, *c*, seen in dotted lines. One end of this skewer turns about the axis, *d*, to allow it to come out of the mortise when the cop is put on.

e (see dotted lines in *fig.* 9) is the spring which keeps the spindle *c* in its place by pressing against one of the sides of the square ends of the spindle. *f* is a projecting pin or little stud, against which the spindle *c* bears when laid in its place. *g* is a hole in one side of the shuttle, bushed with ivory, through which the thread passes, after being drawn through a slit in the centre of a brass plate, *h*. In that side of the shuttle which is furnished with the eye-hole there is a groove extending its whole length for receiving the thread as it unwinds from the cop.

The warp is wound upon the cylinder I, and passes over the roller K; the cloth is formed at the point *r*, passes over the breast-beam M, and is wound upon the cloth-beam N. The delivery of the yarn is regulated, and the warp threads are kept at a uniform tension, by friction produced by a cord with weights attached to it passing round the beam I.

The cloth-roller N bears upon one of its iron axes prolonged, the toothed-wheel, *a*, which works into a pinion, *u* (seen in dotted lines, *fig.* 7), upon the axis of the ratchet-wheel *b*. Hence if the latter be turned gradually by the motion of the lay, as before explained, the cloth-beam N will be revolved very slowly, and thus take up the woven cloth.

The heddles, through the loops of which the warp threads pass (one half through each), are connected together by straps, passing over pulleys, *e*, at the top of the machine in such a manner as to balance each other, the descent of one drawing the other up. At the bottom they are connected to two bars, U and V, which are secured by rods, *o o'*, to two treddles, P P'', turning on a pivot at W. These treddles are alternately depressed by the cams O O'' upon the revolving shaft E, and thus the heddles are alternately raised and depressed, and the warp threads opened to form the shed or angular opening between the threads seen at *r* (*fig.* 6), through which the shuttle passes to carry the woof thread.

Pl. 19, *figs.* 10 and 11, represent the *jaw-temples*, which serve to keep the cloth distended to its full width during the operation of weaving; these temples are attached one on each side of the loom, and consist of spring pincers, which seize the selvage of the cloth immediately in front of the point where it is woven. At each beat of the lay the movable jaw of the temple is opened to permit the cloth to pass the small amount made by the one thread, beat up, and the instant the lay recedes the jaws grip the cloth again, and hold it distended until the lay beats up again.

8. Finishing and Bleaching.

The first operation in the finishing of cotton goods is bleaching, which is not so tedious as with linen, as the cotton is but slightly colored. The size, which was put upon the chain threads before weaving, is first soaked off in warm water, in which the cotton is allowed to remain thirty-six or forty-eight hours, or until a sort of fermentation takes place; it is then washed in running water, and bleached either by exposure to the sun or with chlorine.

The cotton is first singed by passing it quickly over the surface of a red-hot iron, to free the surface from loose fibres. *Pl.* 19, *figs.* 12 and 13, represent the singing-oven: *a* is the oven door; *b*, the fire-grate; *c*, the ash-pit; *d*, the flue. In light goods, muslins, &c., the flame of alcohol or of gas is sometimes used. The cotton then goes to the wash-wheel, represented in plan in *pl.* 19, *fig.* 15; *fig.* 14 *a* is a portion of the front side, and *fig.* 14 *b* a view of a portion of the back of the wheel. This wheel makes about twenty revolutions per minute. A constant stream of clear water is admitted through a tube at *i*, the dirty water passing off through holes in the case *h*; *f* are openings to admit the goods; *m* is a cog-wheel by which the wheel is driven. The goods are then boiled to free them entirely from size and to open the pores.

Pl. 18, *figs.* 17, 18, and 19, represent a washing-kettle of common construction, the upper part, A, of which is for the reception of the goods, and the lower, L, for the water; C is a grating, seen also in *fig.* 19, from the central hole of which rises the tube D. F is the fire-chamber, the grating of which is seen in *fig.* 18. In this kettle the goods are boiled ten hours, being closely watched, as the water should constantly rise through the tube D and pass down through the goods.

Then follows the *bucking* or boiling in a lye of potash, which is thrice repeated, the goods being washed after each operation, and ultimately passed through the wringing-machine (*pl.* 18, *figs.* 20 and 21), consisting of rollers in a strong frame, between which the cotton is passed under heavy pressure, and thus the water is pressed out. Then follows the treatment with chloride of lime, and finally the *sour* bath, the acid of which acting upon the chloride gradually and slowly sets free the chlorine in immediate contact with the cotton.

The goods then pass to the starching and steam-drying apparatus (*pl.* 18, *figs.* 25 and 26), being carried from the roller Q beneath a roller, I, which carries it through the paste-trough, E; it then passes over the hollow cylinders, L, heated by steam, admitted through the tubes, O, from the steam-pipe, N. Ultimately the finished cotton passes out between the rollers, T, and is folded upon the table, U.

We close our observations on cotton manufacture with a few cursory remarks on the kindred manufacture of woollen goods.

Woollen Manufacture.

Nearly all the wool manufactured in Europe and the United States is that of the sheep. The first operation to which it is subjected is washing with soap and water, to free it from sweat, grease, and dust; it is then passed through the drying squeezers, and carried to the drying-room over the boilers of the steam-engine. The wool is then passed through a machine differing somewhat from the willow used in the cotton manufacture, and represented in *pl.* 18, *figs.* 30–33. It consists of a series of rapidly revolving fans upon a shaft, H (*fig.* 33), within a net-work of wire, the whole inclosed within a tight wooden case, A B. The wool is fed to the machine upon the feeding apron, D, running upon rollers, E and G, passes between fluted rollers, and is caught by the teeth, N, of the revolving fans; and as it is carried round is beaten against the wire net-work, separated and opened by the teeth, O, upon the interior of the wire cylinder, and ultimately thrown out at one end of the machine, opened and free from the dust, which has passed through the wire cylinder. After being cleaned in this manner, the wool is again oiled and passed through a wolf of simpler construction, then carded upon machines not essentially different from those already described under Cotton Manufacture, spun, and woven.

VI. COINING.

COINING is the art of making the metallic currency of trade. In civilized countries the currency is partly metallic, partly of paper; the latter having an imaginary value, based upon the credit of him who issues it.

1. METALLIC MONEY.

Gold and silver, the most precious metals, have been used from the earliest periods as the materials for the fabrication of money. Platina has also been resorted to in more modern times, but its value is too fluctuating for a steady currency, and its use has been abandoned. Besides these metals an alloy of silver and copper, and also pure copper, are in use for coins of the lowest denominations, on account of the diminutive size of silver coins of so small a value.

Coins are almost always made in the form of small round plates or disks, on one side of which, called the *obverse*, is the head of the sovereign, the arms of the state, or an emblematic device; and upon the other, called the *reverse*, a suitable expression of its value. As, for various reasons, gold and silver are never coined pure, but with an alloy of copper, the proportions in which the noble metals and copper are used must be accurately prescribed. Almost every state has its own standard. In Germany this is determined by the number of sixteenths of pure silver which a crude alloyed mark shall contain, and the number of coins to be struck from the same. For gold coins, in the same manner, it is fixed how many twenty-fourth parts, or *carats*, of fine gold they are to contain, and how many pieces of coin shall be struck from a given weight of the alloy. Though the just weight and proper alloy are thus fixed for every kind of coin, yet the rule cannot be applied with mathematical precision; a slight variation must therefore be allowed from the regulation. This variation is termed the *remedium*, or the authority to the mint to diminish the alloy. Formerly this was more considerable than it is in the present advanced state of the art of coining. In France it is $\frac{1}{2000}$ above or below the fixed rate for gold, and for silver $\frac{1}{1000}$ for five-franc pieces, $\frac{5}{1000}$ for two-franc pieces, and $\frac{10}{1000}$ for quarter francs.

The value of coined silver is of course somewhat higher than that of uncoined, as those fabricating the coin must be remunerated for their labor. This increase of value is termed the mint tax. In France, where the coinage is most excellent, the mint now reckons coined gold only at about $\frac{1}{3}$ per cent., and coined silver only about $1\frac{1}{2}$ per cent. over the uncoined. The minting of the baser metals is much more expensive than that of gold and silver, as it costs more to coin one hundred cents than one dollar.

1. MELTING. The melting of gold and silver is generally carried on in large black-lead or cast-iron crucibles in cupola furnaces, with charcoal or coke.

The crucible is first heated before the alloyed metal is put in, that any cracks may become apparent; and the metal is covered with a layer of charcoal, to prevent oxidation by exposure to the air. After it is thoroughly melted a specimen is taken out, the alloy tested, and, if necessary, rectified. If the proof is satisfactory, the metal is cast into *ingots*, in moulds of cast or wrought iron. Silver is taken out of the crucible with an iron ladle coated with clay; gold is manipulated with a black-lead crucible held by tongs. In England and the United States the cast-iron crucible is raised from the furnace by the aid of a crane, and set into a peculiar pouring machine, which is gradually tilted by a curved rack and pinion, to allow the contents to flow into the iron forms. *Pl.* 20, *figs.* 1 and 2, exhibit such a machine. As the crucible is tilted, the carriage upon which the moulds are placed is moved along directly under its nose.

2. ROLLING. The ingots having been cast and cooled are next passed through the rolling mill (*fig.* 3). Its construction differs slightly from that of the common rolling mill. M is a cog-wheel, which receives motion from the driving power of the machine; upon the same shaft are wheels, L and O, gearing into wheels, P and K, upon the axis of the rollers; *gg* (*fig.* 3[a]) are the set screws which serve to adjust the distance between the rollers; and *fig.* 4 shows the manner in which these screws are moved together by the screws, H, turning the wheels, F. The rollers are of steel or iron, case-hardened, and are usually from four to twelve inches in length. When the requisite thickness is thought to be attained, a few blanks are struck and tested in the scales; if they are too thick, the rolling is continued; if too thin, the bars must be melted over again. In some cases a flattening mill is made use of to prepare the bars for the rolling mill; *pl.* 20, *fig.* 7, is an end, and *fig.* 8 a front view of the machine. It is, in fact, a rolling mill, but less substantially built than the one already described, and serves to remove the chief inequalities of the bars, and to extend them slightly. H is the driving pulley upon the shaft of the pinion, G, which engages with the cog-wheel, F, upon the lower roller, *b*, upon the other end of which is a wheel which engages with a similar wheel upon the upper roller. A central wheel upon the top of the machine engages with the wheels, *e*, upon the top of the screws which adjust the distance of the rollers, and turns them equally.

The bars then pass to the *drawing machine*, of which *fig.* 10 exhibits a top, and *fig.* 11 a side view; *fig.* 12 shows the pincers and a section of the drawing plate; *fig.* 13 is a top-view of the vice; *fig.* 14, a front view of the drawing plate.

From the driving-pulley L, motion is communicated to the wheel G, on the shaft of which are two polygonal disks, F, which carry the endless chain *l*, upon which the pincer-carriage travels (*fig.* 12). The bars are secured by screws into the jaws of the pincers, and are drawn through the drawing plate. To diminish the ends of the bars that they may pass through the dies to the pincers, they are introduced between the rollers of a machine, seen in *pl.* 20, *fig.* 9, arranged something like the rollers of a rolling-mill. The upper roller is cylindrical, but the lower is formed with three flat sides. The end of a slip of metal is presented between the rollers while they are in motion, not on that side of the roller which would operate to draw in the slip between them, as in the rolling-press above described, but on the contrary side, so that when one of the flat sides of the under roller fronts horizontally the circumference of the upper roller, an opening is formed, through which the bar is to be inserted until it bears against a fixed stop at the back of the rollers. As the rollers continue to revolve, the cylindrical portions come opposite to each other, and press the metal, forcing it outwards, and rendering the part introduced between the rollers as thin as the space between their cylindrical surfaces; thus the end of the slip of metal becomes attenuated enough to pass between the dies of the drawing machine and to be seized by the pincers. The drawing plate is seen in *pl.* 20; *fig.* 14 shows the die-box; the dies are adjusted vertically and horizontally, by means of the screws *d d* and *g g*.

The bars are now heated and cut into lengths of about 4 feet, and if, as is the case in the English mint, the breadth is twice or three times as great as that of the coin to be struck, it is also cut through lengthwise. This is effected by means of circular shears, seen in *figs.* 5 and 6; *fig.* 6[a] shows the cutting wheels, with the bars lying between them. G is an adjustable ledge, against which the metal plate rests, to regulate the width of the strip to be cut off.

3. THE CUTTING OUT. *Pl.* 20, *fig.* 15, presents a side-view, and *fig.* 16 a top-view of a coin-punch. E is a hollow cast-iron column, from which the atmosphere is kept constantly exhausted; G is a cylinder with a hollow axis, around which it can revolve on the frame H; by means of the tube K the air can be exhausted from the cylinder when required, and motion imparted to the piston in the same, the pressure of the atmosphere upon the piston carrying the punch, C, down, and the fly-wheel, P, raising it again, and returning it to a position ready for another downward stroke.

The blanks cut out by the above machine are then tested, and smoothed upon the surface.

4. MILLING. The polished blanks are next milled upon the edge, which operation precedes the stamping, and is performed by a machine shown in *pl.* 20. *Figs.* 19 *a* and *b* are the two milling plates, on the edges of which is engraved the device or motto to be impressed upon the edge of the coin; to the plate *a* is imparted a reciprocating motion by the rack bar *e*, and the blank being laid upon the arm *f* is forcibly compressed between the plates *a* and *b*, and passes out at *g*.

A milling machine is seen in *fig.* 20, by which a single workman can mill 20,000 large coins in one day. The two milling plates E and D contain each upon their curved edges one half of an inscription for the edge of the coins; one of these plates is secured firmly to the bed of the machine, the other to the vibrating lever PD, which turns upon an axis, C; *a* is a tube which supports a pile of blanks, and having an opening at the bottom just sufficient to permit one of these blanks to pass out at a time. As the lever PD is moved, the arm CD attached to it carries out the lowest blank of the pile, which is moved from *a* towards K, between the milling plates E and D, and finally passed out at *b*. More recently, in order to improve the appearance of the rim of the coin, the edges are polished by passing them through a machine, seen in *figs.* 17 and 18, similar to the milling machine, the edge of the disk, W, and the corresponding concave being smooth, so that the edges of the coins, as they are carried through by the revolution of the disk, W, are polished and compressed.

5. STAMPING. The coins are now to be stamped with their appropriate devices upon both surfaces. *Pl.* 20, *fig.* 34, is a section of the principal parts of a stamping machine constructed by Gengembre in Paris. A reciprocating rotary motion is communicated to the triple-threaded screw A, within the female screw N, secured to the frame of the machine U; beneath the screw are the dies G and P, between which the blanks are placed, and as the screw A is turned, it descends upon the upper die and presses it down upon the blank, which is thus stamped upon both sides. That the coin may not lose its circular form, the lower die is surrounded by a steel ring, which just incloses the coin at the moment it is stamped, and retires again that the coin may be withdrawn. That no damage may arise to the machine should the coin fail to enter the ring, the latter is placed upon springs that it may be forced down, and only the blank be injured. Sometimes the coin is surrounded by a ring made in sections, which are brought together at the instant the coin is stamped, and thus the inscription upon the rim of the coin is formed at the same time (*pl.* 20, *figs.* 32 and 33).

After the stamping-screw A (*fig.* 34) rises, the upper die and the parts connected with it are raised by the spiral springs S S, to make room for the next blank. In many of the common stamping machines, the blanks are placed upon the lower die, and removed again after they are stamped by hand. In the better machines, however, this is all done by machinery. The apparatus which affects this is called the carrier, and is operated by the vertical motion of the screw-stamp. This carrier first moves backwards to take up the blanks, then forward, gliding across the ring round the lower die, into which it lets the blank fall; after the coin has been stamped, the carrier strikes it and casts it out of the machine. This is effected by a contrivance (*fig.* 27) called the conductor, on the front edge of the carrier.

Fig. 21 is Boulton's stamping mill in the London Mint, which will not require a detailed description; *fig.* 22 is the guide ring and set screws for the top boxes of the stamping screw; *fig.* 23 is the box for the upper die; *fig.* 24 the box which encircles the upper die; *figs.* 25, 25 , 25^b, 25^c, are the details of the stamping ring; *fig.* 26 is the box for the lower die; *fig.* 27 the crescent-shaped conductor on the carrier, which has charge of the prepared coin; *figs.* 28, 29, and 30, show the details of the carrier; *fig.* 31 is the lower box for stamping with a divided ring; *fig.* 32 is a section of the divided stamping ring; *fig.* 33, bottom view of the stamping ring; *fig.* 35 is a view of the stamping machine in which the die is worked by the crank *e*, and levers, *d′*, *c*, and which operates without the violent shaking produced by the machines worked by levers.

In the principal mints the machinery is driven by steam, the pressure of the air being very ingeniously employed to transfer the effective power of the steam to the stamping mill. *Pl.* 21, *fig.* 1, shows an outline of the stamping machine in the mint at Rio Janeiro. Eight stamping mills are arranged around the receptacle, A, in which is kept a constant vacuum. The vertical stamping screws are moved by chains passing round the drums, E, and attached to the pistons in the cylinders, D. The valves bringing the cylinders alternately in connexion with the vacuum and the atmosphere, are worked by pins upon the fly-wheels, F. *Pl.* 20, *fig.* 37, is the cylinder by which the vacuum and the atmosphere are made to operate the stamps. When the bottom of the cylinder is in connexion with the vacuum chamber, the pressure of the atmosphere which is admitted through the holes, *a*, drives the piston to the bottom of the cylinder and operates the stamps; at this juncture the atmosphere is admitted beneath the piston, which, together with the screw stamps, is drawn back by springs. This cylinder, M, is sunk in the vacuum chamber to the fillet, L, and the cylinder is brought alternately in connexion with the atmosphere and the vacuum chamber by the two-way cock, *b*; the cock *d* is for cutting off communication between the vacuum chamber and any one of the stamping mills that it may be desired to stop. *Pls.* 21 and 22 exhibit specimens of the coins of the principal countries. Their names and approximate values will be found in the Table of Contents.

2. Paper Money.

Paper money is the representative of metallic money, and derives its value from the supposed ability and willingness of the individual or company by whom it is issued to redeem it in gold and silver. To avoid the chances of paper money being counterfeited, care is taken through the whole process of its manufacture to make the imitation of it as difficult as possible. The paper is first prepared with water marks, so that without the co-operation of the paper-maker himself, a perfect imitation cannot be made. The engraving is made as complicated as possible, to increase the difficulty of counterfeiting it, and lastly the bills are numbered and signed by the individuals issuing them, or by their representatives. Bank notes have usually been numbered by hand; but machines have been invented which print the successive numbers upon them without aid in making the changes in the numbers. The most ingenious of these machines is that invented by Bramah in London, and which arranges the numbers with such rapidity that it executes threefold more work than can be accomplished by an active penman. *Pl.* 20, *fig.* 36, is a section of the machine. The numbers are arranged upon a series of rings, I, which are turned by wheels, H, actuated by the motion of the handle, F: these numbers are brought successively from 1 to 99,999 or even higher, beneath the tympan, E, in which position they are inked; the note is then laid upon them, and as the handle, F, descends, the impression is transferred from the types to the paper. The next number in order is then produced by the revolution of the rings as the handle is raised, and the same operation is repeated.

VII. MINING.

Having in the preceding pages turned our attention more exclusively to machinery, we will now treat in separate sections of some branches of Practical Technology, and particularly of the subjects of Mining, Smelting, and Agriculture. We will first take a brief view of MINING, as it relates to the extraction of the economical, or, as they are usually designated, the useful minerals.

INTRODUCTION.

All the useful minerals, in those parts of the surface of the earth to which we have access, are distributed into certain distinct groups. These minerals are distributed among other mineral substances, either in beds or veins. They occur either stratified or unstratified. The former are called *layers*, from the laminated structure they present, and beds. The term bed is principally applied to mineral coal, iron, &c. Layers or beds of minerals are sometimes horizontal, sometimes inclined at a considerable angle with the horizon, and sometimes distorted, bent, and broken. The want of stratification and a tendency to a crystalline structure show that the beds belong to an unstratified or massive formation.

In observing a layer or bed of minerals, we notice first its *strike* or direction, that is, the angle which it makes with the meridian line; its dip, or the angle which it makes with the horizon; the position and character of the hanging wall, or the rocks which bound the top of the bed, and of the foot walls, or those rocks which lie underneath the bed, the former being sometimes called the *roof* and the latter the *floor* of the bed; and finally the out-crop of the bed or its termination in the open air at the surface of the earth. Sometimes layers or beds which are horizontal for the greater part of their extent, rise up towards the out-crop and form basin or saddle-shaped folds. They are then called disturbed strata. We often find local dislocations and displacements of the beds, which are here and there interrupted by fissures which have since been filled up by some mineral substance. These fissures run across all the strata of the formation. These interruptions in the continuity of strata in the same plane, accompanied by fissures, are called *faults*, which term is sometimes applied to the rock filling the fissure. These fissures are generally filled with basalt, or some similar rock; the rock which fills the fissure is properly called a dyke. The complications produced by faults are very diverse; the mineral substance which constitutes the rock above and below it, and the fault which has caused the disturbance, being often mixed together, so that the character of the bed is materially changed. The faults often cause a separation and dislocation of the members of the formation. The thickness of the fault varies from one line to several yards. The strata separated by the fault have frequently suffered therefrom a change of place or a slide of one part below the other. The strata containing mineral coal, intersected by faults, are generally of soft clay mixed with fragments of trap or porphyry.

Pl. 23, *fig.* 4, shows a section of the rocks containing mineral coal in the region of Newcastle upon Tyne. The scale of the perpendicular is double that of the horizontal distance, so that in fact only half the dip is represented. The line *i i i* represents the great bed or seam of coal, which has a thick bed of sandstone for its roof. The Holywell shaft, to the left of the profile, the Carsdon shaft, *a*, the Algernon shaft, *c*, the Chirton shaft, *d*, the Percy shaft, *e*, the Howdon shaft, and nine others, are cut through beds and seams parallel to each other. The part lying south from the River Tyne, *g*, below the morass of the Jarrow, *h*, some hundred feet or more, is not represented, but may be estimated from what is shown in the section. The dotted lines and the roof of the bed or seam, *i i*, serve as the horizon to aid us in judging respecting the dislocations occasioned by the many faults which have destroyed the continuity of all the strata. In passing from the lowest southern point below the Jarrow morass, the roof of the seam or bed uprears itself at an angle of 10°, and is there interrupted by the first fault; afterwards by the second, which raises it about twelve yards. A third fault meets the bed at D, which sinks it about thirty yards, whence the bed mounts at about the same angle up to C, where it is raised about eighty yards by the fault, so that merely the lower strata of the formation appear. Later it sinks again at B about 22 yards, and then passes on horizontally to a thick fault or dyke, A, which throws down the whole bed about 280 yards, from whence it gradually rises again.

Pl. 23, *fig.* 3, is a section of the coal strata of Ronchamp, A, in the department of the upper Saone. The distinctly marked seams are suddenly broken through by a porphyritic mass, B. In the plains of Champagne, lying beyond the interruption, there has been found a continuation of the red sandstone, C, which forms the roof of the bed of mineral coal, D D; E is the transition slate, and at B, we again find the porphyry. The boring works, *b b*, and the shaft, *a*, are carried down even to the porphyry, B, but the bed of coal has not again been found.

A *vein* is a more or less thick mass of rock of proportionably small dimensions compared with the rock in which it is found, which differs in kind from the rock which incloses it, even when the inclosing rock and vein belong to the same species. We also apply in relation to veins the terms strike, dip, roof, and floor. Although the strata on both sides of a vein have the same successions, they are for the most part dislocated, and therefore do not form opposite continuations. Veins too have their disturbances and contortions, frequently more than beds, and are likewise often pierced through by other veins.

1. Experimental Works.

The existence of localities of beds or veins is usually indicated by outward signs. We trace the head or outcrop of the bed by the *shoads* or loose fragments which have been accidentally detached from it. It is only in particular coal formations that the localities of beds of coal are so clearly indicated as to furnish sufficient grounds for working the mine. If the miner has found the locality of a bed or vein, he must closely examine the region around in order to judge of the changes the formation has undergone. Springs which contain hydrochlorate of potash in solution are usually indications of the presence of beds of coal. Naphtha and asphaltum springs indicate also localities of coal; jets of carbonic acid, or carburetted or sulphuretted hydrogen gas, frequently indicate beds of coal, as well as masses of mineral salt.

If any one, by means of any of the indications above mentioned, has come upon the outcrop of a bed or vein, he must attempt to uncover and display it. He must examine its dips and determine its strike by those parts which are uncovered, and also determine its extent by sinking pits in the vicinity of the bed or vein, and driving transversely to intersect it. The experimental work should be carried on until the miner shall consider himself justified in commencing the real working of the mine. In those cases in which saline or gaseous exhalations serve as indications of the presence of beds of minerals, BORING is the most suitable experimental work.

The earth-borer, or *auger*, is an instrument for boring, in any soil, holes of small diameter, in order that we may not be obliged to sink a shaft or drive a level to learn the nature of the soil. We have already spoken of Boring when treating of Artesian Wells (Vol. I. p. 626), and have represented the principal boring tools, so that we shall here content ourselves with a short enumeration of the same.

An auger consists of an upper piece, which always remains above the hole bored, and of a lower piece, or the auger proper, which takes hold of the bottom of the auger-hole and its sides. The middle piece, or shaft, unites the two pieces above named, according to the depth of the auger-hole. The auger is suspended by means of the upper piece to the rope in the boring frame, and must be so arranged that a person can turn the auger without twisting the rope. The middle piece or shaft is cylindrical, octagonal, or square. The last form is best, because it is cheapest and at the same time admits of manipulation by means of handspikes. The size is according to the depth of the hole to be bored. The diameter is usually 14 lines, but for the greatest depths is as much as 21 lines. Its length is from 16 to 19 ft. Each end is enlarged for the purpose of joining the middle piece to the parts above and below. The most common method of uniting the different pieces of the auger is by means of a male and female screw with triangular threads. The lower end contains the female screw, the upper the male, which is from an inch and a quarter to an inch and a half in diameter. This mode of joining is not so good as the joining by means of a tongue and groove, which admits of turning the auger in all directions.

The boring part of the auger has different forms according to the strata of rocks which are to be penetrated. The chisel auger serves for boring through loose and disjoined strata, like sandstone, &c. In order to fasten upon the rocky strata in turning the auger, use is made of the carp-tongue or serpent-tongue auger, of the riband-shaped, furrowed, and four-cornered auger. For cutting into quartz, pebbles, or rubble-stone, the conical-headed auger answers. The portions of rock bored out, and the earth, are brought to view by means of the soil-borer or loam-spoon, also by the salt or sand-borer, which is a hollow cylinder having a globular valve below. Sometimes the shaft and boring part break in the hole, and they must be again drawn out. For this purpose a hook is used which catches hold of the bands of the shaft, and in this way it is lifted out. The same object is accomplished by a grappling-tool, which is screwed down in such a manner over the shaft broken in the hole or rope that the claws fasten upon the shaft or rope, which is then drawn up.

For facilitating the operations of boring, variously constructed frames are used. A very good boring-frame consists of four posts for suspending the auger with a windlass and lifting-cams. There is a rope for suspending and lifting out the auger, and a swingle or balance-handle to allow the auger to operate by strokes. This swingle is connected with a lever, which is raised by means of cams on the windlass and falls back by its own weight. This windlass is represented in *pl.* 23 ; *fig.* 13^a is a side view of the cams or short levers on the windlass. *Fig.* 13^b is a section at AB of *fig.* 13 *c*, seen towards the side of the windlass. *Fig.* 13^c is a front view. The three cams or lever arms, *aaa*, are fixed to the axis M, and serve to make the lever for the swingle, or auger handle, rise and fall. CC are the cast-iron uprights of the frame; M, the axis on which the rope of the auger winds itself; on the same axis is the lift-wheel, *aaa*, which moves the lever of the boring-rod. N is a cog-wheel which catches in the driver *g* ; *d* is a set of pinion wheels, the teeth of which have a reversed direction, and in which the pawl *k*, which is fastened on the upper rod, is allowed to catch when it is desired to prevent the backward movement of the windlass. *c* is a wooden wheel on which presses the *brake band*, *e*, which is drawn on to it by means of the lever *f* (*fig.* 13^b). *h* is a *stop* placed on the axis of the crank between the upright C and the enlargement of the axis, to keep the wheel in gear with the pinion. If the stop *h* be raised, then the driver may be released from the cog-wheel, by shoving the axis *gh* through its boxes in the frame CC until the pinion *g* no longer engages the cog-wheel N.

The usual process of boring is briefly the following. First, the surface is attacked by the proper boring tools. With conical-headed augers and chisels, the motion of the auger is by strokes, the tool being slightly turned round. The auger is only occasionally lifted when the borings impede its operation. The expense and difficulty increase rapidly with the depth of the hole bored, on account of the weight of the shank of the auger ; for the last few years, therefore, ropes have been used instead of the stiff iron shanks, and with very good success. A tolerably high massive boring-frame, a windlass or vertical capstan, and lever, together with the auger rope and various tools for attacking the rock, are the only things needed in this method of boring, which is represented in *pl.* 25, *figs.* 6, 7, 8, and 9. *Figs.* 6 and 7 represent the boring-frame, the windlass, the swingle, and the preparatory arrangement of the ground for boring, where the hole to be bored is to be six inches in diameter. The frame has four posts, some 12 feet high, and stands over a shaft about 9 feet in depth, which has been sunk at the commencement of the operations, in the axis of which a wooden tube is placed to guide the auger at the outset. The rope passes over a guiding pulley of oak which hangs above the frame, and is wound up around the axis of a windlass, for which a vertical capstan is substituted when the hole becomes deeper. The longer arm of the lever is 12 to 15 feet in length, and the shorter 2 to 3 feet; the latter terminates in a rounded head which serves to raise the rope with the auger. In order to keep the auger rope always taut, the longer arm of the lever is provided with a hook by which it may be fastened down.

The boring instruments used consist of a simple chisel which is fastened on the lower end of an iron rod (*fig.* 8, front view; *fig.* 9, sectional view), which hangs to the rope by means of a swivel. In the middle it is square, but above and below it has a round flange with four incisions, by which the borings may pass up. The diameter of the flange is equal to the width of the chisel. The hook (*pl.* 23, *fig.* 33) is used to give a twisting movement to the rope. A comparison of rope with rod augers shows that in boring a hole 18 inches in diameter and 200 or 300 feet deep, the cost with the rope auger is greater than with the rod auger; and that in using the latter the cost increases greatly with the depth, while with the rope auger it remains nearly unchanged.

2. Mining for Ore.

The tools of the miner differ according to the nature of the stone or soil. In loose substances, such as sand, gravel, marl, &c., he uses a heavy pick with a blunt point. In soft adhesive substances like peat he uses a cutting tool like a gardener's spade, but which is furnished on the sides with two wings, so that the separation of the peat from the mass is rendered easy. This is shown in *pl.* 23, *fig.* 28ᵃ. For digging many mellow substances, such as clay, sand, and decomposed rocks, the pickaxe, crowbar, and shovel are sufficient. The pickaxe used, at one end terminating in a steeled point, and with a handle about 2½ feet long, is represented in *figs.* 14 and 15. The size of the iron part is proportioned to the stone to be worked. In working mineral coal the miner makes a deep furrow or trench in a certain part of the mass to be obtained. The trenching tool is a light pointed sharp pickaxe (*pl.* 23, *figs.* 16 *a* and 17 *a*), having the helve in the middle. For hard stone a heavier tool is used. *Pl.* 24, *fig.* 41, shows the miner at work with the pickaxe in soft stone.

Hard substances are obtained by the mining pick or by the aid of fire. The pick (*pl.* 23, *fig.* 19) is a tool of iron faced with steel or made entirely of steel. On one side it ends in a point of the form of a four-sided rectangular pyramid, and on the other has a flat face. The eye of the helve is in the middle. The miner (*pl.* 24, *fig.* 42) places the point of the pick on the rock which he wishes to obtain, and smites the face of the pick with a short-handled two-faced hammer or mallet (*pl.* 23, *figs.* 20 and 21). The miner has a selection of different kinds of picks, adapted to different kinds of rock. These he arranges on a piece of an iron ring curved like a hook, or has a shap or chain (*pl.* 23, *fig.* 18) with two pieces of hoop iron. Since the employment of powder, the hammer and pick have been used in hard rock only for levelling and digging holes, or where timber-work and machines prevent the use of powder. The mining pick is more useful for working in veins of ore, where also crowbars and large sized steel wedges (*fig.* 29, *a* and *b*) for driving into the fissures of the rock are used.

The use of powder for mining began about the year 1613, and produced an entire change in the mining operations carried on upon solid rock. The first operation in blasting with powder is the drilling of a narrow cylindrical hole, A (*fig.* 9), in the mass to be blasted off. This hole is partly filled with gunpowder, and then, with the exception of a narrow channel needed for firing it off, is rammed down hard, so that the powder which is in the hole on being ignited must exert its force on the rock which surrounds it. *Pl.* 24, *fig.* 40, exhibits a miner busied in the labor of drilling. The holes drilled are from 10 to 48 inches deep, and about half an inch wide. The drill used for boring the cylindrical hole is usually a round iron rod, which ends in a steeled and hardened chisel or cutter (*pl.* 23, *figs.* 22 *a* and *b*). The drill is held in the left hand, and is driven by a hammer. The drill should be occasionally immersed in water to prevent the flying of dust from the hole, and to prevent it from losing its temper by being heated.

In the mines of mineral salt at Northwich, Cheshire, England, they use a drill seven or eight feet long, consisting of an iron rod which bellies in the centre. This drill is held by the middle (*pl.* 23, *fig.* 12). In quarrying gypsum in the vicinity of Paris, they bore with a kind of auger (*fig.* 26). In mining brown coal in Lankowitz, in Carinthia, they make use of an auger (*fig.* 35), provided with a handle like that of a bitt stock, having a flat lance-shaped pod with a small point, the steeled edges of the cutting-tool being slightly twisted. For boring a hole with this instrument three feet, and charging and firing the blast, an hour is sufficient.

After the hole has been freed from the dust and chips by the scraper (*fig.* 23), a dry wad of tow is put on the lower side of the scraper, which absorbs the water in the hole. The hole, when dry, is charged with from two ounces to one pound of powder, wrapped in a cartridge of paper or tarred linen, or if the hole is under water, placed in a well closed leaden or tin cylinder. The cartridge is driven in by means of a rammer (*fig.* 24), which is made of wood, copper, or iron. Previously, however, the priming-rod (*fig.* 25) has been stuck into the cartridge and is introduced with it into the hole. The priming-rod is of copper, and reaches only half way into the powder in the cartridge. The space above the cartridge in the hole is filled with clay, pieces of brick, or pounded slate-stone. This is called the tamping. The first inch or two of the tamping above the cartridge must be only lightly rammed around the priming-rod, and the successive layers be driven firmer and firmer until the hole is entirely closed to the top. The priming-rod is smeared with tallow, and often turned round during the charging, that it may be easily drawn out. When this is done the train is laid to ignite the powder in the cartridge. The most common modes of igniting the powder are the following. First, by using little tubes of elder straw, &c., filled with fine gunpowder, or brandy and powder, and connected with the cartridge by being placed in the hole left by the priming-rod, or inserted at first instead of the priming-rod; second, by matches of rushes, or shavings, or small paper caps covered with powder and stuck into the hole made by the priming-rod. The fire is communicated to them by the sulphur wick, or a thread prepared by dipping it in sulphur. The slow match of sulphur allows the workman time to escape from the blast. In modern times the Beckford safety match is used to great advantage. The electric spark has proved a very safe and suitable means of igniting the charge, especially when a number of charges were to be ignited at the same time. In this way, in the year 1844, in constructing the London and Dover railroad, a part of the Shakspeare cliff was blasted off and thrown into the sea. A good mode of placing the powder at the bottom of the hole is to use the double cartridge of Chenhall. This apparatus (*pl.* 23, *fig.* 11, *a b*) consists of a copper tube about two feet long and of a smaller exterior diameter than the drilled hole, in which a small piston moves with a graduated rod. The piston is drawn back far enough to allow the requisite space for the charge of powder, which is poured into it, and then the tube is stopped up with a paper plug; it is then put into the drilled hole, and by pressure upon the piston-rod the charge is forced out of the tube, which is then withdrawn and the hole is filled in as usual. This method of charging can only be used where the descent is directly down.

The blasting must be so conducted that the axis of the hole drilled shall be parallel with the nearest open side. The surface of the fracture usually runs through the axis of the drilled hole. For example, if one wishes to blast a mass of rock having the profile A B C D (*pl.* 23, *fig.* 10), a succession of oblique drilled holes will be far more effective than perpendicular ones.

Where the rock is full of moisture, cartridges of tarred linen, or paper cartridges, surrounded with tinfoil, and Beckford's matches, are very useful. A mode of filling a drilled hole when the rock is full of moisture, which is employed in Sweden, is represented in *fig.* 8. The ordinary filling is replaced by two wedge-shaped pieces of iron. Each of these pieces of iron ends in a smooth circular face, of a diameter somewhat less than that of the tin canister which serves for the reception of the powder. The charge of powder used is fastened by a cord on the bottom of the first wedge. The second wedge lies with its inclined plane on the first, and is furnished with an iron rod which projects from the upper opening of the tin canister. In the surfaces of the wedges in contact, there is a channel which reaches to the powder and extends into the tube of a hollow wooden staff which is affixed to the end of the iron rod, after a train of powder has been laid in the channel. *c* is the match affixed to the end of the train; B and C are two platforms which serve for boring the hole and firing the charge; D is a piece of stone which prevents the wedges and rod from being thrown too far when the blast is made.

Another mode of detaching portions of a rock or bed is by kindling fires on the mass to be operated upon. This mode is used where fuel is cheap and the rocks are not well situated for drilling. The portions of rock detached by the fire may be easily removed by the pickaxe or crowbar. *Pl.* 25, *fig.* 10, represents the working of the mine in the above manner at Felsö-Banya in Hungary. Preparations are made for working the mine by driving levels, which lie nine fathoms below one another, and are connected by shafts and winces. Piles of wood are erected on the bottoms of the levels, the whole length between the shafts, in order that the fire may operate on the roof of the levels. If the level is so high that the flame from combustibles placed on the floor will not reach the roof, a wooden platform is built up from the bottom of the level and covered with stone to protect it from the fire, upon which the piles of wood are placed. The platform is gradually raised as the roof is mined away.

3. Mining at the Surface.

In many cases the best mode of working beds of minerals is to take off the roof of sterile materials which covers the bed, and to work them under the open sky. Such is the case with respect to beds of peat, many stone quarries, beds of bog iron, and in some cases mineral coal.

In general, the following rules are to be observed in mining under the open sky: In the first place, a sufficient portion of the bed or vein to be mined must be laid bare, in order that the materials to be dug out may be easily procured. We must then descend as far down to the lower part of the bed as can be done without threatening the caving in of the walls. Secondly, we must provide the means of containing water if it collects on the bottom of the mine; all the water should be collected at one point, where the pump is placed. Thirdly, after the first bank or step is wrought out we go on to the next, taking care that a drain is left under the rubbish of the first step to carry off the water. Fourthly, the general rule is to commence at the lowest point in the bed and carry on the mining from below upwards, by cross-cut on the longer line of the bed.

As an example of mining at the surface, we will here give a plan of the operations at the slate quarries near Angers in France. These quarries lie east of that city, on a series of beds of slate which have an average extent of two to three miles, and run in a direction about twenty degrees north of west. In the year 1841, 14 quarries were being worked, with a yearly production of about $4,000,000. The beds dip almost vertically, but usually a few degrees to the north (*pl.* 23, *fig.* 6 D). The separation coincides with the stratification, as the flattened impressions of organic remains which are found abundantly between the layers show.

The slate quarries belong to different companies. The operations of each quarry are under the charge of two superintendents, one of whom directs the labors of the quarry, and the other those above-ground. After the soil and clay produced by the decomposition of the slate, which is often quite thick (*figs.* 5, 6, and 7), have been removed, the rock is worked by steps or banks about 10 feet high each, as is shown in *figs.* 6 and 7, so that an oblong square excavation is formed. Two walls in the quarry are made vertical. On the firmest of one of the upper steps, a wooden platform is erected. This platform carries a pulley, upon which runs the hoisting rope (*figs.* 6 and 7). The platforms are connected by bridges, with sheds, A B C, where the steam-engines are set up. In commencing the quarrying, a notch is made with a pickaxe, and widened into a trench of about 3 feet broad (*fig.* 6), and the slate is taken out on both sides, so that the quarry has always steps upon which the workmen may take their places. To cut in each step, the workmen dig in the fissures of the rock with their pickaxes a series of notches, in which wedges are placed (*pl.* 25, *figs.* 31 *a* and *b*), 25 or 30 of them for every 28 or 35 feet. The workmen all stand in a line, each man to a wedge, and smite with heavy hammers on the wedges, keeping time in their blows. As the slate splits open and the wedges sink, thicker ones are put in their place, until the rock breaks at the bottom and tumbles down. When the rock cannot fall by its own weight, an instrument, represented in *pl.* 25, *figs.* 34, *b* and *c*, is laid on the cleavage of the slate. To this a rope is fastened, and pulled by ten or fifteen men. *Figs.* 32 *a* and 33 show a hand crowbar which is used. The steps cut on each side of the shaft are indicated by the horizontal lines on *fig.* 6. For some time past blasting has been used to advantage, several holes being charged and fired off at once.

When a block is quarried off, it is divided by means of the irons (*pl.* 25, *figs.* 31 *a* and *b*); the drill-wedge and pick (*fig.* 30 *a b* and *fig.* 32 *d e*), the pickaxe and hammer are also used. Each block is divided into pieces of convenient size. The pieces are then loaded into boxes (*figs.* 27, 28, and 29), and carried up to the top of the quarry. The slate is carried from the hoisting-shed to the platforms around the quarry, where it is prepared. This is done in the open air. A working gang consists of three persons, two splitters and one apprentice. The blocks are divided into smaller pieces, having the general form and dimensions of the different kinds of slates. The blocks of slate are divided by placing a flat chisel (*figs.* 32 *b* and *c*, and 35) in one of the clearly marked divisions of the slate, and striking it with a wooden mallet. The slates are then laid flat on a wooden block, and fully smoothed off with a kind of knife.

Another kind of work at the surface is the digging of peat. Beds of peat occur in the flat regions of rivers in the north of France, Holland, and the plains of lower Germany, also on high plains without trees.

The thickness of a bed of peat may be discovered by the peat-borer (*pl.* 23, *figs.* 32 and 34). This is a simple half-opened scoop auger, which is two or three inches in diameter, and is fixed to a pole 15 or 20 feet long, on which is marked a scale for measurement. Peat is usually soft enough to be easily dug by means of a cutting instrument, and from the firmness of the mass may be cut vertically to a considerable depth without any fear of its caving in. Care should be taken that no heavy weight is placed on the edges of the pit. On account of the situation of the peat beds, they can rarely be thoroughly drained without great cost. Where the water can be managed by buckets, small trenches can be dug, and the peat easily obtained by means of the usual spade (*fig.* 27) or the spade with sides or wings)*figs.* 28^a and 28^b). Where the peat-bed is covered with water, and the draining is too expensive, the peat is obtained with nets. For obtaining soft peat a net is used, similar to that with which sand is obtained from the bottoms of rivers. If the peat is firm enough, a rim of hoop-iron is used, on the circumference of which a net is fastened. The rims of the nets used in Holland are from 12 to 22 inches in diameter. The peat obtained by the net can be dried in drying-boxes or moulds.

4. Drifts or Levels.

The excavations intended to reach veins or localities of ore in order to unite them with the surface of the earth, and which have a small sectional area in proportion to their length, are called drifts and levels, or shafts, according as they approach a horizontal or perpendicular direction.

The adit or adet-level is a horizontal gallery, terminating in the open air, and which generally serves for draining the mine. Levels are horizontal excavations driven on the lode. Cross-cuts are levels driven at right angles with others to intersect the lode.

The mode of working the levels, and the tools used for the work, vary according to the condition of the rock to be operated upon. In hard rock the levels are driven without the support of carpentry or masonry. In soft and crumbling rocks carpentry or masonry must immediately follow the mining operations, and frequently precede them. In hard rock the levels are mined by blasting or by means of hammers and picks, or strong steeled wedges or gads (*pl.* 22, *figs.* 31^a and 31^b). A section of the drift or level has usually the form of a trapezium. The upper side is semicircular. The height of the level may be 5 to 6 feet, and the width at the bottom from 3 to 4 feet; but generally the height is 6 feet, and the width at the bottom 4 to 5 feet. The adit level serves at the same time for conducting off and obtaining water. When the water covers the bottom several inches deep, the adit may be divided into two parts by a horizontal partition, which is in fact the roof of the conduit for the water. On this roof is constructed the forwarding floor, and beneath it, on the floor of the adit, the water flows from the mine. The roof of the conduit is 14 or 16 inches above the bottom of the drift, and the gallery above this roof is 5 to 6 feet high. The roof of the conduit consists of boards, which are nailed on beams or sleepers. Drifts or galleries with a very large cross-section, called tunnels, are driven forward by steps, so that part of the tunnel which is being wrought has the appearance of a flight of stairs with several broad steps, each one of which can be occupied by a workman. The obtaining of a cubic foot of rock in a wide drift costs far less than in a narrow one, not only on account of the greater facility of working by steps, but because the extent of space lightens the work. In soft but tolerably compact rock the levels are wrought by means of pick and wedges without blasting. The rock stands long enough to admit of carpentry or masonry being subsequently constructed, to prevent future falling of the walls and roof.

1. Timbering of the Levels. In driving a level which must afterwards be timbered, care must be taken that the requisite space within the timbers is secured. Timber-work is almost always cheaper than masonry, but wood rots and gives way under the pressure of the rock, and therefore requires to be replaced from time to time. In works upon a mine which is to be used only two or three years, timbering is used; while in large drifts or adits which serve for draining the mine, and therefore require to last for a considerable time, masonry is adopted.

Before considering the details of timbering, we may make the following preliminary observations: First, we must observe the degree of compactness of the rock, and determine as far as possible the direction of the pressure. If, for example, the rock is split through in many places, and consists of broken and loose masses of stone, this is a sign that the mass exerts strong pressure, and must be supported by timbering. As the pressure of the rock is not always vertical, but lateral, the resistance furnished must correspond with the pressure. As the pressure which the mass exerts upon several points is less than when the whole mass has to rest on a single point, we must seek to bring the pressure to bear upon as many points as possible.

The ends of every cross-beam used in a mine should lie in the rock. Two mortises or hollows must, therefore, be cut in the rock in which the ends of the cross-beams should lie. These mortises must be 8–12 or 24 inches deep, according to the character of the rock.

The cross-timbers are round, hewed, or split pieces of timber, which are laid in a horizontal position within the level, parallel to each other, and at such distances from each other that from three to five may occupy a length of six yards. The timber-work of the levels further consists of double and single upright posts, standing under the cross-beams. In mining operations it often happens that the roof and sides of the level when it is first excavated are perfectly strong, but in the course of a few years large masses give way both in the roof and sides. Whenever there is any apprehension of this difficulty, double upright posts are chosen for timbering. If weakness in the roof alone is apprehended, the single uprights are used. The double upright posts stand perpendicularly to the bottom of the level, and are connected at the top by a cap or cross-beam. A single upright stands alone under the cap. At Freiburg, in Saxony, where the lodes are not thick, and the levels, consequently, are narrow, all the uprights are placed vertically; but where the lodes are thick and the levels widen, the uprights or posts are placed wider apart at the bottom than at the top (*pl.* 25, *fig.* 11ᵃ). This is made necessary by the width of the levels and the pressure. The uprights are set up slanting wherever the side pressure is greater than the pressure of the roof. After the uprights are placed, covering-boards are fastened upon the caps and upon the sides behind the uprights, in such a manner that they may lap over towards the rock. Where the pressure of the rock is not very great, the second upright is placed about three yards from the first. When the pressure is more considerable, an auxiliary upright is placed half way between the two.

When the level is very wide and the cross-beam does not appear sufficiently strong to resist the pressure, it is strengthened by means of braces of joists, which meet under the centre of the cross-beam and rest on the sides of the uprights. Where a level is employed for ventilation, draining, and often even for mining itself, the timber work has an appearance like that represented in *pl.* 25, *fig.* 13, in which both the uprights lean against each other at the top, and stand below on a horizontal beam or sill. This timber-work is simple and cheap, and requires but little room. This method of timbering is much used in the copper mines of Cornwall. Another kind of timber-work used in rubble-stone which has but little pressure, is represented in *fig.* 11^b^. It consists of four posts or planks, from 2 to $2\frac{1}{2}$ inches thick and 12 or 15 inches broad. These planks cover four sides of the level, and are so placed that the ends of the upright planks are behind the ends of the other two. The planks are held together at the corners by square blocks or pieces of joist, against which the upright planks are nailed. There should be no empty space between the planks and the ground in which the excavation is made.

If the ground is so soft that it will not sustain itself at the least distance from the upright posts, the timber-work must, to a certain extent, precede the mining operations. The process adopted when certain strata of sand or clay are entirely pervaded by water, forming marshy or what is called compressible soil, is as follows. Two upright posts with a cap are placed in the level to be driven. If the bottom is not solid they must be placed upon a sill. When a square frame has thus been set up, a covering of plank piles, or sheeting piles, is driven in around the frame. The sheeting piles must always be introduced at a slight divergency, so that the whole piling may have the form of a truncated pyramid, the smaller end of which embraces the first frame set up. If the ground is not very soft, as soon as the piling is inserted, the level may be driven onward 20 or 24 inches, after which a second piling is placed exactly like the first. In driving the level care must be taken to keep the course perfectly true. The divergency of the piling must be preserved. The piling is kept at some distance from the second frame by wooden wedges, which are driven in between the piles and the frame. The piles are afterwards driven further into the ground by beetles, and then the mining of the level is further carried on until a third frame is set up. The piles should not be longer than 6 or 8 ft., and, therefore, after the fourth frame is set up, new piles must be placed. The second set of piles lie on the frame and below the ends of the first, so that wedges may be driven in between them. As an example of this mode of working in marshy ground, we will describe the operations in the mine of argentiferous lead ore, called the Frederick mine, at Tarnowitz, in Upper Silesia (*pl.* 25, *figs.* 15–17). When marshy ground is met with in driving the levels it is shut in to prevent the caving in of the sand and clay. A square frame, like that described above, is placed against the marshy soil which is to be driven through, and behind it cross-boards, forming a bulkhead, are placed, which are kept up by the frame (*figs.* 15, 16.) If the bottom is bad, the uprights are set on a wooden sill, formed of a half-round board split from a log 16 or 20 inches in diameter. The flat side is placed on the ground. Pieces of board are sometimes placed below the sill to give it more support. The sill is made as long as possible, in order to rest in the earth on each side. After the sill has received its position, the two uprights are set up accurately perpendicular, and are bound together in the usual manner by a cap. The ends of the cap do not project beyond the uprights, as is seen in *fig.* 15. After the frame has been put in place, sheeting piles of plank are placed around the uprights and the cap, and are retained at the requisite distances from the frame by wedges. The wedges lie on the piles already fastened in, and by driving the wedges the position of the frame can be accurately adjusted. The piles are then driven in, commencing with the two which rest on the upper corners of the frame, being made broadest at the end which is driven in. The cap is first covered, and afterwards the uprights. In this mine, where the pressure was very strong, piles formed of plate-iron were used.

To carry on the mining, the topmost of the planks which shut up the end of the level, as is shown in *fig.* 15, is lifted up or moved from side to side, and as much of the earth taken away as can be done without reaching the end of the piling. This plank is afterwards shoved further forward and fastened by two short braces or ties to the last frame which has been set up. The plank when pushed forward is somewhat raised, that it may touch the piling with its upper edge. The section of the planks and side elevation of the braces or ties are shown in *pl.* 35, *fig.* 16. If the ground is very soft or marshy, the water is drained off, and this drainage so regulated that the water may be withheld at pleasure; otherwise it might fill the level and displace the frame. As soon as the workman sees that a sufficient quantity of water has flowed out, he presses back the plank, or stuffs in a bundle of straw. Short braces are driven in by hammers between the uprights and the plank, in order to push forward the latter. When the highest plank has in this way been shoved forward, there remains between it and the one which is under it, and which has not been pushed forward so far, an empty space, through which the mud sometimes flows out. This must be kept under command. In this way by a successive pushing on of the planks, the end of the piling is almost reached. Then another main frame must be forced in and new piling fastened by wedges. If it is apprehended that the framework is not strong enough to resist the pressure, strong pieces or longitudinal beams are placed under the caps, and on the sills and between them perpendicular posts are placed, as is shown in *figs.* 15 and 16.

In ground where the pressure is very great much is accomplished if even a narrow passage can be effected, because by opening and draining the ground it is prepared for subsequent working. For this purpose, at Tarnowitz, temporary posts are erected on timbers placed in a wedge form, and a narrow opening, gradually enlarging, is carried forward in the ground to be worked (*pl.* 25, *fig.* 17). After the ground is drained permanent timber-work is constructed.

2. Masonry of Levels. Masonry is always to be preferred to timbering if the adit or level to be driven is to remain open for several years, and cheap and durable materials are at hand. Masonry is indispensable where the adit or level is driven in very soft or marshy ground, where the object is not only to resist the pressure but to prevent the flow of water into the mine, and in all wide galleries or tunnels, such as are made on canals or railroads. All kinds of hard stone are used as materials for masonwork. When bricks are used they must be burnt very hard. The stone obtained in the mine is rarely suitable for the masonry of the adits or drifts. For dry masonry only rubble-stone and moss are used. For cementing the mason-work common lime and sand mortar or hydraulic mortar are used.

There should be no empty space behind the masonry, or between it and the walls or roof of the drift. If this essential condition is secured, mason-work will receive a pressure on all parts of its exterior surface, and therefore can only be destroyed by falling into the inside of the drift. In ground where there is no very strong pressure, and where at the same time the roof and the walls or sides of the drift are to be sustained, the masonry generally consists of a semicircular vault, or a right cylindrical arch resting on two piers extending perpendicularly along the walls of the drift. If the bottom of the drift is incapable of supporting the piers, the following means of obviating the difficulty are adopted. 1. The piers are placed on sills of oak wood, as in *pl.* 25, *fig.* 12. 2. Beneath this sill is constructed an inverted or *reversed arch.* 3. A perfectly closed elliptical arch is constructed, the longer axis of which is vertical (*fig.* 14). The first method is adopted when the side pressure is weak. The second and third are resorted to when the drift is of large dimensions and the pressure is very considerable. The lower curve of the ellipse may be flattened to prevent the gallery from being too high.

We will now refer to some examples of the appropriate masonry of mines. In loose ground, like clay, sand, &c., and at a slight depth below the surface, where the excavation is afterwards to be built in with masonry, the walls and roof are temporarily supported by props and cross-beams. In this kind of ground, dry walls filled in with moss are often used, which are made 29–24 inches thick. These walls are better in marshy ground than those cemented with mortar. If the pressure is very considerable, and the ground at the same time marshy, hydraulic cement is used, and small canals are left here and there, by which water may flow into the adit.

If the proper curve for the arch of the masonry is fixed upon, centrings, constructed according to the condition and weight of the masonry, are placed for supporting the arches while being built.

The most general rule for constructing arches in the adits or drifts of mines is, that the chord of the arc should be perpendicular to the direction of the pressure. If the bottom and sides of the drift are capable of sustaining pressure, but the rock above or in the roof exerts a perpendicular pressure, an obtuse or surbased arch is employed. If parts of the walls of the drift are cracked and loose, the abutments of the arch should be laid deeper into the rock or ground on the sides of the drift, or so far that a solid point is found for them to rest on. If the sides of the drift are so broken that no solid support can be found for the abutments, the span of the arch may rest on the firm bottom of the drift, or strong slabs of stone. The section of the arch then forms an ellipse compounded of many arcs of a circle. If the sole or bottom of the drift is so yielding that no firm ground can be found even by excavations, then ground or foundation arches must be constructed. These are flattened arches the chords of which lie in the direction of the drift, the impost of each arch being on points of the sole which have been ascertained to be perfectly firm (*pl.* 25, *fig.* 20 *a b*). Upon these foundation arches the side walls are constructed. Various means of remedying the want of firmness of the sole of the drift may be resorted to. The sole may be covered with large slabs of stone, or an inverted or counter-arch may be constructed, and on its springings the side walls may be erected. If the sole is wholly excavated and peculiar strength is to be given to the gallery, sustaining arches may be thrown across the drift under the bottom of the gallery which is to be constructed. The arches should be at a distance of from four to eight feet from each other (*pl.* 25, *fig.* 21 *a b*). Against the springings of the sustaining arches, and at right angles to them, the ground arches above described (*fig.* 20) should be constructed, and upon them the walls of the gallery or adit are built. Rubbish should be placed so as to fill up the space beneath the sustaining and ground arches. If, finally, there is nowhere any solid rock, and the bottom of the drift is wholly soft and yielding, continuous elliptical curves must be used to form the gallery (*pl.* 25, *fig.* 14).

Pl. 24, *fig.* 2, represents a mode of constructing the masonry of an adit where the foot-wall furnishes the only firm support. The foot-wall forms part of the bottom of the adit, and a partial ellipse of mason-work is made to rest on steps or projections of the firm foot-wall.

Recently whenever practicable, an entire or partial ellipse has been used in the masonry of levels and adits. One advantage in using the ellipse is that it may be constructed within timber-work and piling, which is first constructed when the ground is soft and compressible (*pl.* 24, *fig.* 1).

In building the roof arch, centrings are necessary, as in masonry above ground, and the work is carried on in the same manner, except that the confined space makes it more difficult and tedious. The laying of the key-stones in such cases requires particular care and skill. After the completion of the section of an arch, such as is shown in *pl.* 24, *fig.* 6, the centring should remain several days before it is removed.

A peculiar method has been adopted in the lower levels of the mines of Freienwalde in Prussia. Here an iron supporting-arch was made use of to preserve the roof and sides of the gallery while the arch was being constructed, to keep out the water. The walls of the galleries are vertical, and covered with a semicircular arch. The sole, where it consists of sand, and there is not an excess of water, stands very well. When it is very wet it becomes necessary to turn a reversed arch, upon which the walls of the gallery are built. Only one iron centring is used while constructing the arches, which is moved forward as the work proceeds. It is made of wrought-iron, and consists of three ribs which have the form of the outside of the walls (*pl.* 25, *fig.* 18). These exterior centrings, if they may be so termed, consist of three parts, the bottom piece, and two similar half arches which lap over each other in the middle, and are fastened together by means of screws. The iron sole rests upon another of wood, and the three ribs of the centring are placed nearly two feet apart. Upon these ribs lie about forty iron plates, seven to eight feet long, half an inch thick, and four inches wide. By this means the walls and roof of the excavation are secured for a distance of seven feet, and when the arch is completed the supporting frame is moved on to support the next stretch.

Most of the machine-chambers below ground consist of rooms for the water-wheels which are connected with the pumps, the steam-engines being very seldom beneath the surface. These chambers require to be walled up, partially or entirely, and great care is necessary in their location, as serious accidents may occur, entailing costly repairs. In *pl.* 24, *figs.* 3, 4, and 5, is seen a wheel-house as usually walled up in the Saxon mines, the wheel being indicated in *fig.* 3 by the dotted circle. The water is admitted through suitable openings in the roof if the wheels be over-shot, or through the side walls of the chamber if under-shot wheels be used.

5. Sinking of Shafts.

When a shaft is to be sunk into solid rock it is done by blasting. In this work great inconvenience is caused to the workmen by the water which issues from the clefts in the rock and falls down upon them. In order to prevent this a gutter is cut in a spiral form along the sides of the shaft (*pl.* 25, *fig.* 22), emptying into a small excavation in the solid rock, calculated to contain the water discharged in twenty-four hours, from which the water is raised in buckets when it is full.

In England, especially in the vicinity of Newcastle, the shafts are made circular, the smallest being ten feet in diameter. The circular form is well adapted to shafts in strata of a small dip, and is also much used in the Liège coal-mines, and in some parts of France. For shafts in rocks of great dip, the rectangular form is preferable, particularly when they are to be timbered; in Germany therefore the rectangular form is generally used, and the masonry is executed in four arches abutting against each other in the corners.

1. Timbering of Shafts. The timbering of the shafts is the woodwork necessary to support the sides. In shafts which are to serve for a short season only, a temporary timbering is made use of, constructed in the following manner. Green oak, birch, or beech, is bent into hoops, which are placed one beneath the other as the shaft proceeds, and serve

to support the sides for a limited period; this method is not expensive, and is not resorted to in excavations of an enduring character.

In permanent shafts timbering of a more substantial character must be made use of. The shafts intended to be stayed with timber are usually square or rectangular, as this form renders the timbering easier. Where the pressure of the earth is not excessive, the timbers are placed three or four feet asunder; where the earth is moist, it becomes necessary to place them closer. *Pl.* 25, *figs.* 23 *a* and 24, show the arrangement of the woodwork in elevation, and *fig.* 23 the same in plan; *fig.* 25, vertical section of the timbered shaft. As seen in *fig.* 23 *b*, the shaft is divided into three divisions, one for the service of each of the tubs, and another for the ascent and descent of the miners.

Pl. 24, *fig.* 7, shows the first steps to be taken in sinking a shaft. The lower and stronger beams of the frame for supporting the windlass are parallel with the short sides of the excavation. 6 or 8 feet below the surface the first rectangular frame of the timbering is placed, which serves as a guide for the balance of the shaft, the sides of which, as the work progresses, are supported by similar frames at suitable distances from each other, and have joists driven down behind them, the spaces between which and the walls of the shaft are filled with blocks and wedges of wood, to give them a firm bearing, and the longer sides of the framework are strutted with stout cross-timbers, the ends of which are seen in *pl.* 25, *fig.* 26; these timbers are more clearly seen in *fig.* 23 *b*. *Pl.* 24, *figs.* 8 and 9, represent different methods of shaft-timbering.

In very wet mines it becomes necessary to dam out the water, which is done either with oaken frames, with cast-iron cylinders, or with masonry laid with hydraulic cement. *Pl.* 24, *fig.* 18, is a section of a shaft of a coal mine in Belgium thus walled up.

It often occurs that shafts pass through strata of coarse sand filled with springs; in this case the excavation is opened much larger than it is ultimately to remain (*pl.* 24, *fig.* 21), and lined with a double timbering, the intermediate space being puddled with tenacious clay; this, however, can only be accomplished when on penetrating the sand a firm impermeable stratum is reached.

As an example of damming out with cast-iron, we will give an instance which occurred in a coal mine near Newcastle, England. At a depth of 42 feet from the surface, a spring was encountered which poured in 200 gallons of water per minute; the workmen having succeeded in penetrating to a firm impermeable stratum below, a carefully prepared ring of oak was laid at the bottom, upon which segments of cast-iron were placed, the joints between the segments being chinked with strips of wood, and the space being well puddled, by which the water was completely shut out, and a foundation was furnished for the masonry above, which was placed directly upon the iron segments.

Further down a copious spring was encountered, which required a similar dam of nearly 40 feet in height, the segments being rather thicker than those above.

At a depth of 216 feet a third tubing became necessary for a distance of 24 feet, and at a still greater depth a fourth was required. *Pl.* 24, *fig.* 19, is a vertical section of a portion of this dam. Above these cast-iron cylinders the shaft was lined with stone masonry.

There is another species of damming, in which, instead of lining the gallery or shaft, the point from which the spring has burst is plugged up as it were. This occurs most frequently in a gallery, the whole of which, in such cases, is often closed by the dam. A bed of moss is first laid upon the sole, and the timbers of the dam are then built in, wedged, and caulked with moss. *Pl.* 24, *fig.* 28, shows an instrument used for enlarging the openings between the timbers, and *fig.* 29 the chisel for driving in the moss; *figs.* 26 and 27 are sections of such a dam, propped upon the front side to prevent bending; *figs.* 22 and 23 are instances of the same in vertical shafts.

Sometimes the wall of the shaft is built upon an iron shoe, sharp at the bottom, and the excavation is made upon the interior, the shoe cutting its way down as the work proceeds, and sinking gradually with the wall. Between the wall and the sides of the shaft are scantlings, placed vertically to prevent interference between the masonry and the sides of the cut (*pl.* 24, *fig.* 20). At other times the sides of the shaft are supported at the time it is sunk by a temporary timbering of scantling (*pl.* 25, *fig.* 19), which gives place where the shaft is entirely excavated to the masonry walling.

2. Shaft Masonry. When shafts are to be kept open more than six or seven years, masonry is preferred to timbering. The masonry is either laid in common or hydraulic cement, or is carried up dry where the ground is free from water. When one or more sides of a shaft are to be secured by masonry, arches are sprung over the level below the shaft (*pl.* 24, *fig.* 13), and on these arches the masonry is carried up, presenting either a straight face to the shaft (*pl.* 24, *fig.* 10), or the concavity of an arch (*fig.* 11) when the rock is rather loose, and exerts a considerable pressure on the wall. The empty spaces behind the walls are packed with rocks. *Figs.* 12 and 14 are sections of a rectangular shaft, all four sides of which are secured by masonry; *fig.* 15 is the plan. In shafts of great depth a partition-wall is built, separating the ascent-shaft from the service-shaft, and affording additional security to the masonry of the long sides of the shaft. Wooden partitions are also often made of boards nailed against cross-pieces fixed in the masonry; the boards are tongued and grooved, and closely fitted, the division of the shaft into two spare spaces serving for ventilation. *Figs.* 24 *a*, 24 *b*, and 25 *a*, 25 *b*, show a wooden partition; at the lower end (*fig.* 24 *b*) it is inclined to the side of the shaft, in order to prevent the buckets from catching under it. The ladders stand in the smaller portion of the shaft on foot-boards (*fig.* 25 *b*), which occur every 30 feet; each foot-board has a man-hole (*fig.* 25 *a*), through which a man can pass freely.

In inclined shafts the masonry of the short sides is made in the same manner as in vertical shafts. The upper side is secured by a flat arch, or according to the dip and pressure of the strata by arches of more or less rise, resting below on strong supporting-arches (*pl.* 24, *figs.* 16 and 17), which span the gallery into which the shaft enters. When the shaft is very wide, as when the ascent-shaft, service-shaft, and water-shaft, are contained in one, a single arch would require a great excavation into the strata over-head, and great thickness; it is preferable, therefore, to build one or two partition-walls, and to arch each part of the shaft separately.

When at any part of the mines a powerful spring is encountered which cannot be cut off at a higher point, it may sometimes be backed up by a dam or bulkhead until it breaks out at the surface. This method can only be resorted to when there are no clefts in the formation through which the water might issue at another point, or perhaps even at a greater depth. A bulkhead for this purpose consists generally of strong beams of oak timber, closely fitted and caulked with moss or oakum with the aid of caulking-irons (*pl.* 24, *fig.* 29), and then wedged with wooden wedges, which are inserted by the aid of a kind of chisel, shown in *fig.* 28. A bulkhead of this kind, built in the lead mine of Huelgoet, in France, is represented in *figs.* 26 and 27. For the purpose of caulking on the water-side, a hole was left in the centre, which was afterwards closed with a wedge-shaped block of beech wood. The space behind the bulkhead was filled with concrete made with hydraulic cement. The ends of the beams bear against a rectangular offset in the rock on both sides of the bulkhead, which is, moreover, stiffened by braces on the outside.

When a shaft in a wet mine is abandoned, it is often necessary to shut off the water from the mine by a bulkhead, across the shaft below the wet strata, in the solid formation. The part of the shaft above the bulkhead is generally filled up with rock. A horizontal dam or bulkhead of this kind may be built of masonry or timber; in the former case the spherical form is to be preferred; a bulkhead of timber is represented in *pl.* 24, *figs.* 22 and 23. The ends of the beams and the side beams are bevelled, and rest on a shoulder in the rock, as seen in the plate, where they are wedged tight; the centre or key-beam is held in its proper position by means of a strong iron eye-bolt, *b*, while the whole bulkhead is caulked and firmly wedged up. Any subsequent strain of the timber is prevented by bracing on the top of the bulkhead.

6. Working the Mines.

Mines may be divided into two classes according as they are worked. In the first the economical minerals are found in connexion with the *gangue* and sterile rocks, which are separated in the mines, and are suitable for walling and protecting the passages. The second class embraces those mines in which the *deads* are not serviceable for the above purpose. To the first class belong most metallic mines, and to the second, mines of coal, salt, &c. Mines may be worked either by *open* or *subterranean excavation.* The former are the least expensive, when not pushed to a great depth; and are preferred for mineral deposits lying near the surface, for building materials, lime, &c.

Pl. 24, *fig.* 43, exhibits a general view of the subterranean operations as conducted in steps, which is called *stoping;* by this process the sole of an existing *level* is cut down by steps, or the work may be commenced directly from the foot of the shaft; after the work has proceeded for some time, the excavation presents the appearance of a series of steps, as seen in *fig.* 43. The height of a step is generally to its length as one to three or four; a similar method is adopted in the gold mines of Morro Velho in Brazil (*pl.* 25, *fig.* 4). The thin coal-seams near Mons are worked in a similar manner, a main shaft for the working of the vein and another for the pump being the first sunk (*pl.* 26, *fig.* 3); these shafts are then united by a cross-gallery and two principal levels are then driven, the one upon a level with the bottom of the pump shaft, and which serves to carry the water to the sink, called the *sump*, *c*, the other serving as a working level for the seams above. In *pl.* 24, *fig.* 32, the levels are run parallel with the vein. Upon the left is seen the water shaft, and above it the working shaft, from which leads out the working gallery; *b* is the ground level, which leads the water to the sump.

Pl. 26, *figs.* 4 and 5, show a mode of operation practised in lieu of stoping, in horizontal or slightly inclined veins. P is a working shaft, and P′ serves for the pumps and also for ventilation; AB is the principal working level, either horizontal or slightly inclined towards A.

A variety of methods are adopted in the working of those mines which do not furnish the material with which to support the roofs of the excavations. Pillars are left which are just sufficient to support the strata above, or massive columns are left, a large portion of which is removed when the regular working is finished. In other cases levels are driven forward and the pillars are cut away by working backwards, allowing the whole superincumbent strata to fall down and follow the miners in their retreat. In highly inclined veins covered levels or galleries are oftentimes necessary for ventilation (*pl.* 26, *fig.* 26 *b*), in which *a* is the gallery, *m* a pillar, and *r* the passage for the draught.

Pl. 25, *fig.* 5, represents two coal seams, one immediately above the other. In such cases the upper seam is first worked and the pillars removed, and two years afterwards the lower seam is worked by long pillars and galleries running in the direction of the dip; the pillars are then removed, and the whole is allowed to fall in after the miners.

Pl. 24, *fig.* 31, is the plan of a Sunderland mine in an immense field of a million square fathoms. The whole is set upon pillars, and the work is driven as far as ventilation and the power of removing the coal to the main shaft will permit. A are the large safety pillars; B is the ventilating shaft; C, a shaft or inclined level.

Pl. 25, *fig.* 3, shows the method adopted in the silver mines in the vicinity of Freiberg, and in the iron mines of Müssen in Rhenish Prussia.

7. Ventilation of Mines.

The air in mines becomes unfit for respiration either by the consumption of oxygen by the miners and lights, or by the development of gases which are dangerous or at least do not sustain life, as carbonic acid, hydrogen, sulphuretted and carburetted hydrogen, carbonic oxide, sulphurous acid, and the fumes of mercury and arsenic. When there is no reason to apprehend the presence of inflammable gas in a mine, the condition of the air is readily investigated by lowering down a burning candle, which will only burn in respirable air; the presence of sulphuretted hydrogen is recognised by the smell, or by the blackening of strips of paper dipped in a solution of acetate of lead. When carburetted hydrogen, called *fire-damp*, is suspected, a safety-lamp is lowered, the wire cylinder of which will become entirely filled with flame when the air contains one sixth of the gas; when one half of the volume of the air is composed of carburetted hydrogen the lamp will go out. The practice of setting fire to the inflammable air in mines, which was formerly often resorted to, is very objectionable, being not only dangerous to the workmen engaged in doing so, but also to the mines which are set on fire, besides having the disadvantage that two volumes of oxygen are consumed for each volume of inflammable gas.

The only effectual way of purifying the air in mines is by the copious introduction of pure atmospheric air, a continuous current of it being made to enter the mines at one point, and passing out at another after circulating throughout the excavations. This ventilation may either be produced solely by the difference in gravity of the external air and that in the mines, aided by a judicious arrangement of the excavations, when it is called *natural ventilation:* or else it is caused in part or entirely by machinery, producing *artificial ventilation.*

1. Natural Ventilation. In mines with but one surface opening, whether a shaft or a gallery, the ventilation is very much assisted by large dimensions which allow two opposite currents of air to be formed without interfering much with each other. In shafts the dripping of water at the sides promotes a downward current of air, while an upward current takes place in the centre. By dividing a shaft or gallery into two parts by a closely fitted partition, the ventilation is much augmented; one of the parts may be advantageously connected with an air-chimney. The wind may also be temporarily made use of by means of a windsail.

The natural ventilation generally exists in a sufficient degree in mines with two surface openings, between which there is a considerable difference of level, which may be increased by erecting an air-chimney over the higher one. In winter the currents of air are often inconveniently strong, and are therefore diminished by doors which partially shut off the draught.

2. Artificial Ventilation. As the natural ventilation depends on the difference of temperature of the exterior and that in the mines, it may be effectually assisted when it is found insufficient by a furnace placed at the bottom of a shaft, by means of which a brisk draught is created.

Machines for injecting or exhausting air are also employed extensively. *Pl.* 24, *fig.* 35, represents an exhausting engine driven by steam, erected at the mine of Bois de St. Ghislain. The exhausting cylinders have ten feet diameter; they are made of oak staves hooped with iron hoops, their bottoms as well as the pistons are of cast-iron, and have each ten valves which are counterpoised. At each stroke of the engine one of the cylinders exhausts air from the mine while the other is descending freely.

The centrifugal ventilator is also frequently employed in ventilating mines. *Pl.* 26, *figs.* 6 and 7, represent half sections of this apparatus: six curved rings or guides, *a*, *a*, are attached to a disk at the upper end of the vertical axis; on the lower side of the guides is attached the annular disk, *cc*, which lies in the plane of the head of the cylinder, DD, which covers the opening of the shaft. To *cc* is attached a sheet iron cylinder, *ee*, dipping into water contained in a circular trough, *ff*, in order to prevent leakage; the difference in the height of water on both sides of the cylinder, *ee*, is due to the difference of pressure between the exterior air and the interior, which is set in motion by the rotation of the ventilator. *Figs.* 8 and 9 represent a similar apparatus, which revolves on a horizontal axis. *Fig.* 10 is a ventilating screw, which will act either as an exhauster or a blower, according to the direction in which it is turned.

The manner in which the circulation of air to the furthest extent of a mine is insured by regulating its course by means of doors, is shown in *pl.* 23, *fig.* 33. The air comes in at the shaft A, circulates through all the working levels by following the course indicated by the arrows, and escapes again through the shaft B; the dark portions of the figure are exhausted workings which are separated by air-tight partitions. At *a*, *a*, *a*, is shown how the current is guided into the foreheads of the mine. *Fig.* 34 represents another system of working and ventilation, which is in general use in coal-mines. The current descends through the shaft A, and is divided into two parts, which remain separate throughout the whole mine until they unite again near the shaft B, through which the air rushes out; D is a furnace which keeps up the ventilation.

In most mines there are persons whose sole duty it is to examine constantly the state of ventilation. An anemometer, which is frequently used for the purpose of ascertaining the velocity of the air-current, is represented on *pl.* 26, *figs.* 13, 14, and 15, in two side-views and a top-view. To the axis, A, are attached four wings of gold-foil, making an angle of 30° with a plane perpendicular to the axis: an endless screw, V, drives a wheel, R, of 100 cogs, which by a small lever, *c*, moves the wheel R′, having fifty teeth, one tooth for every revolution of R. Thus for 5,000 revolutions of the fans the wheel, R′, makes one; when the axis of the instrument is presented to the draught, the number of revolutions of the fan counted by the indicators, *i*, *i′*, will show the relative velocity of the current.

3. Illumination of Mines. The pit-bottoms only and the straight galleries of transport are lighted by stationary lamps (*pl.* 23, *fig.* 36, the bottom of the engine pit of a Newcastle coal mine). The miners either carry small tallow candles, which when at work are fixed in front of their hats, or oil

lamps suspended from a hook by four chains. Since the invention of Davy's safety lamp it has been universally employed in all mines in which inflammable gas is developed. On *pl.* 26, *fig.* 12 *a*, it is represented; it consists of a common lamp covered with a cylinder of very fine wire gauze, which was found by Davy to interrupt the flame of carburetted hydrogen, unless the air is agitated. An improvement upon Davy's lamp was made by Messrs. Upton and Roberts, by covering it with a glass cylinder in such a manner as to admit the air which feeds the flame only under its bottom, first through holes and next through a disk of wire gauze. The air which surrounds the wire-gauze cylinder will therefore not be set in motion by moving the lamp, or by currents of air. *Figs.* 12, *c*, *b*, *d*, represent this lamp.

Another safety-lamp, invented in 1838 by Dumesnil, is represented in *figs.* 12, *e* and *f*; the oil-reservoir is at the side, the flat wick passes through the cylinder plate, *p*, and air for the flame is supplied at both sides through the tubes, *c c*, covered with wire gauze. The flame is encased in a strong glass cylinder, MM, and at the top is a double chimney with a contracted orifice, but not covered with wire-gauze.

Fig. 11 represents a breathing-tube which is made use of to enter the mines when they are filled with noxious gases, in order to save persons in danger of suffocation. It consists of a tube of cloth or cotton kept open by a wire spiral, and is provided with a mouth-piece fitted closely to the face, which has two valves, one admitting the air from the tube, the other opening outwards when the air is exhaled. With a tube of three quarters of an inch diameter respiration can conveniently be kept up at a distance of 100 feet from the respirable air, and with larger tubes at a greater distance.

8. Transport of Ores to the Surface.

In irregular and short levels the ore is carried on the back of the workmen in bags or convenient vessels. In many mines in France the ore is dragged in a kind of sledge (*pl.* 26, *figs.* 16 and 17) on the floor of the level. In the larger levels wooden or iron tracks are laid, on which the ore is transported in vehicles called dogs or rolleys (*figs.* 19 and 20). Another mode of constructing these cars is seen in *figs.* 21 and 22, each wheel having a separate axle, which affords some advantage on curved tracks. A two-wheeled car (*fig.* 18), with props like a wheelbarrow, is also frequently used.

In working deposits of considerable dip the coals or ores are simply thrown down into the main level of transportation from the upper working levels through planked openings, which are frequently provided with a valve at the lower end, by opening which the cars placed below it will be filled.

When the rolleys cannot be brought to the surface through the gallery, they are unloaded at the bottom of the engine-pit, either by being tilted over or by opening one of the sides of the car, which moves on hinges. The material is then drawn up in buckets or *corves*, the size of which depends upon the power of the machinery employed to raise them. For raising ore from a moderate depth a common windlass (*pl.* 26, *fig.* 28) may be employed. For greater depths and larger loads horse and steam-power are used. *Fig.* 27 represents the application of a steam-engine for the purpose of raising coals. It works in two shafts at once, the empty corves descending in one while the full ones are coming up in the other. In this way the weight of the material only is required to be overcome by the engine, the descending and ascending corves balancing each other, an arrangement which should always be attended to.

In cases where a mine has a capacious adit, or when material must be introduced to fill up the spaces from which the ore has been removed, the ascent of the corves is caused by the descent of vessels filled with water or rocks; the velocity is regulated by brakes. The same means are employed to draw up the ores on inclined planes, the lower part of one of which is seen in *fig.* 26 *a*, which also shows the manner of loading the car, M M. A dog, G, filled with ore is weighed by an apparatus indicated in the figure, and is then allowed to tilt over and discharge its load into the car, M, by withdrawing the bolts which hold it down to its truck.

Fig. 23 represents a car which is frequently used on inclined planes, *Figs.* 24 *a* and 25 show the usual contrivance for unloading large cars. The last sills of the railroad on which the car runs are movable about pivots, *j*; when the car comes on them, they are held in the horizontal position by the hooks *x* and *y*; after attaching the car by the chains, *c*, and drawing the bolt, *n*, of the end of the car, the hooks, *x* and *y*, are thrown out by means of the lever *d*, when the frame will be tilted by the weight of the car, and the load discharged. It requires but little force to replace the frame afterwards in the horizontal position, when the car will again be on the track.

The descent and ascent of the miners take place on single or double ladders (*pl.* 24, *fig.* 37) on winding stairs (*fig.* 36), in the corves (*fig.* 38), or on an especial seat attached to the rope (*fig.* 39). In France, Belgium, and England, the latter modes are common, but in the Prussian coal mines, in the Hartz, and in Cornwall, the common ladders are in general use, in consequence of which much time and force are spent by the miners in the ascent, more particularly through shafts of a depth of 1,200 to 2,000 feet.

9. Drainage of Mines.

When the workings are above the level of a valley at no great distance, the drainage is generally effected by an adit level, which is a slightly inclined subterraneous canal emptying the waters of the mine near the lowest level of the valley. Such a slope only should be given to it as is just sufficient to make the water run, in order to drain the mine at the lowest possible level. This method of drainage is always the surest where it can be effected, and notwithstanding the great first outlay is generally the most economical.

Whenever the workings are driven below the natural means of drainage, or below the level of the plain, recourse must be had to mechanical power. The water is sometimes raised in buckets or tubs, but most frequently by pumps of various construction. The common suction-pumps are used for inconsiderable depths; for great depths forcing-pumps with hollow pistons or solid plungers are employed, all of which have been fully described in a former article. We add the description of an excellent lifting-pump in the mines of Huelgoet, which is set in motion by a hydraulic engine (*pl.* 26, *fig.* 29). C is the working barrel, closed at the top, but open at the lower end; P is the piston, LL′ the valve-box; when the piston descends, the water ascends through the suction-valve, *s*, into the valve-box and the barrel, and by the upward stroke of the piston it is raised through the lift-valve. Both valves are conical, without any packing. The leather packing of the piston-rod, X, is seen in *fig.* 33; that of the piston, which is a spring-packing, in *figs.* 31 and 34. A small lateral tube, *u′ u″ u‴*, provided with stop-cocks, connects the suction and lifting-pipes and the barrel, and serves to fill the suction-pipe with water when the pump has not been in action for a length of time. A small valve, W, which is loaded with the pressure of one atmosphere, shows at all times whether the suction-valve is in good condition, as, when it does not close perfectly tight, the pressure of the upward stroke will cause the valve, W, to open. *Fig.* 32 shows the joining of the several pieces of the lifting-pipe.

Water containing copperas in solution is injurious to leather packing by rendering it hard. In such cases plungers of solid metal without any packing are to be preferred (*fig.* 30), and in the copper and zinc mines in Cornwall they are generally in use.

Before closing this article we must say a few words about some mines which claim our attention, either by the peculiarity of the mode of working or by their picturesque appearance. Among these are the Swedish mines at Falun and Persberg; of the former we have given an exterior view (*pl.* 23, *fig.* 1), and a view of the great cauldron with the head of the working-shaft (*pl.* 25, *fig.* 2); and of the second the exterior view (*pl.* 23, *fig.* 2) and the interior view of the rock chambers (*pl.* 25, *fig.* 1). The copper mines at Falun and Persberg have long been celebrated, but are now nearly exhausted. In the time of Gustavus Adolphus they yielded yearly over 5,000,000 pounds. The principal entrance, which we have represented, is 240 ft. deep and 60 ft. wide, and was formed by a terrible caving in which occurred in 1687. It was then resolved to suspend the working, but upon a revolt of the miners the labors were resumed.

A singular impression is made upon the beholder by the interior of the mill-stone quarry at Niedermendig on the Rhine (*pl.* 26, *fig.* 2), with its colossal arches and pillars. The quarrying of the stones is quite simple. The hardness of the stone is such that neither masonry nor timbering is required, but immense pillars are occasionally left to support the roof. The stone is blasted in large blocks, which are first worked cylindrical, and split with wedges into disks of the required thickness; the stones are then dressed, the hole is cut, and they are sent up to the surface completed.

The salt mines at Wieliczka (*pl.* 26, *fig.* 1), in Galicia, are justly considered one of the wonders of Europe. They extend not only beneath the town, but also to a considerable distance on each side; and their treasures still appear to be inexhaustible, though they have been worked between five and six centuries.

The depth of these mines is upwards of 2000 ft.; there are eleven openings to the surface, and the aggregate length of all the galleries is said to be over 250 miles. Many exaggerated stories are told of whole families living in the mines and never coming to the surface, but these are entirely without foundation. The workmen are divided into three bands, which relieve each other alternately, spending eight hours of the twenty-four in the mines and the balance above-ground with their families. In 1570 and also in 1614 the mine suffered very much from fire, and since then all timbering has been discarded, the roof being supported upon pillars of rock-salt; the steps are also cut out of the same material. St. Anthony's Chapel, upon the first floor, about 300 ft. from the surface, is also hewn out of the salt rock, as is also the great hall, which contains lustres hanging from the roof and all the curiosities, crystals, petrifactions, &c., which have been found in the mine. The effect of illumination is said to be truly magical in these spacious rooms, and to be enhanced by the varied color of the salt, white, pink, grey, and black.

These mines are supposed to be connected with the salt formation in Walachia, having an extent of upwards of 500 miles.

VIII. METALLURGY.

Metallurgy, equally with other branches of art, requires its own peculiar implements and tools, the most important of which we shall notice in the sequel. As our limits will not permit us to speak of all the metals, we shall select iron, indisputably the most important one, and carry it through the different processes to which it is subjected, from the ore to the merchantable metal.

1. General Preparation of Ores.

Metals, united with other mineral substances, in the form of ores, are found distributed throughout the crust of the earth, and we have seen them extracted therefrom in the foregoing article, by the operations of mining.

Before the final reduction, the ore is more or less separated from foreign substances by mechanical means; this it is not, however, possible perfectly to accomplish, and the further the operation is pushed the greater will be the waste of the ore.

The preparation of the ore commences with the picking or sorting, which takes place in the mines; and consists in separating those pieces of rock which apparently contain no ore, from those which contain more or less of it.

The richest portions are to be subjected to the dry stamping; the next in grade, which are too rich to be subjected immediately to wet stamping, are first sifted, and thus are made to yield much pure ore. There are, then, two other qualities of ore distinguished, which are subjected to wet stamping and sifting.

Sifting serves to separate the rich ore from the fragments of sterile rock, the whole having first been subjected to stamping, either wet or dry, and to distribute and separate the ores in the order of the coarseness of the grain. The sieves are plunged into vessels of water, and violently agitated by a series of up and down motions, and thus the mineral substances are raised up and fall nearly in the order of their specific gravity, the metallic portions sinking to the bottom; those particles which pass through the meshes of the riddles settle at the bottom of the vessel, and are afterwards exposed to washing, when they are worth the trouble.

The powdering of the ores is performed in stamping-mills. The stamps are raised by wipers or cams on a revolving-shaft, and are permitted to fall upon the material in troughs; the stamps are shod with iron at their lower ends, and weigh from two to three hundred pounds (*pl.* 27, *fig.* 21). A stream of water passes constantly through the trough, and the pounded ore passes with the water immediately to a series of shallow receivers united by channels; the richest portions of the ore, being heaviest, settle nearest to the stamping-trough, and the lighter particles next, until the water arrives at the last receiver, where the lightest particles are thrown down.

2. Roasting.

The ore prepared as above is submitted to another operation, called *roasting*, before coming to the furnaces.

Iron ore, which requires only to be pulverized to assist its melting, is roasted to render it friable, and disengage its water and carbonic acid. Sulphur, antimony, and arsenic are also volatilized by the process of roasting, and by their union with the atmosphere various products are formed. At a low temperature sulphates are formed, which, as the heat is elevated, yield sulphuric acid gas; the metallic oxides remain behind.

3. Furnaces.

The different furnaces made use of in metallurgic operations may be divided, according to their construction, into *open furnaces*, *stack furnaces*, *reverberatory furnaces*, and *crucible furnaces*. In the two first classes the fuel is mixed with the ore; in the third, only the flame operates upon it; and in the fourth, the material to be heated is inclosed in crucibles, which are exposed either to immediate contact with the fuel or to its flame. In some of these furnaces a blast of air is used to urge the fire, and increase the heat.

1. Open Furnaces. Open furnaces are the simplest used in metallurgic operations. *Pl.* 27, *fig.* 1, is an example, in which the walls are but 2 or 3 feet high; strictly, this should be considered as several furnaces, with division walls between them. The roasting of minerals is performed in these furnaces in the following manner: The floor is covered with a layer of fuel, upon which the ore is placed and the fuel is lighted. Those ores containing sulphur and bitumen require but little fuel, as when once heated to a certain point they take fire and burn of themselves. Others, as iron ores, which contain no combustible matter, require considerable fuel to effect the roasting. Ores are often roasted in pits in the earth, in which case a high and dry locality must be chosen; frequently the operation is performed in heaps in the open air, which is often considered the most available method. *Pl.* 27, *fig.* 2, shows the liquation furnace used for separating silver from lead ores; the walls, *a*, are inclined towards each other, and on the top are covered with plates of iron, which leave narrow openings between them, their whole length. The material to be operated upon is placed upon the inclined plates, and the fuel beneath and all around it; the lead, as it melts, drops through the openings between the plates, and collects in the receptacle *b*. *Figs.* 3, 4, and 5, represent a blomary or forge-fire for the reviving of iron; it consists of low masonry work, with an excavation in the hearth, to contain the metal to be operated upon. *Fig.* 3, *a b c d* are four cast-iron plates, the bottom of the hearth forming a fifth; *e* is the opening through which the tuyere passes; three or four inches above the bottom of the hearth is a row of holes or a slit to let off the cinders. The hearth and tuyere are hollow, and water is kept circulating through them. An open copper furnace, seen in *fig.* 6, differs from the blomary principally in having a spherical hearth; *a* is the crucible. The masonry, which partially surrounds the hearth, is for the purpose of better concentrating the fire; *b* is the tuyere; *c*, the black wall through which the tuyere passes; *d*, a partition wall dividing the space above the hearth.

Pl. 27, *fig.* 7, is a view of an open silver refining furnace; *a*, the opening for the tuyere; *b*, the cupel crucibles. The cupel consists of a crucible of iron, in which the wood and bone ashes are rammed, on the surface of which is a depression for receiving the silver which is to be refined.

2. Stack Furnaces. The signification of the word *stack* sufficiently explains the general character of this class of furnace, the interior space being open at the top, and entirely closed with masonry, forming a shaft or stack which receives the material to be heated, either alone or mixed with the fuel, the atmosphere necessary to combustion being supplied at the bottom, either by the draught or by a blowing apparatus; those operated by draught alone are used for roasting only. *Pl.* 27, *figs.* 11^a and 11^b, are vertical sections, at right angles to each other, of a Swedish furnace of this description; *a* is the stack which is to be filled with the material to be operated upon; *d* is the fire space, at the bottom of which is a grate; *e* the ash-pit. The fire space is covered with massive iron bars, laid close to each

other, which, however, permit the flame to pass through. *b*, the openings from which the ore is withdrawn as it is roasted; *g*, inclined iron plates, over which the iron is withdrawn from the furnace. The ore to be roasted is supplied from above, at the top of the stack. *f* are openings in the ash-pit, to supply draught and for the withdrawal of ashes.

Fig. 8ᵃ is a vertical and *fig.* 8ᵇ a horizontal section of a furnace for roasting iron ore; *a* is the shaft, lined with fire-proof stone; *b* is the grate. The roasted ore is withdrawn at the openings, *c*, into the spaces, *e*, and thence to the arched chambers, *f*; *d* is the ash-pit. The operation in this furnace is continual, the material being constantly supplied at top, and withdrawn below as it is roasted.

Pl. 27, *figs.* 9ᵃ and 9ᵇ are sections of an ellipsoidal furnace for roasting iron ore; *b′* are three fire doors; below each grate is an ash-pit, *d*; *c* are openings for withdrawing the ore.

All stack furnaces used for the purpose of smelting metals, and which require a high heat, are furnished with a blowing apparatus; they may be divided into *blast furnaces* and *blue ovens*.

Fig. 10ᵃ is a vertical section and *fig.* 10ᵇ a horizontal section of an iron blast furnace; *a* is the shaft; *b* the boshes; *c* the crucible; C and D are the tuyeres, of which there may be one, two, or three; *e* is the hearth-pit, where the melted iron collects; *g* is the dam-stone, which closes the hearth-pit, except at a single point, which is closed with clay, through which an opening is made to let off the melted iron; *f* the timpstone, which is protected by the timp-plate, imbedded in fire-clay. The upper portion of the stack is seen at 10ᵃ, above *fig.* 7. *h* is the fauld-plate, over which the cinder is run out; A is the working side, B the back, C and D the blast sides of the furnace. At *fig.* 20 are seen the tuyere chambers. Every part of the wall exposed to a strong heat is constructed of fire-proof stone.

Pl. 28, *figs.* 1ᵃ, 1ᵇ, are sections of a blast furnace, through the dam-stone and hearth, upon a large scale. The stones *a* rest upon a layer of sand, *p*, and form the hearth; beneath the sand is an iron plate, *o*, and beneath the plate is the air passage, *q*; the cheek stones, *b*, the back stone, *c*, and the dam-stone, *d*, form the walls of the hearth-pit; *f* is the timp-iron, *g* the timp-plate, *e* the timp-stone; *h* and *i* are the tuyere stones, *k k* iron plates to support the wall above; *l l* are the wall stones between the timp-stone and boshes, *m* the openings for the tuyeres. *Pl.* 27, *fig.* 19, is an interior view of a blast furnace house in the department Aveyron. *Fig.* 12 is a so-called *blue oven*, which is worked with a closed breast, and has an opening below to let off the iron and cinders; *a* is the shaft, *b* arched openings through which enter the blast tubes; *e* is an opening which, when the furnace is in operation, is walled up as high at the tap hole. When the furnace is started the breast is closed, with the exception of a hole at the bottom to let out the iron, and a hole six or eight inches above the first through which the cinder flows out; it is filled to the top with coal and iron, the supply of which is renewed as the charges sink. This furnace is kept in continuous blast for three, six, or nine months.

Pl. 27, *figs.* 13ᵃ, 13ᵇ, and 13ᶜ, represent a crucible furnace with closed breast; *a* is the shaft, *b* the crucible for the metal and slag. The sole, *d*, consists of cement, and rises towards the tuyere opening at the back.

Figs. 14[a] and 14[b] are sections of a furnace in use at the Falun copper works. The shaft terminates in the sink in the clay at *f;* the fore-hearth in front of the breast-opening, *k*, communicates by a canal with the crucible *o*. The layer, *e*, is firmly rammed clay, *d* cinders, *m* iron plates in front of the hearth.

There are also blast-furnaces from which the iron runs uninterruptedly through the tap-hole, which is never closed. *Pl.* 28, *fig.* 2[a], is a furnace of this description, constructed something like the German blue oven. *a* is the shaft, *c* the crucibles into which the metal flows, *e* the openings for the tuyere.

3. Reverberatory Furnaces. Those furnaces in which the fuel does not come in contact with the metal, but operates upon it by its flame, are called reverberatory or puddling furnaces. In furnaces of this description the ore is placed upon a level or concave hearth, and the walls and arch are so constructed as to throw back the flame upon the metal to be melted. In *pl.* 28, *figs.* 3[a], 3[b], 3[c], and 3[d], is represented a double roasting furnace on the reverberatory plan, in which there are two hearths one above the other, *h* and *h′*. This furnace may be used in two different ways: either each hearth may be used with its separate blast, or the blast may be applied to the lower hearth only, passing thence with the stream of hot gases to the upper one. In the former case the smoke passage, *f*, is closed with an iron plate, and the smoke passes immediately to the chamber x, and the double roasting furnace performs the functions of two reverberatory furnaces, with this difference, however, that the upper one is easier to heat. Where it is used as a double roasting furnace, the passage *f* is opened and there is but one fire, viz. upon the grate *r;* the upper hearth then serves for preparatory roasting and the latter for finishing the operation. The working openings, *o* and *o′*, are upon opposite sides of the furnace, that two laborers may be employed at the same time without interrupting each other.

Pl. 27, *figs.* 15[a], 15[b], 15[c], represent a puddling-furnace used for converting cast-iron into wrought-iron; *a* is the ash-pit, *r* the grate, *b* the fire-bridge, *h* the hearth upon which the pig metal is placed. The bridges *b* and *d* are hollow, having each in its centre a cast-iron pipe through which a stream of water is kept constantly running; *l* is an opening beneath the chimney, through which ashes which collect there may be withdrawn; *t* are cast-iron columns which support the stack. Beneath the hearth is an open space, and the openings, x, are for the purpose of giving access to the same.

4. Crucible-Furnaces. Those furnaces in which the substances to be acted upon are confined in a crucible which is exposed to the action of the fire, are called crucible-furnaces. Their construction is very various, according to the use to which they are to be applied. Of this class are muffle-furnaces made use of for various metallurgic processes, in which the material is to be kept from immediate contact with the fire. *Pl.* 28, *figs.* 7[a], 7[b], represent a furnace for roasting or distilling arsenic with muffle-formed chamber. A is the ash-pit, B the grate, D the hearth of a double layer of fire-

bricks upon which the finely stamped arsenic mineral is spread. The fire passes from the grate beneath the hearth out at the opening, *q*, thence back through the channels, *i*, to the double chimney, *g*, and thus the flat muffle-formed space above the hearth is heated without bringing the flame into contact with the arsenic, and the arsenic acid passes by the passage, *h*, to the condensing-chamber. Whilst the furnace is in operation a second charge is being warmed upon the top of the furnace, and is fed to the muffle at the hole, *e*.

Crucible-furnaces, which serve simply for melting, are of the simplest construction. *Pl.* 28, *figs.* 8^a and 8^b, is a Sefstrom furnace, and consists of two cylinders of sheet-metal so united by the ring, *e*, as to leave a vacant space between them. The interior cylinder is lined with fire-clay, and there is also a support of the same material for the crucible; at *a* is an opening for the entrance of the blast, which passes through a circle of holes, *b*, to the fire on every side.

For handling the crucibles in this and other similar furnaces, the tongs shown in *pl.* 27, *figs.* 17 and 18, and *pl.* 26, *figs.* 9 and 10, are used. *Pl.* 28, *figs.* 6^a and 6^b, represent an English muffle of sheet-iron lined with fire-clay; *a* is the fire space, *c* the fire grate, *e* the fire door. The box, *d*, in the space, *b*, is the muffle.

Fig. 5^a is a longitudinal section, and 5^b a transverse section of a muffle-furnace used for burning enamels and colors upon porcelain and glass; *a* is the ash pit through which the draught passes to the fire; *b* is the fuel; *g* the grate. The muffle, *h*, is shoved into the furnace from front. When the operation is completed the chimney is closed at *d*, and the whole permitted to cool gradually.

Sand-baths are another species of furnace of this general character. They are used where materials are to be warmed or heated to a moderate degree without coming in contact with the fire, for which purpose the vessels which contain them or the substances themselves are buried in the sand, or simply laid upon its surface. *Pl.* 28, *figs.* 4^a and 4^b, represent a sand-bath-furnace, in which *a* is the ash-pit, *f* the grate, *b* the fire space, *h* the fire door; behind the fire space is a bridge over which the flame and smoke pass to the chimney, *c*, which may be closed by the plate, *d*, to regulate the cooling of the sand-bath. Over the fire space is a cast-iron plate, and upon this a frame, *i*, which supports the sand-bath.

4. Chemical Metallurgic Apparatus.

The apparatus used in the chemical processes of metallurgy are the same as those required for this branch in the laboratory, modified only by the amount of materials operated upon in each case. As an example, however, of the difference which occurs in the construction of some of the apparatus, we will present the amalgam mill (*pl.* 27, *fig.* 16) used for extracting gold from auriferous sand. As but a portion of the metal can be extracted from the sand by a single mill, it is usual to unite several of them together, that the gold sand carried by the water from one mill may be conveyed to the other. Two such machines are seen together in the drawing. *a* is the mill-basin secured to the frame, *h*, and having a hollow tube in its centre through which the shaft, *d*, driven by the wheel, *g*, of the runner, turns. Upon the top of the shaft, *d*, is a cross-bar, *b*, which is connected with the runner by two arms; in the centre of the runner is a funnel-formed opening which receives the stream of water and sand, which in its passage beneath the runner is brought into contact with the quicksilver at the bottom of the basin *a*, which is also kept in motion by iron plates upon the bottom of the runner, and which amalgamates with a portion of the gold, the sand and water passing on to a similar mill where the process is continued.

5. Working Iron.

No metal is of so great importance to man as iron; on this account we have selected it to give a rather detailed description of its manufacture. As it leaves the furnace after the operation of smelting, it is known as raw-iron or pig-iron, of which two kinds are distinguished, white-iron and grey; the former has a silver white color, and is used in the manufacture of steel; the latter is of every shade, from black to light grey. Wrought-iron is of a light grey fracture, running partly into white, partly into grey. Steel has a greyish white fracture, is harder than iron, and is worked with more difficulty.

We have already spoken of the furnaces made use of in extracting iron from the ore, and will now say a few words upon the process itself. The ore having been broken into small pieces and roasted, is ready for the smelting process, which reduces the oxygen and separates the compounds of silicic acid in the form of slag. Charcoal, stone coal, or turf, may be used according as they are to be obtained to advantage.

The furnace is first slowly heated, to prevent it from cracking, and is then charged lightly with coal and ore alternately. When the first traces of metal show themselves the crucible is cleaned, the tap hole closed, and the blast is let on, lightly at first, and gradually increased for five or six days, when it has its full power. The labors of the blast-furnace then consist in renewing the supply of ore and coal from time to time, and keeping the furnace free of slag.

When sufficient metal has collected in the crucible, the tap hole is opened and it is suffered to run off; in blast-furnaces with open breast this takes place every twelve, eighteen, or twenty-four hours; the tap hole is then cleaned out and again closed.

Within the last twenty years many experiments have been made with *hot-blast-furnaces;* in these the blast is heated before it is supplied to the furnace. Many methods have been adopted for effecting this purpose; sometimes the air is heated in separate furnaces, at others the waste heat from the furnace itself is employed; generally it is made to pass through heated cast-iron pipes, the convolutions of which are surrounded by fire; at others it is accomplished in air-tight chambers (*pl.* 28, *fig.* 11).

Wrought-iron is produced immediately from the ore or from pig-iron; in the former case, where the blomary fire is made use of, the iron ore, roasted or not, is mixed with coals, and melted down upon an open hearth under a blast produced by bellows of the common form, or more generally by wooden cylinders urged by water-wheels.

The production of wrought-iron from pig metal is accomplished in finery fires, or puddling furnaces. In finery fires the metal is partially melted under the blast, and the carbon and foreign substances measurably expelled before it is taken to the squeezers.

The puddling-furnace is undeniably the best adapted for converting pig-iron into bar-iron. The iron hearth of the furnace already described is covered to a depth of three or four inches with cinders from a charcoal forge, from another puddling-furnace, or from a re-heating-furnace. If none of these can be obtained, cinder from a blast-furnace will answer. The furnace is then fired, and when the cinder is melted, and the bottom and sides are properly protected, cold cinder is thrown in; and when the bottom is so far cooled that the tools make no impression on it, the iron is charged. As the latter begins to get red it is turned and worked over, and as it becomes white and commences to melt, it is broken with hook-formed instruments, and mixed with the partially melted cinder; after a further heat it is divided into lumps twelve or fifteen inches in diameter, and carried to the hammer or squeezers. These lumps, called balls, are then subjected to the operation of *shingling,* which is performed under the hammer or in the squeezers, and which converts them into blooms or more regularly formed masses; these blooms then pass to the rough rollers. Sometimes no hammer or squeezers are employed, but the balls are taken directly from the puddling-furnace to the rollers. The roughing rollers take the bloom and reduce it into billets of a size proportioned to that of the bars to be drawn. The rollers for the final preparation of the iron are seen in *pl.* 28, *figs.* 12^a, 12^b, and 12^c; *fig.* 13 represents them in plan; *figs.* 14 and 15, cross-sections; *fig.* 16, the cog-wheel driving the rollers; *fig.* 17, a front view of a sheet-iron rolling machine; *fig.* 18, a view from above, and *figs.* 19 and 20, details of the same; *fig.* 21 shows the operation of rolling; and *fig.* 22, the cutting off of railroad rails by circular saws. The rollers are set in strong cast-iron frames, and are adjustable more or less near each other by screws; they are furnished with round or angular grooves according to the size of iron to be rolled.

After the balls are prepared in the puddling-furnace they are carried in the tongs (*fig.* 10) to the hammer, or, where no hammer is used, to the first set of rough rollers (*figs.* 12^a and 14), where they are drawn into billets or plates. The hammer is, however, to be preferred, as the cinder falls freer and the welding is more perfect.

The iron thus prepared either by hammering or by passing many times through the rough rollers, is cut, bound into parcels, re-heated, and taken to the finishing rollers.

Sheet-iron is made directly from the bloom upon the rollers (*figs.* 17 and 18), which are made to approach each other slightly after each passage of the iron, by means of the set screws moving the upper rollers; the iron is repeatedly heated during the operation, which is continued until the sheet is reduced to the required thickness.

IX. AGRICULTURE.

Agriculture is that art by which the earth is rendered capable of ministering to our necessities. It treats of the growth of plants and animals, as mutually dependent branches, the latter being always founded upon the former. Its legitimate aim is not the production of the largest and finest animals, the heaviest crop without regard to cost, but the reaping from a certain capital the surest heaviest income.

Agriculture may be taught or studied in three different ways: as a trade or mechanically, as an art, and as a science. Mechanically considered, agriculture does not differ from other trades, and consists in the imitation of practice and the exercise of judgment. As an art it takes a wider range, and follows fixed rules and precepts, which are the result of long-continued observations upon nature. So long as these rules are founded upon nature, they are of value; but in most cases they spring from isolated observations, are not in accordance with first principles, and are unworthy of confidence. The insufficiency of such rules, without distinction of cause and effect, is never more apparent than in the case of an agriculturist who has followed them with advantage in one district, and who, when he moves to another of different character, finds they but mislead and deceive him.

Science, on the contrary, fixes no positive rules, but developes the principles to be followed in every variety of case that may arise, teaches us to dive to the bottom of nature's springs for the foundation stones of a rational theory, and is in fact itself the only true basis on which a system of agriculture can be erected. Theory alone, however, can never make an agriculturist, but only when hand in hand with practice.

1. Tillage.

A. The Soil.

The surface of the earth, the grand workshop of the vegetable kingdom, produces everywhere, when left to itself, those plants to the growth of which the soil and climate are congenial. The original elements of the soil, silex or sand, clay, lime, and iron, now one now the other preponderating, constitute, as it were, the vessel in which is prepared the food necessary for the growth of plants and in which it is offered to their roots.

These elements impart certain qualities to the soil, according as they preponderate, one producing a light, dry soil, with but little power of retaining moisture; another, a close, moist soil, having strong affinity for water, and retaining it for a great length of time. A certain medium between the two extremes, to a depth of nine to twelve inches, is most favorable to the growth of cultivated plants. In general the greater the preponderance of sand the lighter and more easily moved is the soil, while a preponderance of clay gives it exactly opposite qualities.

The food of plants consists of water and the remains of decayed vegetable bodies, which in the state in which it is found in the soil is called *humus*. Soils may be divided into, 1. *very stiff clay;* 2. *moderately stiff clay;* 3. *sandy clay;* 4. *moist, fine-grained, sandy soil;* 5. *dry, coarse-grained sand.*

1. STIFF CLAY is in best condition when, either by nature or liberal treatment with manure, it contains a rich supply of humus, or when the decomposition of the humus has been effected by cultivation which has brought every portion of the soil in contact with the atmosphere, and which at the same time has eradicated the weeds. As such soils, however, on account of their impermeability, are liable to suffer from an excess of moisture, care is necessary that good water-furrows be provided to carry off superfluous water, which otherwise might stand in pools upon the surface. Attention to this is important to the prosperity of every plant, but indispensably necessary to the growth of the cereals.

2. MODERATELY STIFF CLAY OR CLAY LOAM. In general, what has been said of stiff clay holds good of this soil also; it is, however, easier to work, suffers less from moisture, and thus is better adapted to the growth of grain. On the other hand, it is more easily deprived of its humus by a succession of crops; but by the admixture of lime the assimilation of its elements is promoted, and even when there is a lack of humus, with favorable weather, good crops may be expected.

Each of these grades of soil is, however, easily baked or hardened upon the surface by the sun: on this account a covering of vegetation is of great importance to the development of the strength of the soil.

3. SANDY CLAY OR SANDY LOAM. This soil permits the ready entrance of the air, and in consequence its cultivation presents comparatively few difficulties; its natural products, weeds, require a corresponding greater degree of care. This soil may be said to be in the best order when the manure applied to small grains is decomposed and mixed with the earth. Care is requisite to retain the surface water instead of leading it off, and to compact the soil during its cultivation by the use of the roller. Furthermore the ready access given to the atmosphere causes a constant decomposition of its humus and manure until interrupted by frost, and consequently such soils should never be left without some growing crop. On this account such land should not be fallowed, as the air thus carries off its useful gases and the soil soon becomes sterile.

4. MOIST, FINE-GRAINED, SANDY SOIL. The peculiarity of this soil consists in the extreme fineness of its sand, which exists in a state of dust so minutely divided as to resist the entrance of the air to an equal degree with those soils containing too much clay. Water is thus prevented from escaping, and weeds grow with great luxuriance. The sun hardens this soil so as to render ploughing extremely difficult, and the atmosphere is completely

excluded. This so-called *cold soil* must be so managed in cultivation as to destroy knot-grass, charlock, and other weeds which are apt to infest it, and to forward the decomposition of its humus. This is accomplished not so much by fallow as by cultivation in hills upon long manure. Potatoes and garden vegetables, when used for food, are not so well adapted to the purpose, as the coldness of the soil retards them, and they flourish only in very warm days. Naked fallows evaporate the gases which should nourish vegetation. As this soil also suffers from too much moisture, the *lands* should be laid off narrow and the furrows be well cleaned out, particularly for winter grain.

5. DRY, COARSE-GRAINED, SANDY SOIL. This is the direct opposite in all respects of clay soil, and must be managed in an entirely different manner. If in the latter the entrance of the atmosphere is resisted, in the case before us it is too much encouraged, and the ceaseless evaporation may impoverish the soil before it has borne a single crop. This soil is only fit for grain when it can be shaded by a heavy cover of foliage, which impedes the evaporation of the gases. Its weeds are eradicated by leaving it for many years in meadow, when they are prevented from perfecting their seed, and thus ultimately are extinguished; even knot-grass, the worst and most troublesome of all weeds, cannot endure many years after the ground is laid down to meadow. As with the soils in which clay predominates care is not necessary to conduct off superfluous water, in this case every means must be resorted to, to retain the moisture for the use of vegetation. Neither land nor water furrows are necessary, and the roller must be used with every crop, to compact and consolidate the soil as much as possible.

This classification of soils is important only so far as the decomposition of humus and the growth of weeds are concerned; thus far it is sufficient. A classification as regards fertility requires that other attendant circumstances be noticed, as the subsoil, the character of the surface (whether flat, rolling, or otherwise), and the presence of other chemical and mineral substances. The knowledge of soils thus classified is taught by *Agronomy*, which treats of the different elements of soils and the relation they bear to each other.

There are also exterior signs to be noticed in judging of soils. Their tenacity, as manifested in ploughing and harrowing; its excess in one case, while it is entirely wanting in another; their different powers of absorption and retention of moisture; their color when wet, and their peculiar odor indicating the presence or the absence of humus.

We will now turn our attention to some of the most common agricultural tools.

B. Agricultural Tools.

1. THE PLOUGH. Ploughing serves to open the soil for the admission of air and moisture to the organic matter which it contains, and which is thus decomposed and fitted to serve as food for vegetation. The operation is more or less necessary, more or less difficult, according as the soil is stiff and tenacious, or loose and porous. Another object to be accomplished by

ploughing is, the destruction of weeds, which are turned under with the surface soil, and covered with the layer immediately beneath it, which is brought up in contact with the atmosphere and laid in narrow parallel ridges. This turning up and separating from the subsoil is performed by a sharp horizontal plate of iron called the *share;* the dividing into narrow ridges is the work of a vertical iron called the *coulter;* and the turning over is done by a board shaped for the purpose, called the *mould-board.* Every plough consists of these three elements, arranged in proper order, the coulter preceding the share and mould-board. Ploughs may be divided into two great classes: those with wheels, called *wheel-ploughs*, and those without, called *swing-ploughs.*

In *pl.* 29 ploughs of different construction and for various purposes are represented. *Fig.* 1 is a swing-plough in use in Belgium, the share and mould-board of cast-iron, and forming an uninterrupted and continuous curve; *fig.* 2 is a Brabant plough, also of cast-iron, which runs very steadily and may be set to cut deep or shallow, narrow or wide furrows; *fig.* 3 is a Flanders cultivating plough; *fig.* 4 is a Belgian plough, used for breaking up sod-land; *fig.* 5 is a Bohemian plough; *fig.* 6 is a form of subsoil plough or deepener, for increasing the depth of the soil and moving the subsoil; *fig.* 7 is a shovel plough, for cultivating growing crops; *fig.* 8 is a small plough, used also for cultivating and hilling potatoes and other crops; *fig.* 9 represents a plough so arranged as to keep the furrows without the aid of the ploughman; *fig.* 10 is an old Thuringian plough; *fig.* 11 is the so-called champion plough, with the guide wheels of unequal diameter, the right wheel running in the furrows; *figs.* 12 and 13 are right and left hand views of a German plough, which nearly resembles the Belgian; *fig.* 14 is a simple form of subsoil plough, which breaks up the subsoil without bringing it to the surface; *fig.* 15 is a hand plough, for working between the rows of seed beds; *fig.* 16 is a plough with wheels behind the sole, to diminish the friction upon the subsoil; *fig.* 17 is a light plough, used for covering stubble before winter.

In no part of the world, perhaps, have the mechanics of agriculture made such rapid advancement as in the United States. The plough has been made much lighter and of easier draught, whilst its cost has been materially lessened. Amongst others an ingenious instrument has been invented for digging potatoes, which promises to be a great labor-saving machine. Improvements have also been made in ploughs for cultivating upon the sides of hills, and in the common cultivator.

2. The Harrow. The object of the harrow is three-fold: more completely to pulverize the ground after it is left by the plough, to eradicate and destroy the roots of weeds and grass, and to cover seed when sown broad-cast. It consists of a strong wooden frame filled with wooden or iron pins, each of which as the harrow is moved makes a small furrow, or breaks the clods it may encounter.

Pl. 29, *figs.* 18 and 19, are old forms of the Scotch harrow, with horizontal and oblique teeth; *fig.* 20 is a harrow with hooked teeth, for the purpose of eradicating weeds and grass; *fig.* 21 is a form of cultivating harrows invented in Saxony, for working between the rows of crops; *fig.* 23 is a Norwegian harrow, as improved in England; *fig.* 22 is the so-called English extirpator, which nearly resembles the cultivator in common use all over the United States.

3. SOWING AND PLANTING MACHINES. Many machines have been devised for planting and sowing, which differ essentially from each other, according to the nature of the seed they are intended to plant. *Pl.* 29, *figs.* 32 and 33, are instruments used in the preparation of the ground; *fig.* 28 represents a simple instrument used for marking the lines in which to deposit those seeds planted by hand, and may be drawn forwards either by the hand or by an animal; *figs.* 34 and 35 are instruments for transplanting.

Sowing machines were first invented in Germany about the middle of the 17th century; since then they have been much improved in England and the United States. With nearly every machine for this purpose is united one or more small ploughs, to open the furrows, in which the seed is regularly distributed; they are so arranged that they may be placed to run deeper or more shallow, according to the nature of the seed to be planted, and to cut the furrows at such a width as may be required. There is also some arrangement attached to most of them for covering the seed. That portion of the apparatus which strews the seeds in the drills generally consists of a series of tubes reaching almost to the ground. Into these tubes the seed falls from a cylinder filled with holes, or is thrown in by small scoops upon an axis made to revolve in the seed-hopper; they are so arranged as to be adjustable more or less near to each other, and receive a slight shaking motion to secure the passage of the seed. In a seed-sower represented in *fig.* 30 the seed is fed to the funnel by a revolving cylinder, and there is an arrangement to stop the feed when the machine is turned. Hornly's seed-planter, seen in *fig.* 36, is intended to sow all kinds of small grain, as also to distribute dry or liquid manure; it has ten seed-tubes, with the same number of ploughs or drills. The furrows are opened at the required distance apart, the seeds are dropped in them either continuously or at proper distances, and immediately covered. *Fig.* 29 is a more simple machine for drilling beans, which are dropped at certain required distances from each other; *fig.* 31 is a machine used for sowing clover-seed, and consists of a series of short perforated cylinders from which the seed is distributed with great regularity as it is drawn along the ground; this is said to be a labor and seed-saving machine, which performs its work well. *Fig.* 27 is a simple machine for drilling turnips, in which the feed-roller receives motion by a band from the axis of the machine.

When seed is sown by hand it is covered by a drag seen in *fig.* 24. *Fig.* 25 is an instrument for the same purpose, which leaves the surface very smooth, and may be loaded with stones to increase the pressure. *Fig.* 26 is the common roller sometimes used when the field has been well harrowed, to cover the seed.

C. Grain Crops.

After the grain is cut it is bound into sheaves and put up in shocks (*fig.* 39), and when sufficiently dry it is stored in stacks or barns. These stacks are so formed as to shed the rain, and are thatched with long straw, the more effectually to exclude the rain. *Pl.* 30, *figs.* 25 and 26, are common forms, the former as put up in Germany, the latter in England. Before the general introduction of threshing machines, the grain was beaten out upon a threshing-floor, generally formed in the barn itself. The threshing-floor was prepared by first covering it with stiff clay, which was moistened, trodden, and beaten; when dry it was wet with bullocks' blood, and after further beatings, suffered to harden. *Pl.* 30, *fig.* 32, shows an English grain-barn and threshing-floor beneath the same roof. *Fig.* 33, another arrangement of the same with corn-loft, potatoe-bin, and tool-house added. Movable grain-barns are sometimes made use of, which are brought up to the side of the stack which is to be threshed (*pl.* 30, *fig.* 34). In most parts of Europe grain is still threshed by hand with the flail; in the United States threshing-machines are in almost general use for the purpose, and usually consist of a cylinder of wood or iron, studded with teeth, which revolves rapidly within a concave also filled with teeth, so arranged that the rows of teeth on the cylinder fall into the spaces between the teeth upon the concave; the grain being fed into this machine is carried round by the cylinder and violently beaten between its teeth and those of the concave, and the grain thus threshed falls out at one end of the machine, while the straw is carried out at the other end by the centrifugal action of the cylinder and the draught which it occasions.

Where the grain is threshed by hand it is much mixed with chaff and the dust of the threshing-floor; to separate it from these it is passed through the *winnowing machine* or *fan* (*pl.* 29, *figs.* 37 and 38). The grain is put into the hopper, *h*, from which it is delivered gradually upon a vibrating sieve which permits the grain, but not the larger pieces of straw, to pass through; it then descends into the inclined board, *k*, to the back of the machine, whilst the dust and lighter particles of chaff are blown out at the other end by the revolving blower or fan, *d*, *e*, *f*, *g*.

In some parts of Europe grain intended for grinding is first coarsely broken up on a mill seen in *pl.* 29, *fig.* 40, in which the grain is crushed between revolving rollers.

When the straw, after the grain is threshed out, is used for feeding, it is first cut into short lengths, the better to be mixed with the grain or other food used with it. This is performed upon the straw-cutter. Upon small farms this machine consists of a trough three to four feet in length, through which the straw is fed beneath the edge of a knife worked by hand. On larger establishments more effective machines are in use; in one represented in *pl.* 29, *fig.* 41, the knives are secured to the arms of a fly-wheel, which is made to revolve rapidly and thus cut the straw as it is fed from the end of the trough.

Before we proceed further it may be well to say something upon the preservation of the various products of the farm.

In some parts of Europe many kinds of grain are kiln-dried before being threshed. *Pl.* 30, *figs.* 40 and 41, show an arrangement used for this purpose. The same building contains the threshing-floor, the stove, and the shelves for the sheaves of grain which are replenished from the stacks without continually, as the grain is threshed.

D. Root and Fruit Crops.

Root crops, such as potatoes, turnips, and the like, are preserved in cellars or in holes in the ground, or even, where the cold is not too severe, in heaps raised above the surface and covered with earth. *Pl.* 30, *figs.* 31 *a* and 31 *c*, represent such an arrangement. The roots are heaped and covered first with straw, then earth to a depth sufficient to exclude the frost; in the centre of the heap is a hole usually filled with straw, in which a thermometer (*fig.* 24) is placed. This thermometer is occasionally examined, that frost and fermentation may be guarded against; sometimes the roots are heaped upon the surface covered with light frames (*fig.* 31 *b*), and then with straw, the ends being filled with straw that access may be had to the roots. Clover hay requires peculiar management, otherwise the leaves fall from the stalks and its value is diminished. It should be mowed when a majority of flower-heads are developed, and left one day in the swath. The next day the swaths are to be turned so that two fall together; it is then left until nearly dry, and when the stems on being bent cease to show any moisture, it is gathered in when the dew is upon it. Upon the continent of Europe it is sometimes cured upon frames made for the purpose, called clover-horses (*pl.* 30, *fig.* 27). *Fig.* 28 is also a form of frame used for the same purpose, the object in both cases being to secure a free ventilation amongst the clover, which is arranged with the flower heads inside, that they may not suffer so much from the rain.

The drying of fruit can only be performed in dry weather, when this is done in the open air. When it is carried on upon a large scale, kilns built for the purpose become necessary. In *pl.* 30, *fig.* 35, is a plan of such a kiln, on the line, GH, of *fig.* 36; *fig.* 36, a vertical section upon the line, RS, of *fig.* 38; *fig.* 37, a transverse section on the line, GL, in *fig.* 38; *fig.* 38, a horizontal section on the line, GH, in *fig.* 36; and *fig.* 39 is a perspective view of one of the sliding frames for holding the fruit. Beneath the drying chamber is an oven, and at *m* are openings for the entrance of air which passes through tubes, *x*, to the fruit-chamber, and is again drawn off by the tube, L, and carried beneath the fire-grate to save fuel, and to increase the draught in the drying-chamber.

E. Under-Ground Drains.

When from the nature of the subsoil an excess of moisture exists in the soil, excluding the atmosphere, the evil must be corrected by under-ground drainage. Soils of this moist, cold nature, are unsuited to the growth of any cultivated plants, though particularly congenial to that of weeds. Surface draining does not accomplish the desired end; indeed this can only be effected by deep under-ground drains, which, lying beneath the surface, collect the water from a considerable distance, whilst the cultivation of the ground is not inte rupted.

The first thing to be attended to in laying out drains is to give them a sufficient fall or descent to carry off the water which collects in them. The operation commences with the construction of a main drain through the lowest portion of the field, to receive and carry off the contributions of the minor drains. This main drain is best left open, and in general should be at least three feet wide at the bottom, and three feet deep; from this radiate over the whole surface of the ground to be drained, the under-ground branches, which, having been dug to the requisite depth, are filled with stones, bushes, straw, reeds, or similar substances, as they may be at hand.

If stones be made use of, care should be taken that none are so large as to fill alone the bottom of the drain; in general the stones should lie hollow, so as to permit the passage of the water, and not dam it up at any one point. *Pl.* 30, *fig.* 29, is not an unusual arrangement, the drain being covered first with a layer of straw, rushes, &c., then with the soil. Where reeds and straw are made use of, *fig.* 30 shows a common arrangement. When the drain itself is filled with these materials, there should be a space above of at least one foot, which is to be filled with the surface soil; this should be heaped over the drain, that as the ground gradually consolidates it may not sink below the general surface.

In England, where draining is extensively practised, the plough is made use of in opening the drains, which materially lessens the cost of excavation. The following tools are also made use of in England: The drain shovel (*pl.* 30, *figs.* 10, 11, and 12), and drain hoes of various forms and sizes (*figs.* 8 and 9). The earth-borer is often made use of to advantage to ascertain the nature of the ground beneath the surface, as the labor of draining may often be reduced by finding a stratum of gravel beneath, into which the surface water may be conducted. For minor depths, the auger shown in *fig.* 15 is quite sufficient. When a greater depth of auger is required, an instrument, shown in *fig.* 16, is made use of. *Fig.* 17 is the shaft of the auger; *fig.* 18, the handle; *fig.* 19, the guide for directing the rod of the auger when a considerable depth is to be attained.

Whilst we are speaking of English operations, we will take occasion to mention a few instruments in use in England for cultivating and hoeing vegetable crops. *Pl.* 30, *fig.* 14, is a hoe used to thin out plants where they stand too thick; *fig.* 13 is a double-pointed hoe, of Portuguese origin, and serves to cultivate on both sides of a plant. The treble-pointed hoe (*fig.* 22) is for working between the rows of garden vegetables; *figs.* 23 and 21 are other forms of hoe used for the same purpose; *pl.* 30, *fig.* 20, is an instrument for cutting and grubbing up roots of trees and small shrubs.

F. Double Crops.

Not unconnected with the present article is the subject of double crops. We shall limit ourselves, however, to the consideration of a method practised with success in Austria, for obtaining a crop of small grain and a crop of roots from the same ground each year.

The field (*pl.* 30, *fig.* 1) is ploughed and harrowed in the usual manner, and planted with small grain, wheat, rye, or oats, in rows two feet apart;

before the grain is up the field is rolled and harrowed, which leaves it in the state seen in *fig.* 2. Upon the appearance of the grain (*fig.* 3), the cultivator or some other instrument is made use of between the rows. At the moment the first crop begins to show its ears, the second crop, which may be potatoes, turnips, or beets, is planted between the rows (*fig.* 4). *Fig.* 5 shows the grain ready for the harvest, and in *figs.* 6 and 7 the second crop has possession of the ground.

G. Flax.

This useful plant is harvested when ripe by pulling up the roots, tied in bundles, and dried in the field. It is then freed from seed by passing the heads through an iron comb, bound in small bundles and *rotted*, that the woody portion of the plant may be separated from the *harl* or fibrous portion. After the rotting is completed, it is dried and broken upon a simple machine called a *flax brake* (*pl.* 30, *fig.* 44). In the lower or stationary part of the frame there are three slats on edge, between which work two similar slats upon the movable frame which vibrates upon a pivot in the frame of the machine. The flax is laid upon the lower slats, and is broken by the motion of the upper frame, which is worked by the hand of the operator.

A great variety of machines have been invented for braking flax, which have in a measure replaced the hand machines. After the flax is broken, it is submitted to an operation called swingling, to remove the woody portions which have been broken up by the brake; it is laid upon a bench and beaten by the swingle (*pl.* 30, *fig.* 45 *c*), then it is *heckled* upon the coarse heckle (*fig.* 45), and lastly upon the fine heckle.

Pl. 29, *fig.* 42, is a machine for cleaning flax after it comes from the brake, which makes better work than the above manual operations. It acts in the following manner: two reels, *a* and *b*, revolve rapidly, nearly in contact with each other; the flax is attached to rods and hung at the frame at c, and is gradually lowered and raised between the revolving reels until entirely freed from the *hurds*, when it is fit to be spun.

H. Cider.

An important branch in the economy of the farm is the making of cider, which may be prepared from apples, pears, or plums. The ripe fruit is ground or mashed in a mill (*pl.* 30, *fig.* 47) driven by horse power, or upon a small scale in an apparatus represented in *fig.* 48, in which the fruit is crushed by a conical roller, pivoted in the centre of the table. Upon a larger scale, the fruit, after being ground in the mill (*pl.* 30, *fig.* 47), is carried to the press (*fig.* 49), the screw of which is worked by the rope *e*, or otherwise. The cider is received from the press in barrels, which are kept entirely full until the fermentation is ended. Its flavor is improved by the addition of strawberries, raspberries, or other small fruits, before the fermentation; lime or chalk is sometimes added, to check the too rapid fermentation. By the evaporation of sweet cider a syrup or molasses is obtained, by many preferred to that made from sugar-cane.

2. Live Stock.

A proper choice of stock is a matter of much importance. Whether the most improved or the common breeds are to be selected, depends upon climate, soil, and other circumstances. Good, sufficient food, shelter from the severity of the weather, and faithful attendants, are indispensably necessary to the thriving of all farm stock.

A. The Horse.

We shall here treat of the horse as a farming animal, and refer to the article Zoology, in the second volume of this work, for a scientific description of him, which would be out of place here. *Pl.* 31, *fig.* 19, represents the skeleton of the horse with the outline of his form; *fig.* 18, the appearance of the same immediately beneath the skin; *fig.* 21, a side view of the bones of the head; *fig.* 20, a top view of the same; *fig.* 30, a healthy knee-joint of the hind leg; *fig.* 31, the ligaments and blood-vessels of the same; *fig.* 32, the healthy bone, and *fig.* 33, a spavined bone of the same joint; *fig.* 34, the hoof of a five-year-old mare not yet shod; *fig.* 35, the same after having been shod a year; *fig.* 36, a section of the fore hoof, and *fig.* 37, a section of the hind hoof.

As the age of a horse is determined by the condition and appearance of the teeth, it becomes necessary to observe these closely.

They are divided into *incisors*, *tushes*, and *grinders*. In the full-grown horse there are twelve incisors, six in each jaw; the two front incisors, *aa* (*fig.* 24[a]), are popularly called *nippers* or gatherers; the two next adjoining, *bb* (*fig.* 24[a]), separators, or middle teeth; and the outer, the corners, or corner teeth, *e* (*fig.* 27[a]). The tushes are between the incisors and grinders, *dd* (*fig.* 25[a]). The horse has also twenty-four grinders, twelve in each jaw. There is, besides these, another or temporary set of teeth, called *milk teeth*; some of these are apparent at birth, others are developed in the first years afterwards. The horse is foaled with six *molar* or grinding teeth in each jaw; the twelfth day after the two front nippers appear above and below, and in fifteen days the two intermediate; the corner ones are not cut till three months after. At ten months the incisors are on a level with each other, and have a very sensible cavity; at twelve months this cavity becomes smaller (*pl.* 31, *fig.* 22), and the animal shows four molar teeth on each side above and below, three of the temporary or colt's, and one horse tooth; at eighteen months the cavity in the nippers is filled up, and there are five grinders, two of the horse and three of the colt's; at two years (*fig.* 23) the first of the colt's molar teeth in each jaw are displaced, and the cavities in the corner teeth are not yet quite filled up; at two years and a half or three years, the front nippers fall and give place to the permanent ones; at three and a half the middle nippers are likewise removed, at which period the second milk molar also falls (*pl.* 31, *fig.* 24[a]), and the four corner teeth continue to protrude themselves more and more (*fig.* 24[b]).

At four the horse has six molar teeth, five of his new set and one of his last; the corner colt's tooth, seen from the side, has become very small (*fig.* 25[b]); at four and a half years these corners are replaced by the permanent teeth, and the last temporary grinder disappears. At five years the principal indications are found on the corner teeth and tushes; the corner teeth have their inner and outer edges upon a level, and the tushes are developed (*figs.* 26[a] and 28[b]); at five and a half they are completely out, and the internal wall of the upper nippers, which was before but incompletely formed, is now on a level with the rest; at this period the nippers or incisors have all of them a cavity formed in the substance between the inner and outer walls, and it is the disappearance of this that marks the age; at six years those in the front nippers below are filled up, while the cavities in the corner teeth are still deep, the tushes well grown, and their points more or less worn off (*figs.* 27[a] and 27[b]). At seven years the mark or cavity in the nippers is filled up, and the tushes are a little more worn (*figs.* 28[a] and 28[b]). It often occurs, however, that there is a depression in the cavity of the nippers, and also, in the middle teeth, no real cavity, but a slight brown depression. At eight years the cavities have entirely disappeared, and the tushes are still more worn (*figs.* 29[a] and 29[b]); at this period the horse is said to be *aged* and to have lost his mark, but among good judges the teeth still present sufficient indications. At nine years old the groove in the tushes is nearly worn away, and the nippers become rather rounded; at ten these appearances are still stronger; at twelve the tushes only exhibit a rounded stump, the nippers push forward, become yellow, and as age advances appear triangular and usually uneven. There are also other indications of great age in the horse, such as rough, uneven hoofs. *Pl.* 31, *figs.* 38 to 47, show the foot of the horse in several diseased forms; spavin, windgall, malanders, ring-bone, club-foot, &c.

B. Neat Cattle.

The raising of neat cattle is an important branch of husbandry, even considered independently of the usefulness of the ox as a beast of burden. The flesh and the milk, either in its natural state or in the form of butter and cheese, serve as food, the hide and other portions of the animal as articles of commerce. From the wild ox of Europe have descended many varieties, much modified by taming or cultivation. We shall figure a few of the most noted of these varieties: *pl.* 31, *fig.* 2, is a Swabian cow; *fig.* 4, a Sussex bull; *fig.* 5, a Sussex cow; *fig.* 6, a Herefordshire cow; *fig.* 7, a Devonshire ox, and *fig.* 8, a Kiloe ox; *fig.* 1 is a Swiss cow of the mountain race; *fig.* 3 is a Swiss bull. This latter race is of medium size, not remarkable for its fattening qualities, but superior milkers.

The ox is very generally used as a beast of burden. When an animal is stubborn and refuses to pull, he should be yoked to a heavy weight, as seen in *pl.* 32, *fig.* 1, in such a position that in order to reach the food trough he must haul up the weight, and thus he becomes gradually accustomed to the strain upon his shoulders. The question of the relative profit of the horse and the ox as beasts of draught is still undecided, and must be determined for each locality by existing circumstances, climate, &c. The horse is much more subject to disease than the ox, while the latter is more easily fatigued, particularly in warm latitudes. Amongst the diseases to which horned cattle are subject is that very dangerous one caused by eating too greedily of green food; this produces such a quantity of gas as to endanger the life of the animal, which oftentimes is only saved by opening a vent for the gas from the stomach. *Pl.* 32, *fig.* 3, is the knife used for this purpose, and at *fig.* 2 is seen the manner in which it is applied. The knife is plunged into the animal with its sheath, which is left in the opening when the knife is withdrawn, to prevent the immediate closing of the wound.

Particular cleanliness is requisite in the management of neat cattle, also light, well-aired stalls, such as are represented in *pl.* 32, *fig.* 4. *Pl.* 29, *fig.* 44, is a plan and elevation of a cattle-barn. The cattle-stalls are in the centre of the building, with a passage-way between the cribs and the wall for the purpose of feeding without disturbing the animal. The building should be furnished with a chimney, with a valve for purposes of ventilation.

The milk as it comes from the cows is strained immediately into cans (*pl.* 32, *fig.* 4), and is then set away in shallow pans in the dairy room. In large establishments an especial house is devoted to the milk, butter, and cheese (*pl.* 30, *fig.* 42). *Fig.* 43 is the plan of such a house. *a* is the milk-room, with shelves around the walls for the milk-pans, and a table in the centre. This portion of the building has very thick stone walls, and only one window, *d e*, which runs slanting through the wall, and is glazed on both interior and exterior. There is also a ventilating chimney to keep the room well aired. In the room *b* the butter and cheese are made and the utensils kept; *f* is a fire-place used in making cheese. In the room *c* the butter and cheese are preserved; the centre of the room may be partitioned off for an ice-house, which can be filled through the passage *g h*, and the exterior space, *i k l m*, remains for the butter and cheese. In this room is kept the *lactometer*, which should be found upon every milk farm; it is seen in *pl.* 32, *fig.* 5, and consists of a row of cylindrical glasses of equal size and similarly graduated. The best milk is first poured into the glasses, and when the cream has separated from the milk, its thickness or quantity is noted on the graduation; this serves then as a scale with which to compare the milk of the other cows.

By butter-making is understood the process of separating the oleaginous portions of the milk by means of a rapid and violent shaking; this is ordinarily accomplished in the churn represented in *pl.* 32, *fig.* 6^a. *Fig.* 6^b is the dasher. A more convenient churn for large establishments is represented upon the same plate; *fig.* 7 is a barrel-shaped vessel resting in the frame (*fig.* 9). The dasher (*fig.* 8) is hung upon an axis within the barrel, and is worked by a crank. *Pl.* 30, *fig.* 46, represents an English churn, in which the dasher, at the same time that it is raised and lowered, is rapidly revolved, by which arrangement the cream is much more violently agitated. After the butter has separated from the buttermilk, it is worked and beaten by the hand or by wooden implements until all the buttermilk is worked out; it is then salted, and if intended for transportation or keeping, is packed into firkins or jars, to preserve it as much as possible from contact with the atmosphere.

Cheese is also another product of milk; the solid portion of the milk or curd is caused to separate from the whey or watery portion, by the addition of rennet, which is the stomach of the calf dried and preserved for that purpose. The curd is first drained in a bag, then salted, pressed, and set away in the cheese-room to dry. *Pl.* 32, *fig.* 10, is a common form of cheese-press.

C. The Sheep.

So easily does the sheep accommodate itself to differences of climate and situation, that every country has its peculiar race. In *pl.* 31 are represented some of the most important varieties. *Fig.* 9 is an improved Merino ram, *fig.* 10 a ewe of the same; this breed has fine short wool, particularly adapted to fine cloths. The Saxon Merino or Electoral race is a cross between the Saxon sheep and Spanish Merino; it produces light fleeces, but of the finest, softest wool. The English breeds have run into great variety by crossing, some furnishing long, others short wool; of the latter are the Southdown sheep (*fig.* 11). *Fig.* 12 shows the Leicester breed, *fig.* 13 the Herefordshire. In most countries the sheep are driven in at night and confined in stalls. Sometimes they are permitted to remain all night in the open air, but in this case they are confined in a movable inclosure or hurdle *pl.* 32, *fig.* 12); or as the night air is considered to injure sheep in the climate of England, movable sheep stalls are sometimes made use of (*figs.* 11^a and 11^b). At other times stationary shelters are erected for them, into which they are driven every night. *Pl.* 32, *fig.* 13, is such a sheep-fold or stall, so arranged as to serve the purpose of sheltering the sheep at night, while it is furnished with shelves on which silkworms are fed.

D. The Hog.

Next in importance to the sheep comes the domestic hog. In form it varies but little from the wild hog of Europe, from which it is descended. Its teeth are rather remarkable; they are 44 in number, twenty-eight back teeth, and above and below six front and two corner teeth. By cultivation it has run into numerous varieties, a few of the most important of which are figured in *pl.* 31. *Fig.* 16 is a boar, *fig.* 17 a sow of the Berkshire breed; *figs.* 14 and 15 are of the Chinese race, which have been more or less introduced into England and on the continent of Europe. Everything which can be digested is devoured by this voracious animal. Roots, fruit, grain, or carrion, nothing comes amiss; its own young are not safe, even when other food is plenty, but the character of the flesh depends upon the nature of its food. Where this is flesh or oily nuts, the flesh is very inferior; but where fed entirely upon milk and grain, the meat is extremely delicate. Where potatoes are used for feeding hogs, they are first washed in a machine (*pl.* 29, *fig.* 43) and cooked, which process is found to add greatly to their nutritious qualities. The above machine consists of a cylinder revolving in a frame; the cylinder is partially filled with potatoes and revolved until the friction has loosened the dirt from them; it is then filled with water, or a stream is kept running through it, until it flows clean from the machine.

E. The Silkworm.

Silk is an animal production, spun by the so-called *silkworm*, the larva of the *Phalæna bombyx mori.* The animal is furnished with a collection of vessels in which is secreted, about the time of spinning, a glutinous liquid which hardens on exposure to the atmosphere, and forms the silk thread, which is usually about two thousand feet long, and is strengthened for use by doubling. In the raising of the silkworm the first care should be to provide the food; many substitutes have been tried for the mulberry, but nothing has yet been found to take its place.

The white mulberry, the leaves of which furnish the best food for the silkworm, is indigenous in Syria, Persia, China, and southern Germany. That the leaves may be gathered with ease, the tree should not be permitted to grow very tall, but be shortened in every season, for several years after it leaves the nursery. *Pl.* 32, *fig.* 31, may be cut in, as seen in *fig.* 30; the following year the branches which it has pushed (*fig.* 33) are headed down, as seen in *fig.* 32, and so on each succeeding year, as seen in *figs.* 34, 35, 36, and 37, until the tree receives a low bushy form, from which the leaves may be easily gathered. Recently the mulberry has been grown in hedges, from which the leaves may be gathered without trouble. The *Morus multicaulis* is best adapted to this mode of culture. The rooms in which the worms are fed are furnished with shelves one above the other; or more properly removable frames made of plaited willow roots or coarse netting (*pl.* 32, *figs.* 16 and 17); they should be well ventilated, and capable of being darkened when required. There should also be arrangements for heating the apartments, that an equable temperature may be maintained, and the air kept constantly dry; should the air become too dry it may be corrected by placing vessels of water in the rooms.

The first care of the silk-grower is to procure good eggs; cocoons are selected of a white or yellow color; the female cocoons (*pl.* 32, *fig.* 24) are rounder in the middle than the male (*fig.* 25), which have a deeper depression in the centre. Equal quantities of both are selected. The cocoons inclose the *pupa; fig.* 26 is the female, *fig.* 27 the male. A temperature of 50° to 80° Fahrenheit is necessary to bring them out, and a period of two to three weeks is required; this should take place in a tolerably dark room.

Figs. 28 and 29 are the perfect insect, the former the female, the latter the male. Soon after hatching they are permitted to come together. After a few days the male dies, and the female, after laying five to six hundred eggs, dies also. These eggs are permitted to hatch at a time when the young leaves of the mulberry are tender. The eggs (*fig.* 18) are placed in boxes (*fig.* 15), which in eight or ten days are placed in frames covered with paper, and pierced with holes, upon which some young mulberry leaves are strewed; from the tenth to the fourteenth day the eggs hatch, when they are carefully carried to the feeding apartments. Several distinct periods are distinguished in the life of the silkworm; during the first (*pl.* 32, *fig.* 19) the worm is sparingly fed with cut leaves. In the second period (*fig.* 20) the supply of cut leaves is increased; during this period the first skin is cast. In order to clean the frames, tender branches of mulberry are laid over the worms, and when they have crept upon them they are removed to a clean frame. On the fourth day of this period the second skin is cast. In the third period (*fig.* 21) the worms are again removed, and on the fifth day the third skin is cast. On the sixth day of the fourth period (*fig.* 22) the fourth skin is cast, and the frames are again cleaned. In the fifth period (*figs.* 23^a and 23^b), the feeding increases until the tenth day, when it again decreases gradually. On the 11th day the worms cease eating, the body becomes transparent, and the thread is visible. The spinning-chamber is now arranged with branches of birch, upon which the worms creep and wind their cocoons (*pl.* 32, *fig.* 14). This operation occupies six or seven days, though the cocoons should not be removed until the tenth day.

The chrysalis is then to be killed, which is effected by exposing the cocoons to a high heat, to steam, or the vapor of turpentine. They are then thrown into hot water to loosen the glue which binds the threads together, and the silk thus loosened is wound upon a reel eight to twenty-four threads together. Nine or ten pounds of cocoons give 1 pound of silk.

F. The Honey Bee.

The rearing of bees, though not generally pursued by agriculturists, is one of the most interesting employments of the husbandman, while there is none in which he can engage which affords so large a profit upon the capital invested, or the labor and attention required.

In a wild state, bees occupy hollows in trees, living in families of from 20,000 to 40,000. In a tame or cultivated state, however, they are kept in boxes or baskets made of straw or willow roots, called hives. A complete swarm of bees consists of one queen, the mother of all the other bees (*pl.* 32, *fig.* 43), differing in form and shape from them all; her wings are much shorter, and her legs are without the brushes and cavities with which the working bees are furnished. The queen is the object of the attention and solicitude of the whole hive, and alone lays the eggs which produce the working bees; the latter (*fig.* 45), which are the smallest and most numerous in the hive, are produced in small cells, and are but sparingly fed at first. When fed with the food prepared for the queen they lay eggs, which, however, produce only drones (*fig.* 44). The working bees have stings, and upon their legs brushes, with which they collect the pollen which adheres to the hair of their bodies from the flowers, and pack it away in small cavities or baskets on their legs; this pollen is thought by most naturalists who have turned their attention to the subject, to be made use of by the bees only for the purpose of feeding their young, their own food being exclusively honey, or sugar in some other form. The drones are the males; like the queen, they have neither brushes nor cavities on their legs.

The impregnation of the queen is effected by the drones on the wing and without the hive. *Pl.* 32, *fig.* 55, is a sheet of honey-comb; *a* is a closed drone cell; on the left is seen a queen's cell, and on the right another half completed. Within their hive the bees close all openings and cracks with a substance called *propolis*, which they gather from resinous or other trees in the state in which it is used, and then commence the building of the combs. The cells destined for the queens are many times larger than the others, and require 100 to 150 times as much wax. There are also about 1200 to 2000 drone cells and smaller cells in which the working bees are hatched. Besides these there are others less regularly formed, and used only for storing honey.

The queen lays during the summer from 16,000 to 18,000 eggs, the care of which devolves upon the working bees, assisted, it is believed by some, by the drones. The larvæ produced from these eggs are fed with honey mixed with the pollen of flowers, called bee-bread; in seven to eight days the first transformation takes place; the pupa is then shut up in its cell, and after thirteen or fourteen days the perfect animal comes out, and an hour or two afterwards is ready to start out on its labors. Those which are crippled or disabled are immediately killed and carried out of the hive. When two queens exist in the same hive, one of them leaves with a portion of the family, and the bees are said to *swarm; pl.* 32, *fig.* 42, shows a swarm of bees, hanging one to the other upon a branch of a tree.

When the bees have completed their labors and the hive is filled, they are smothered with sulphur, and their store of honey and wax is taken. Many hives have been contrived by which the surplus honey is taken without destroying the bees, and the lives of these interesting insects are spared. *Pl.* 32, *fig.* 56, is a hive contrived by Thorley for this purpose; the lower box is the habitation of the bees, and has a hole in the top over which a straw hive or other box is placed; when the lower box is filled, the bees ascend and fill also the one above it, and at the close of the season the upper box may be taken from them, leaving sufficient provision for the winter in the lower one. On top is seen a glass globe in which the bees may be watched at their labors; it is, however, necessary to keep the globe covered with another box to exclude the light. *Pl.* 32, *fig.* 57, represents the collateral hive of White, consisting of wooden boxes placed side by side, with openings for communication in each box; they are represented in the figure as separated from each other, to show the openings; when the labors of the bees are over for the season, one of these boxes with its contents may be removed, leaving them the other for their winter support. The most common material of which hives are constructed in Europe is straw; the form most usual is seen in *pl.* 32, *fig.* 38; in the United States wood is almost exclusively made use of. *Fig.* 52 is a style of straw hive much used in England; several of these are placed one above the other, and the top one is furnished with a cover. One or more of these boxes is taken from the bees in the fall, leaving, as usual, sufficient honey to carry them through the winter

Besides the straw cover which surmounts the whole, each hive is furnished with a wooden cover composed of slats (*figs.* 52 and 53); these bars should be 1⅜ inches wide and placed at a distance of half an inch from each other, and are for the purpose of supporting the combs attached to them. Other hives have been used with glass windows (*figs.* 48–50), through which the operations of the bees may be watched; *fig.* 54 is the cover of the hive seen in *fig.* 50, showing the openings through which the bees pass to the glasses above. The better to observe the bees at their labors, the bottom or sides of the hives may be made of glass (*fig.* 51); *figs.* 40 and 41 represent a barrel hive, much used in Europe, where the bees are managed on the depriving system; at the close of the season the hive is opened and the surplus honey is cut out; to facilitate this operation, the division boards, which in *figs.* 47 *a* and *b* are horizontal, are in this hive placed vertically.

Bee-stands are the shelters in which a number of hives are placed, and may be either large wooden boxes, containing a number of hives (*fig.* 46), or masonry structures (*fig.* 38), or detached sheds, open upon one side or entirely closed (*fig.* 39), the object in every case being to protect the hives and bees from the sun, rain, and cold winds.

X. HUNTING AND FISHING.

1. Hunting.

Hunting is the art of chasing and capturing the various kinds of wild animals, either with a view to their destruction as vermin, or as affording sport in the pursuit, or as furnishing food, clothing, or other economical results. The classification sometimes adopted in professional treatises of different degrees of the art, varying with the kind of game, will here be unnecessary.

Hunting in Europe differs very materially from the art as practised in America, if indeed it deserves the name of an art upon the latter continent. There the noxious animals have become scarce, comparatively speaking, and *game* properly so-called is in most places protected by law, and killed only by the privileged classes. In many parts of America, on the contrary, bears, wolves, jaguars, &c., are still to be found in abundance, and game may be taken by any one who has the inclination to seek and possesses skill in finding and capturing. Whilst in Europe hunting has become an art usually practised by the rich and noble or their retainers only, in America the field is open to all, and in most cases hunting is practised in a very unskilful manner. In presenting the following article, therefore, our object is not so much to afford instruction to our American readers, who will probably derive from it little or no information of practical importance, as to show the manner in which hunting is carried on in the civilized parts of the Old World, to give an account of the implements used, the different species of animals pursued, &c.

The animals sought after in Europe are Bears, Deer, Roes, Wild Boars, Hares, Foxes, Badgers, Beavers, Otters, Martens, and Wild Cats, among quadrupeds, and Wood Grouse, Moor Fowl or Red Grouse, Pheasants, Partridges, Woodcock, Snipe, Quail, Swans, Wild Geese, Wild Ducks, Buzzards, Curlews, Plover, Corncrakes, Fieldfares, &c., among birds, and the order in which they are mentioned will indicate their relative importance in the eyes of the hunters and sportsmen of that country.

A. Aids in Hunting.

Success in hunting depends in a great measure upon the sagacity and training of the dogs employed to discover the trail of game and other animals. Hence it is necessary that the hunter be provided with good dogs, the training of which should, whenever possible, be superintended by himself. At the head of hunting-dogs stands the slow-hound, by means of which the trails of wild animals are discovered and followed up. The education of this kind of dog is a task requiring great care, and three years are usually consumed in the process. If the animal is not perfectly trained at the end of this period of time, the blame should rest upon the trainer, provided the dog is of a good stock. The slow-hound may be trained upon stags and wild boars. For baiting-dogs, the Bull-dog, Danish Mongrel, Wolf-dog, and Pomeranian Boar-hound are employed; they also require a very careful education, and should be taught not only to catch a wild animal when wounded, but to seize it at the proper place, and not to make the attack from behind. In addition to those already mentioned we may also name the Boar-finder, the Pointer, Setter, and Spaniel, the Greyhound, used in catching hares, the Badger-dog, employed in searching for foxes and badgers in their subterranean retreats, the Otter-dog, and even the Poodle, which may be trained as a water-dog. Horses are also of assistance in hunting, and are used either as stalking-horses, behind which the hunter conceals himself in order to approach within proper distance of game, or as saddle-horses mounted, upon which the hunter follows deer, &c. In this connexion we mention, finally, Hawks, although falconry at the present day has been almost entirely abandoned. For this description of hunting all the species of hawks are employed, but a careful education is required to render them serviceable. Immediately after the capture of a hawk its talons are cut off, and a cap of strong leather (*pl.* 33, *fig.* 48), made in such a manner as to cover the eyes completely, without, however, causing a painful pressure upon those organs, is clapped upon the head, and removed only at bathing and feeding times. The wings are confined by means of the collar (*fig.* 50 *b*, *c*), a strap of fourteen inches in length, provided with a slit, whilst the feet are shackled with the catching shoes, rings nearly four inches long with loops supporting the bill. To the catching-shoes are attached leather straps used for keeping the hawk at a greater or less distance. Hawks are kept in a mews or house arranged for the purpose, on hoops or horizontal poles, are attended to very carefully, and now and then bathed; the Jer Falcon requiring to be frequently sprinkled with cold water. The training of hawks is a work troublesome in the highest degree.

They often fly away, even those that are best trained. When this occurs the falconer throws up a lure (*pl.* 33, *fig.* 49), which is an imitation of a bird, or merely two wings fastened together, or even a live pigeon is made use of in order to bring back the wanderer to the proper course. Herons, cranes, buzzards, crows, pies, hares, ducks, partridges, and quails, may be hunted with hawks. Falconry has never been practised to any great extent in North America, though some American falcons, the duck hawk and pigeon hawk (*Falco peregrinus* and *columbarius*), might be usefully employed.

B. *Practical Hunting.*

In order to convert a heath or forest into convenient *hunting ground* it is divided into exact squares by means of alleys intersecting 900 paces from each other, the distance ascertained to be the best. On each quadrangle six toils of cloth or some other stuff are needed, being part of the apparatus of hunting practised in artistic style. On *pl.* 33, *figs.* 1 and 2, are exhibited *toils* of the ordinary description, which should be ten feet in height each, and 150 paces in length, calculating three feet to a pace. Two breadths of linen usually reach to a height of nine feet, to the upper edge of which a network one foot high is attached, the meshes of which are made of strong twine or packthread. A strong cord is sewed to the top and bottom of the cloth, and furnished with short sticks and rings. When network is not used, a very broad cord, or rather binding, is attached. *Fig.* 3 exhibits a rolling or drawing toil, which is almost indispensable in many cases, as, for instance, in hunting wild boars. A toil of this description is disposed (as shown in the figure) across the place through which it is supposed the game will pass, in case any should be driven out of the woods. When the animal has passed through, the toil is stretched out. Several poles belong to a drawing toil.

Nets of different descriptions have been in use for a longer period of time than toils. Nets for stags are much stronger than those employed in the capture of smaller game. *Fig.* 6 exhibits a deer-net of this description. Tossing nets (*fig.* 5) are called also mirror nets because the threads cross each other at right angles. The meshes are six or seven inches square. Boar-nets are only half as high as stag-nets, and those used for taking roes are likewise somewhat lower, the rope being of the thickness of a quill, and the width of the meshes four inches. Wolf and hare nets are also used; the latter, however, are lower, with meshes of three inches square. *Rows of patches* are also employed for the same purposes. The patches (*fig.* 4) are about three quarters of a yard square, and, that they may blind more readily in the dark and in the forests, which is the only end in view, consist of bleached linen or cotton cloth. In cases where the apparatus employed in the more artistic kind of hunting is not sufficient, the patches come into use; and when they are not placed too near, and the game is not too tightly entangled, the animal prefers receiving the shot to passing through the patches. Besides the cloth rags, *bunches of feathers* (*fig.* 7) are very useful. The latter are composed of feathers of birds of prey, amongst which those of geese may be mixed. In making this apparatus, two feathers (*fig.* 6) are fastened together by the quills, which are split for that purpose. They are then passed along the rope by means of loops. The bunches are always ten inches apart, and the row when finished is placed upon the reel, where they are spread and stretched. Another mode of making the bunches is shown at *fig.* 9, *a* and *b*, in which the feathers are soaked, so as to enable the manufacturer to tie them into knots in threes, two on one side and one on the other. They are then looped up on the rope, and firmly stretched by means of gags. They are likewise placed at distances of ten inches from each other and reeled up.

Besides the foregoing our plate exhibits other implements which complete the hunting apparatus. *Fig.* 10 represents a pole of beech-wood, with a branch at top, *a*, and a similar pole furnished with iron hooks at the upper end, *b*. *Fig.* 11 is a pole of fir or pine, very light, having at top a hole or notch, through which the cord passes. A pole for a high toil must be ten feet long. *Figs.* 12 and 13 represent two net sticks, the upper extremity of the one at *fig.* 12 having a straight branch to it, while the one at *fig.* 13 is merely notched. The former are more conveniently arranged, as the cord might easily escape from the notches of the latter. The accompanying propping poles (*fig.* 14) are three feet long, and furnished at the two ends with iron hooks or rings. *Fig.* 15 is a straight fork for elevated apparatus. It is six feet high, and provided at top with a fork, one of the prongs being somewhat shorter and slightly bent, the other a little longer and bent outwardly. *Fig.* 16 is another rod, indispensable where riding is necessary. These rods are stouter than the poles referred to above, are eleven feet three inches in length, and furnished at top with a hole, through which passes a handle or very strong ropes reaching on both sides down to the hooks or pins, to which they can be fastened. At top is an iron ring with a hook to it to receive the upper ropes of the cloth and one of the winding ropes. For raising and lowering the toils a brass bar is added above, through which passes a cord three fathoms in length, and furnished at one end with a piece of wood. *Figs.* 17 and 18 represent hooks, on which roe and hare nets are stretched and fastened; they are four feet long and pointed below. A complete hunting apparatus, moreover, must include a paling and punching iron (*fig.* 19) for making holes for the poles, *a*, and another instrument, *b*, used in setting up the nets and patches, which consist of a rounded piece of wood tipped with iron. Pins (*fig.* 20) of oak, beech, or any hard wood, should always be at hand, as also small hooks with which to fasten the toils to the ground; also a mallet (*pl.* 33, *fig.* 21) for driving down hooks and pins. *Fig.* 52 is the needle used in making the net. *Fig.* 53 represents the pack starting for the hunt, and *fig.* 54 the chase of the wild boar.

C. Shooting, Trapping, &c.

Under this heading we include the methods of hunting in which neither toils, nets, patches, nor feathers are employed. Hence we shall consider

1. Shooting. The best way for a hunter to approach his game is to move

against the wind. Wild animals, birds especially, possess so delicate a sense of hearing as to render it a difficult matter to come within shooting distance by going in the direction of the breeze. When the haunt of game has been discovered, the sportsman stations himself in the vicinity, and to the leeward, early in the morning or in the evening, and waits until the animal sought for appears. But if unsuccessful in this way, the ground must be explored to the leeward and search made. Wild boars are hunted with good boar-hounds also to the leeward, and when the animal appears, may either be shot in front of the dogs or killed with the hunting-knife, whilst the hounds hold it fast. Roes are brought within shooting distance by imitating the cry of the doe to her young, by means of a leaf or a piece of birch bark. The roe soon approaches and is slain.

2. Catching the Badger. When the winter retreat of the badger, or the passage through which it goes in and out during the summer season, is discovered, a piece of heavy wood is placed before the entrance, and fixed in such a manner in connexion with another piece, that upon the animal's entering or leaving it must necessarily fall down and crush the badger by its weight. Another mode of capturing the badger is by means of the hood, which is a network of packthread furnished with iron rings. The hunter, having placed the hood at the entrance of the retreat, watches until the badger leaves it, and after the animal has got his head into the apparatus, it is closed around his neck. When the hood has been placed in the proper position, it is necessary that the badger should be driven from his hole by dogs. The badger may also be taken by means of the iron apparatus exhibited at *fig.* 25. Plates of good iron are used, which are placed before the entrance of the retreat, and covered slightly with earth. The plate, however, should be rubbed with the acicular leaves of the fir tree, or foliage of the oak or beech, and even then the badger ventures to run over the plate only when all other passages are closed. The plate should be well fastened to the spot or the animal may take it with him into the hole, in which case it would become necessary to dig him out. Another implement is exhibited at *fig.* 24. In order to protect the hunter from the blows of the badger, the animal is seized by means of the nippers (*fig.* 33).

3. Taking the Fox. In the first place, foxes may be shot whilst running. They are also caught in holes dug for the purpose, or taken in their dens by means of badger dogs, and finally, may be driven into nets placed at the entrance of their retreats. The best mode of catching the fox is by iron traps (*figs.* 22 and 23). Foxes may also be caught by means of the iron plate (*fig.* 25). A wooden trap (*fig.* 40) is used for the same purpose. Two pieces (*a* and *d*), each four feet in length, are placed on the ground, and at one third that distance apart. Both are fixed firmly, and slightly covered with earth. An upper piece (*c*) is five feet and a half long, and sustained by small poles. A transverse rest (*d*) is placed near the summit of two solid supports, and each movable piece of the apparatus rests upon appropriate sticks. At the other end, the upper pole slopes in such a manner as to form a slightly-opened hinge, and is attached to a stretched string

(*h*) extending the whole length of the trap. This apparatus is made at leisure, and allowed to stand out during winter and summer, without apparent design, so that the foxes may become familiar with its appearance. As soon as the fur of this animal becomes good again, the trap is put up and baited, when the fox happens to be in its retreat during rainy or bad weather. In attempting to go out he is caught under the trap and crushed. It must be understood that a trap of this description should be placed at the entrance of each fox-hole. In taking foxes with iron hooks, either the kind exhibited at *fig.* 27, called the German hook, or the Lorraine hook (*fig.* 26), or the French hook (*fig.* 28), may be used. These figures are so beautifully and minutely drawn, that it is unnecessary to describe the instruments particularly.

4. The Otter. The otter is taken either in the water or upon land, by means of the iron plate, on which the bait is to be fixed. Or the snare (*fig.* 29) may be used, constructed much like *figs.* 22 and 23, the only difference being this, that instead of beams, barbed blades are employed. The otter-trap is represented at *fig.* 37. The clod-trap (*fig.* 38) is used for the same purpose.

5. The Wild Cat and Marten. The wild cat is caught by means of the iron plate baited in the same way as for the fox, or may be shot whilst running. Martens are fond of frequenting the same places as foxes, and are taken in the same kinds of iron traps; the wooden trap may also be employed. For tree martens the wooden trap (*fig.* 39) is in general use, being fixed at a height of from three to four feet. The bottom pieces are firmly fixed on two forked poles or on two branching young trees. Martens are taken with nets also and with board traps. Of the latter we shall say a word when we speak of the polecat.

6. The Polecat. The polecat is generally caught in the same manner as the marten and also with polecat traps (*figs.* 35, 36), the latter being used also for taking the marten. Polecat traps are constructed of boards, and are so simple that a glance at the figures will show the method of making them. Before setting up the trap, the animal must be rendered familiar with the locality by depositing from time to time food relished by it. After this has been done a dead bird or raw egg is laid upon the tongue-piece of the trap, which must be set doubled in such a manner as to oblige the animal to pass through it in order to reach the bait. A plain trap should have a grating of iron wire at its posterior end. Polecats may be taken also in spring-traps (*figs.* 33, 34). Being constructed at a small expense, great numbers may be scattered about. A small bird is suspended between the loops, and when the animal attempts to take the bait, the loop is detached and incloses the game.

7. The Weasel. The weasel is most readily taken in the double board-traps exhibited in *pl.* 33, *fig.* 36, and which are laid for the most part in hen-houses and pheasant walks or preserves. Weasels will also go into the wire loops exhibited in *figs.* 33 and 34.

8. The Pheasant. In places where wild pheasants are to be found pheasant dogs are employed to search them out. When they come upon a

bird, it rises and alights upon a tree, and the dog runs round and round, barking at it, until the sportsman makes his appearance and shoots the game (*fig.* 55). Pheasants may be hunted without dogs on a bright starry night, or when the moon shines faintly. These birds are taken also in thorn nets or tunnel nets, and finally, with the *pheasant trap* (*fig.* 44), which consists of a large box resembling a house, on the outside of which one or several silk nets, or linen walls, fall down when the trigger or holding-piece of the apparatus is pulled in the attempt of the pheasant to take the bait.

9. WILD GEESE AND DUCKS are caught in nets of different kinds, on land or water, or (especially the ducks) with fishing tackle. They are also procured by shooting. For this purpose a cabin of leaves is constructed upon the shore, towards which the ducks are attracted by means of the bird-call, or they are killed from a boat (*fig.* 56). In boat-shooting the gun is rested upon a support (*fig.* 51), and the skiff rowed cautiously from place to place. Ducks, however, being difficult to approach, it is better to make use of decoys, or even the shooting horse, behind which the sportsman hides himself until the birds come within distance.

10. PARTRIDGES were formerly taken in nets made of thorn bushes, but having now become scarce (in Germany) are reserved for shooting, or caught in the partridge-trap (*fig.* 43), constructed upon the same principles as the pheasant-trap described above.

11. FIELDFARES AND OTHER SMALL BIRDS. In taking fieldfares and other small birds the apparatus most in use is the gin (*fig.* 30) or horse-hair loops, tripled or quadrupled according to the necessity of the case. The bait consists of berries. *Fig.* 30 represents the bow-gin. Snares somewhat similar to those used by boys in America for rabbits are also in use for catching snipes. *Figs.* 31 and 32 represent spring snares in which birds are strangled. Another mode of taking birds is by means of the trap exhibited in *fig.* 45. A very useful contrivance for catching singing birds in numbers is the fowling-floor (*fig.* 46). This is a mound, *a*, of 18 or 20 feet in length by 12 feet wide, and 3 feet in height, covered with sods on which little twigs with berries and trained decoy birds are placed. Other decoy birds are hung in cages in neighboring trees, BB. Around the mound is fixed in the ground a large net with small meshes, which is carefully folded down on the ground. Its upper edges are fastened to a double frame, *gg*, capable of being closed round the hinges, *ff*, and whose extremities are held firmly to the ground between stretched ropes passing crosswise from the spring-poles, *ee*, through rings at the end of the frame, to the pegs, *dd*, driven into the ground. Two lines, *hh*, are passed under the frame and over the blocks, *cc*, and are united into one line, *b*, which is governed from the hut, C, where the fowler is stationed, and which has only small loopholes on the side towards the mound, the door being on the opposite side. A pull at this line will lift the two sides of the frame a little from the ground, when the spring-power of the poles, *ee*, will immediately act, and rapidly draw the two halves of the frame into a vertical position over the fowling-floor, causing the net to be lifted and closed over the mound. This

contrivance is chiefly in use in Thuringia, a district in Germany, which annually exports many thousands of the finest singing birds.

12. Birds of Prey. Birds of prey, besides being shot and destroyed in other ways, may be taken with the gin net, which also proves of service in catching other birds. *Figs.* 41 and 42 exhibit two kinds of traps, *fig.* 41 for partridges, *fig.* 42 for smaller birds. When intended for rapacious birds they are constructed on the plan of *fig.* 42, but much stouter.

2. Fishing.

A. Fresh Water Fishing.

1. Fishing with Hook and Line. The general principles of bait-fishing are so well known that it is scarcely necessary to mention them here. The apparatus is exceedingly simple and within the reach of almost every one, but in many cases great skill is necessary to capture the so-called game fish.

The instrument usually employed for hand fishing is the rod and line (*pl.* 34, *fig.* 1) held in the hand, and the baited hook cast into the water. Sometimes a swimmer or float is attached to the line, to show more readily the attack of the fish, or to regulate the depth to which the bait ought to sink. The bait varies with the fish to be captured, with the season, and with the condition of the water. It may consist of a worm, caterpillar, grasshopper, bit of meat, small fish, frog, and indeed animal matter of almost any kind. Sometimes a number of short baited lines are attached to a longer one, which is then stretched out in the water, and allowed to remain over night.

2. Fishing with Nets and Weirs. This mode of fishing affords more abundant results than the preceding, but its machinery is much more complicated and expensive. The forms of nets are very various, differing with the species of fish, locality, &c. A simple kind is that known as the *scoop* or *hoop-net*, consisting of a netted bag attached to a hoop with a long handle (*pl.* 34, *fig.* 2). The *dip-net* is a square piece of netting, stretched by the corners between two semicircular hoops, which cross each other at right angles, and are suspended from a long pole. The *fish-weir* is represented in *figs.* 4 and 5, the *set-net* in *fig.* 6, the *seine* or *haul-net* in *fig.* 3. *Fig.* 7 shows the construction of what is usually called a *fish-pot* or *basket.* The *casting-net* is much used on the Southern sea-coast of the United States. This consists of a circular net with weights around the circumference, and a long rope attached to the centre. This is cast into the water, and the circumference sinking more rapidly than the centre, any fish which happen to be beneath are immediately inclosed.

3. Fishing by Fire. This consists in attaching an iron vessel containing burning splints to the bow of a boat, or carrying it by hand close to the water. The light attracts the fish, which are then taken either by hand or by means of scoop-nets, spears, gigs, &c. (*pl.* 34, *fig.* 8).

B. Marine Fishing.

It will already have been understood by our readers that fishing includes not only the capture of fishes, but of aquatic animals in general. Under this head, therefore, may be given the catching of whales, crabs, oysters, lobsters, &c., in addition to that of herring, cod, tunny, mackerel, &c. We have, however, presented the general features of the whale-fishing under the head of MAMMALIA, and those of the fishes above-mentioned under FISHES, and shall, therefore, conclude this part of our subject by a brief reference to the figures on plates 34 and 35.

Pl. 35, *fig.* 1, represents a party of fishermen in the act of capturing tunnies, according to the method practised in the Mediterranean. The entire apparatus is shown in *pl.* 34, *fig.* 9, consisting of huge nets, arranged in a succession of chambers, in one of which the scene first mentioned is supposed to be taking place. *Pl.* 35, *fig.* 2, shows a scene of the whale-fishery; a party of men about to harpoon a whale, with the ships in the distance, from one of which is streaming the smoke evolved in trying out the blubber. The dead whales, previously captured, form part of the picture. In *pl.* 35, *fig.* 3, we see fishermen catching herrings by means of an enormous net. The number thus taken amounts sometimes to 120,000 or 140,000 at a single haul.

Pl. 34, *figs.* 13 and 14, present incidents in cod-fishing. Oysters are taken by means of the *rakes* (*pl.* 34, *fig.* 11), and sometimes by a kind of *dredge* (*fig.* 12). Crabs and lobsters are caught in *pots* (*fig.* 10) baited with meat.

INDEX TO TECHNOLOGY.

[The numbers refer to the top paging of the text.]

www.ingramcontent.com/pod-product-compliance
Lightning Source LLC
LaVergne TN
LVHW011238110826
845150LV00006B/1678

* 9 7 8 1 4 2 5 5 1 4 0 2 0 *